NEW WORLD ORDER
ASSASSINS

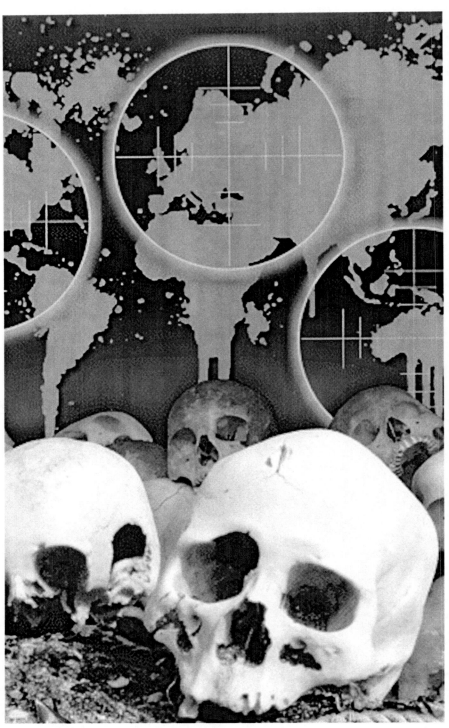

ILLUSTRATION BY PETER CURRENTI

NEW WORLD ORDER
ASSASSINS

By Victor Thorn

Published by American Free Presss

NEW WORLD ORDER ASSASSINS

ISBN: 978-0-9846350-0-9

First edition 2011

AMERICAN FREE PRESS
645 Pennsylvania Avenue SE #100
Washington, D.C. 20003
1-888-699-NEWS toll free
www.AmericanFreePress.net

in conjunction with

SISYPHUS PRESS
P.O. Box 10495
State College, Pa.
16805-0495
sisyphus1285@cs.com

Front and Back Cover Art: Peter Currenti
Manufactured in the United States of America

Order more copies of this book from:
AMERICAN FREE PRESS
645 Pennsylvania Avenue SE, #100
Washington, D.C. 20003
1-888-699-6397 toll free charge line
$30 plus $5 S&H inside the U.S.

TABLE OF CONTENTS

BY WAY OF DECEPTION

In 2003, my first political book appeared in print. Epic in size at 570 pages with quite possibly the most exceptional artwork to ever appear on a cover, *The New World Order Exposed* stands as a testament to the power of conspiracy theories. I use the word "power" because that's what lies at the root of this phenomenon—a desire to control via the accumulation of power.

What strikes me most about this subject are those who refuse to even consider the possibility that infinitely powerful individuals *don't* conspire to maintain and expand their empires. Imagine the sheer naivete of such an outlook. Worse, consider how utterly boring and stunted their lives are. These people actually rely on the government and corporate-owned mainstream media sources to deliver their news. On top of that, they seemingly trust them (as opposed to any alternatives). It's inconceivable that anyone would turn exclusively to CBS News or a White House spokesman for their information—then swallow it hook, line and sinker.

Ironically, those who rule atop their global control pyramids laugh with glee at these myopic, infantile, close-minded patsies who've surrendered their minds to a lapdog press which licks the boots of their masters (i.e. international bankers, greedy CEOs and corrupt politicians). This organized crime syndicate steals their paychecks, murders at will, engages in narcotics trafficking, launders money, kills their children in war and engineers megalomaniacal crimes like 9-11. Yet, compliant and submissive, the masses actually stand-up for their oppressors and defend them.

Like brainwashed lemmings led to slaughter or driven over a cliff, they recite the elitist's mantra: "There aren't any conspiracies." When asked why, they reply: "Because the government and those newscasters on TV say so." Naturally, the controllers chuckle even more vociferously, amazed that such large groups still swallow their fairy-tale nonsense. After all, any person with even a high school student's understanding of basic physics would realize that two 110-story skyscrapers can't fall the way they did on Sept. 11 unless a controlled demolition entered the equation.

But they still keep bowing at the altar of ignorance. Why? Because cognitive dissonance doesn't allow the collective to inherently accept one crucial point—their rulers are absolutely and positively evil. No, not simply crooked—but psychopathically evil.

This information leads us to the book at hand. After seven long years, the third installment in this trilogy is finally completed (with *The New World Order Illusion* published in the interim). To anyone contemplating the title—*New World Order Assassins*—it's not difficult to ascertain the subject matter. What I'm covering are high-profile killings which occurred between 1962 and 1999.

I must disclose, however, that this collection is not comprehensive. Rather, I've covered other infamous events in previous books, including 9-11, Israel's attack on the *USS Liberty*, Jonestown, JFK's slaying, Waco, Oklahoma City, the "suicides" of Vince Foster and Ron Brown, journalist Danny Casolaro's silencing, plus the "Boys on the Tracks" case. Furthermore, I plan on chronicling other similar occurrences in the future, such as JFK Jr.'s untimely demise, Chappaquiddick, the Unabomber and Zodiac serial killings, plus the elimination of reporter Dorothy Kilgallen.

However, prior to delving into the chapters that follow, I'd like to briefly discuss the subject of Manchurian candidates. To understand this subject, we need to fully comprehend that these fall guys are nothing more than a distraction. None of these "mind-controlled" patsies killed anyone. They merely served as red herrings in an elaborate, sadistic, magical ritual.

Here's how it works. Picture a magician appearing on stage. "Government" as a concept fills the role of master illusionist, with a traumatic murder (such as that of Bobby Kennedy) serving as the "trick." Now, to successfully accomplish this amazing feat, they need to use misdirection and sleight-of-hand, like any magician would. So, here's where Sirhan Sirhan enters the picture. Of course he underwent hypnotic brainwashing, but this guy didn't shoot RFK. Simple logic and a preponderance of evidence show it to be impossible.

Does anyone really think these cold-blooded killers would let such a pivotal event rest solely in the hands of a mind-numbed zombie? Hell no. Real shooters did the actual dirty deed, while Sirhan fumbled and bumbled around like an incapacitated automaton.

Here's where it gets really freaky. Without any doubt, a conspiracy took place when Kennedy was riddled with bullets (from behind, nonetheless) at the Ambassador Hotel in L.A. But who augments the conspiracy of Sirhan Sirhan? Conspiracy theorists do! Instead of pointing to the *real gunmen*, they aid and abet the criminal syndicate by continually pushing the MK-ULTRA angle. But Sirhan's duping is merely a symptom—not the real cause.

Then, to muddy the waters even further, researchers of every shape, color and stripe jump in with the standard line "the CIA did it." But let's pause a moment and decipher who comprises the CIA. Originally, the OSS handled America's most clandestine services. But following World War II, the Central Intelligence Agency emerged. Prior to that time—while the war still raged—a dirty little secret had developed. Namely, purported enemies—Nazis and Zionists—were actually working hand-in-hand with each other behind the scenes. The reason why is obvious: they wanted the same outcome—to move Jews out of Europe into a new homeland in the Middle East (i.e. Israel).

This skullduggery is vitally important because the CIA became an amalgamation of many different factions. Specifically, it amassed (over the course of a decade) its core membership from: Project Paperclip Nazis; the Mossad; MI6 (descendants from Cecil Rhodes's Round Table); and the P2 (Vatican)

On top of that, the OSS worked closely with Sicilian Mafioso during WW II (a trend the CIA carries on to this current day). Then, of course, we must factor in secret societies (Freemasons and Yale's Skull and Bones), the Council on Foreign Relations and Wall Street financiers, psychiatric mind-benders (Ewen Cameron, Jolly West etc.), occult elements and prominent crime families such as the Bushes. All of these influences helped "create" the CIA *per se*. So, to pinpoint only one ruling factor is a difficult proposition, and I'm always wary of attempting to pigeon-hole these operations, for extremely complex organizations are at work using numerous techniques to distract the masses (not to mention a varying host of agendas).

On that note, I'd like to finish by addressing one other topic—the commonalities which exist in all of these cases. Although obviously each factor listed below isn't inclusive to every case, a thread does weave through the overall tapestry. Thus, I've organized an alphabetical lexicon of sorts which can be used to analyze not only the contents of this book, but other assassinations—either past, present, or future.

Arrests—Shortly before a specific incident, the perpetrator is arrested, then inexplicably released with a slap on the wrist. Or, law enforcement officials are told to stand down and not touch the patsy-to-be. They are subsequently given free rein to create a legend and carry out the plan at hand.

Blackmail—One of the most prevalent reasons why governments elect to murder a target, especially when the information's immediacy isn't easily squelched.

Bodyguards—Prior to a hit being performed, the FBI and CIA often obtain crucial data from plants inside a target's inner circle. Bodyguards are the easiest way to infiltrate.

Cointelpro—A notorious FBI program used to infiltrate, distract, divert, and divide/conquer.

Cults—Group think on an isolated, closed-off collection of people, such as religious sects who have the same core beliefs. Or, the cult can become an institutionalized facilitator, like Scientology.

Diaries—These are either used as an immediate, direct threat toward a powerful individual, or faked to create a legacy for the fall guy in question. One other possibility is as "evidence" that the Manchurian candidate underwent hypnotic brainwashing.

Drugs—A tremendous source of black budget money for intelligence operations, also a method to mind-control specific patsies.

Gatekeepers—The mainstream media has long been an essential purveyor of cover-ups. They create the "official story," along with other government representatives. Local newscasters also dramatically change their initial reports to fit the official story once the feds swoop in.

Guns—Often, multiple shooters are placed at the death scene to carry out the operation, while invariably a "lone nut shooter" is blamed for the deed. After the fact, this fall guy will have purported expert knowledge of firearms, even though he is many times a complete novice or amateur.

Lurkers—Persons such as George Bush Sr., Richard Nixon, J. Edgar Hoover, and James Jesus Angleton always seem to be somewhere in the shadows of these criminal acts. Names change as time goes by, but these "fixers" are always present. In my works, an undeniable crossover of interchangeable characters can be traced from the Bay of Pigs to the murders of JFK and RFK, Vietnam drug running, Watergate, Iran-Contra and 9-11.

Mafia—The CIA has perennially interacted with both Jewish and Italian mobsters to do their dirty work (i.e. murders, drug trafficking etc.).

Magic Bullets—An amazing number of inconsistencies are reported in regard to fingerprints (or a lack thereof), forensics and physically impossible trajectories.

Mind Control—Although the CIA's MK-ULTRA program has "officially" been discontinued, the role of psychological manipulation will remain prevalent with government cut-outs (i.e. psychiatrists and psychologists) utilizing techniques such as hypnosis, brainwashing and psychic driving.

Money—More specifically, the mysterious source of money that patsies seem to obtain with no visible means of support (or any feasible method of obtaining it).

Mossad—Their motto says it all: "By way of deception. . . ."

Occult—Playing on the sensationalism card, the "devil made them do it" is always an easy way to arrive at a motive. In addition, "magickal" icon Aleister Crowley seems to appear at the most opportune moments.

Patsies—Mind-controlled Manchurian candidates used as red herrings to divert attention away from the actual shooter, in addition to the primary motive.

Premonitions—Victims often feel to the innermost crux of their existence that they're soon about to be killed.

Project Paperclip—The United States clandestinely imported Nazi scientists and mind-control experts into this country following World War II. They became an integral part of the CIA and our fledgling space program.

Racism—Used as a convenient "motive" or the actual motive *is* racism by the power elite in regard to the individual targeted.

Scientology—A black, wicked mind-control cabal that exerts horrific negative energy. This den of deception was founded by a complete sham named L. Ron Hubbard, who ripped off his original partner, Jack Parsons of JPL fame.

Sex—One of the ultimate manipulation tools. "Honey pots" (women agents/infiltrators asked to have sex with the men they are monitoring) have been used since ancient times.

Trigger Mechanisms—The "mark" will carry a book upon his arrest (such as J.D. Salinger's *The Catcher in the Rye*), or movies like *The Wizard of Oz* or *Taxi Driver* can be utilized to implant certain trigger words, or as a scapegoat in the crime.

War—Vietnam provided a pervasive backdrop for much of the social unrest that plagued America from the early 1960s to mid-1970s. Later, Iran-Contra filled that role, followed by our war in Afghanistan. The constant theme in each is widespread drug trafficking by the CIA to finance black budget operations.

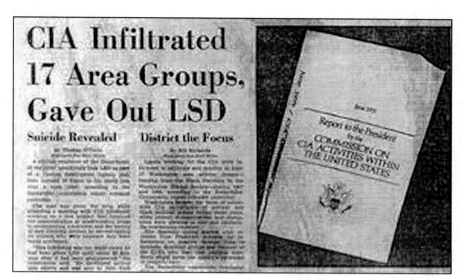

Left, a newspaper headline confirmed CIA experimentation with LSD. At right, a presidential report from the Commission on CIA Activities Within the United States, published in 1975, exposed many clandestine CIA "black ops." The report was commissioned by President Gerald Ford and overseen by none other than Vice President Nelson Rockefeller. (See chapter 10 of this book for more on Rockefeller.)

Admittedly, this list could be greatly expanded, probably into an entire book. But it suffices for the time being as a general outline of what researchers should take notice of whenever one of these murderous events takes place in the future.

—Victor Thorn
Happy Valley, Pa.
November 2010

CHAPTER 1

PRESIDENTIAL MODEL

THE MURDER & DESECRATION OF MARILYN MONROE

On the evening of Aug. 4, 1962 three men entered Marilyn Monroe's residence and killed her. This tragic murder (as opposed to the suicidal overdose official historians led us to believe occurred on the morning of Aug. 5) served as the first of many high-profile political assassinations of the 1960s. In the following pages, you'll discover the identity of these powerful figures that wanted to silence Hollywood's most glamorous movie star. This work is primarily based upon three books: Donald H. Wolfe's *The Last Days of Marilyn Monroe*; Matthew Smith's *Marilyn's Last Words*; and Milo Speriglio's *Marilyn Monroe Murder Cover-up*.

Although these men arrive at different conclusions, I've compiled the best evidence from all of them to reconstruct what happened to Ms. Norma Jean Baker, and why.

THE WALLS HAVE EARS

When news of her death sped like a meteor from L.A. to the rest of America, Attorney General Bobby Kennedy claimed to have spent the entire weekend in San Francisco. That statement was a categorical lie. Initially, the *San Francisco Chronicle* reported on Friday, Aug. 3 that Bobby Kennedy "arrived without his usual smile and shook hands woodenly with those who welcomed him." The reason for his preoccupation is simple: he'd been sent by his brother—President John F. Kennedy—to take care of some business that could get very messy. He most certainly didn't look forward to it.

Rather than stay in San Francisco, Kennedy flew south and checked in to the Beverly Hilton Hotel later Friday night. He then commenced to have dinner with Marilyn Monroe at La Scala, where the two argued about their relationship, as well as her affair with another former lover, President Kennedy. The heated exchange involved some potential information that could have sunk both brothers in a heartbeat.

During a Friday afternoon call to close friend Robert Slatzer, Marilyn threatened, "I'm going to blow the lid off this whole damn thing! I'm going to tell everything! Everybody has been calling trying to get the story anyway—Winchell [and] Kilgallen. And it's clear to me now that the Kennedys got what they wanted out of me and then moved on!" After pausing for a moment, she continued, "Well, I've told a couple of people already."

Marilyn made this call from a pay phone out of fear that her home lines were bugged. She had good reason to be suspicious. Kennedy enemy Jimmy Hoffa hired private eye Fred Otash to bug in-law and Rat Pack actor Peter Lawford's Santa Monica house, which served as the Kennedy's playground for sexual liaisons. [Lawford was married to Bobby and Jack's sister, Patricia.] Here, Marilyn was recorded making love on different occasions with John Kennedy and later his brother, Bobby. Realizing the windfall of blackmail material at his disposal, Hoffa next hired "King of the Wiretappers" Bernard Spindel, to tap her phone and all the rooms in her newly purchased home.

Hoffa's "ears" weren't the only ones present at this address. J. Edgar Hoover also had Marilyn's house bugged, as did CIA Counterintelligence Chief James Jesus Angleton (whose name appears on a cover sheet to authorize the surveillance). In addition, Marilyn also recorded home tapes of herself free-associating about the sordid details of her

complicated life. She spoke in very explicit terms about her sexual relationship with JFK.

The reason why various researchers have been effective over the
years in piecing together what happened to Marilyn is because the walls
had ears (many ears)—and everybody was listening.

SATURDAY AFTERNOON—ARGUMENT NUMBER ONE

Unable to adequately convince Marilyn to see things his way Friday
night, RFK returned to San Francisco. He then took a helicopter back
to L.A. on Saturday afternoon, landing at Fox Studios in Hollywood,
where a car driven by Peter Lawford awaited. [Fox was producing a film
version of his book, *The Enemy Within.*]

Some prominent individuals, as well as those nearest to Marilyn,
contradicted his alibi that he remained in San Francisco all weekend.
L.A. Mayor Sam Yorty confirmed that Bobby was in L.A. on Aug. 4, as
did future LAPD Police Chief Daryl Gates. In his book, *Chief: My Life
in the LAPD*, he wrote, "The truth is, we knew Bobby Kennedy was in
town on Aug. 4. We always knew he was here." Marilyn's housekeeper,
Eunice Murray, also admitted years later that RFK visited Ms. Monroe's
house on Aug. 4. Her words were confirmed by handyman Norman
Jeffries, who adamantly stated that RFK and Lawford arrived at Marilyn's residence between 3 and 4 p.m.

After clandestinely securing a room at the Beverly Hilton Hotel Saturday afternoon, Kennedy and Lawford did indeed drive to Marilyn's
home. Utilizing a different technique than the previous night (i.e. using
honey instead of vinegar), Bobby first made love to Marilyn. But by
this time, Marilyn had wised-up to their tactics, especially when Bobby
demanded the incriminating evidence that she kept in her possession.

As Bobby rampaged from room-to-room searching for letters, photos and other documents, a violent struggle broke out. Slamming doors
and arguing, Bobby demanded, "Where is it? Where the hell is it? I have
to have it! My family will pay you for it!"

Standing up to him, Marilyn shot back. "I'm tired of this whole
damn thing, of being a plaything!"

Panicked by their heated argument, Bobby began wailing like a falsetto-voiced old woman. "Where is it? Where is it? Where the f*** is it?"

Instead of answering, Marilyn threatened to hold a press conference and spill the beans on them.

Out of control, Bobby grabbed Marilyn and pushed her to the floor, bellowing, "If you threaten me, Marilyn, there's more than one way to keep you quiet."

Marilyn had become a serious problem, but before she kicked Bobby and Lawford out of her house, they called Dr. Ralph Greenson (Marilyn's personal psychiatrist) and told him to come over. He did, subsequently giving Marilyn a shot of pentobarbital to calm her nerves. By this time, Kennedy and Lawford had stormed from the premises, leaving Marilyn with Greenson until he left at 7 p.m.

BOOK OF SECRETS

What did Bobby Kennedy so desperately seek that Marilyn wouldn't relinquish? The answer: a little red diary that she began keeping ever since her affair with Bobby began in the summer of 1962. Marilyn kept it partly as a way of compiling notes so that she'd have political topics to discuss with her lover. The other reason, of course—if even on a subconscious level—was as ammunition against the brothers.

This "book of secrets" became such a threat that a CIA document released in 1994 (dating back to the Kennedy era) categorized it as a "national security concern." It also became a great source of interest to James Jesus Angleton. Although some have doubted its existence, individuals such as Mike Rothmiller, an LAPD officer in the Organized Crime Intelligence Division, verify its authenticity. Others do too, such as coroner's aide Lionel Grandison, handyman Norman Jeffries, plus long-time friend and investigator Robert Slatzer. Last but not least, Bobby learned of its existence approximately 10 days before Marilyn's murder.

If this diary sent him into such fits of rage, everyone most certainly wants to know: what did Marilyn write about? In addition to having a photo of President Kennedy with Chicago mob boss Sam Giancana,

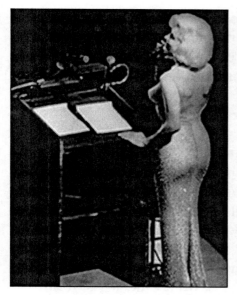 

Left, Marilyn sings "Happy Birthday" to JFK in Madison Square Garden in 1962. Right, a headline from the *Daily News* announces Marilyn's death.

Marilyn's book of secrets revealed:
- Her affairs with JFK and RFK;
- CIA plans to assassinate Fidel Castro;
- A host of mobsters hired by the CIA (and on their payroll);
- Bobby Kennedy's admission that he ran the country on the day of the Bay of Pigs disaster because JFK was ailing with a bad back and under sedation. Bobby was actually the one in charge who foiled the CIA's operation by persuading the president to withdraw air cover—something the Agency never forgave;
- Bobby's plans to imprison Jimmy Hoffa;
- Their conversations about the Soviet Union;
- Atomic test secrets;
- Frank Sinatra's ties to the underworld;
- Giancana and Johnny Roselli on the State Department payroll;
- The CIA's role in the assassination of Dominican Republic President Raphael Trujillo.

In the days before widespread Internet access and scores of conspiracy books, this news promised to be explosive on the grandest of scales. Obviously, nobody—from the president, attorney general, CIA, FBI and the Mob—wanted it to see the light of day, and they'd take whatever steps were necessary to conceal it. Also, although each of these factions had major disputes with each other, their one unifying goal was the danger Marilyn's diary presented to them.

SATURDAY EVENING—PRESS CONFERENCE THREATS

When handyman Norman Jeffries returned after Kennedy and Lawford's departure, he found "Marilyn scared out of her mind. She was in a hysterical rage and looked awful." After Dr. Greenson administered his shot, she began to make a series of phone calls that cemented her fate. The first was to hairdresser of the stars, Sydney Guilaroff. "Bobby Kennedy was here, and he threatened me, screamed at me, and pushed me around." Guilaroff described her as being extremely terrified.

Next, she dialed confidante Robert Slatzer and unloaded everything. "If Bobby doesn't call me, I'm going to call a press conference on Monday morning, and I'm going to blow the lid off the whole damn thing. I've certainly got a lot to say. I'm so angry, I may just show it [the diary] to the whole damn world and let everybody know what the Kennedys are really like."

When next-door neighbor Jeanne Carmen agreed to an interview on *The Reporters Special Edition* program *Marilyn: A Case for Murder*, she told them, "Marilyn was going to talk to the press on Monday, and people might have been desperate."

Marilyn also had other major plans in the works for Monday, including a meeting with attorney Mickey Rudin where she intended to change her will to "get rid of a lot of leeches."

As the night proceeded, Marilyn spoke with Joe Dimaggio Jr. at 7:30 pm, who remembers her being in a somewhat better mood, cheerful and laughing. She then called her hairdresser again at 9 o'clock, this time telling him, "You know, Sydney, I know a lot of secrets about the Kennedys. Dangerous ones." Finally, at 9:30 p.m., screenwriter Jose Bolanos called. The two spoke for a short while until Marilyn heard a commotion at the door and her phone went dead.

MURDER INSIDE THE COTTAGE

Shortly after sunset Saturday evening, three men were seen walking down Marilyn Monroe's street. Neighbor Elizabeth Pollard saw these individuals, including Robert Kennedy. Another woman, playing cards with friends, commented, "Look, girls, there he [Kennedy] is again." Milo Speraglio wrote of this event, "Bobby Kennedy was seen with a man carrying a bag that resembled a doctor's bag entering Marilyn's house."

Norman Jeffries likewise witnessed Bobby Kennedy and two other men at Marilyn's door between 9:30 and 10 p.m. The trio then escorted Marilyn to her cottage out back. The reason they chose this locale is because it was the only area on the premises not bugged. So, what transpired from this point forward is not known, except that shouts were heard, and then the sound of breaking glass (i.e. a window).

The timeline picks up again at 10:30 p.m. when Marilyn purportedly called Peter Lawford before lapsing into unconsciousness. Simultaneously, Murray and Jeffries saw Bobby and two men leave the guesthouse. Hearing her dog Maf (short for "Mafia") barking, they entered the cottage to find Marilyn lying naked on the bed, unconscious, her hand clutching a phone. Frantic, Ms. Murray called an ambulance, and then Dr. Greenson, who told her to also call Dr. Hyman Engelberg.

Shortly thereafter, Peter Lawford and Pat Newcomb arrived, the latter hysterically screaming, "Murderers! You murderers! Are you satisfied now that she's dead?" A melee ensued as an ambulance raced to the scene, followed by police cars and a fire truck.

Donald Wolfe recounts the chain of events. After an ambulance arrived, Pat Newcomb led them to the cottage, where they discovered Marilyn Monroe nude and face up on the bed. With a weak pulse, plus a slight heartbeat and respiration, at least she was still alive. Resuscitating the patient and bringing her back to life, the paramedics considered taking Marilyn to the hospital. That's when a man claiming to be a doctor entered the cottage and gave Marilyn a shot. Within minutes, she was dead.

By 10:45 p.m., calls were already going out that Marilyn had died.

Eunice Murray confessed years later that Robert Kennedy had visited Marilyn Monroe that night, and when the ambulance arrived, she was still alive. Neighbors Abe Landau and his wife also confirmed seeing an ambulance and police car at Marilyn's house earlier in the evening. Lastly, in a July 8, 1964 memo from J. Edgar Hoover to Attorney General Robert Kennedy, he wrote, "You and Miss Monroe were intimate and you were in Miss Monroe's residence at the time of her death."

Although most of the puzzle has been put together at this stage, a few unknown variables do exist. One, who were the other two men with Bobby Kennedy at Marilyn's cottage, especially the one carrying a doctor's bag? Many researchers have speculated that she'd been given a "hot shot" (a lethal injection), but no needles or syringes were found on the premises. Of course, the killers would have wanted to remove all evidence, but another possibility exists.

In her home taped recordings, Marilyn spoke frequently about enemas, including other Hollywood stars that used them, and their popularity throughout history, especially among royal families. At one point she even quips: "Yes, I enjoy enemas. So what?" In this same vein, when asked by Deborah Gould how Marilyn died, Peter Lawford responded, "she took her last big enema."

CLEAN-UP

With the dead body of Tinseltown's most famous movie star now on their hands, a frantic clean-up had to take place, and quickly. The person ultimately in charge of this task was LAPD Police Chief William Parker, who maintained an extremely tight relationship with the Kennedy brothers. In fact, assurances were made to Parker that when they dumped J. Edgar Hoover as FBI director, he would be promoted to that esteemed position.

To facilitate the cover-up, Parker appointed Captain James Hamilton to take charge. Donald H. Wolfe assessed the situation in very clear terms. "Hamilton's Intelligence Division was Parker's version of the FBI. Parker believed that he was the man who would one day succeed J. Edgar Hoover, and Bobby and Jack Kennedy led Parker to believe he was their choice."

Another man known as an architect of the cover-up was consummate public relations man Arthur Jacobs. Attending a Henry Mancini concert at the Hollywood Bowl, somebody contacted him at 10:30 (more than likely Pat Newcomb) and delivered the news about Marilyn's death. Colleague Michael Selsman later revealed that members of the State Department in Washington, D.C. were instructing Jacobs behind-the-scenes. Ms. Newcomb (Marilyn's press secretary and small-time handler) also spoke to Jacobs's wife, telling her she was one of the first to appear at the murder scene.

Determining that the risk factor of leaving Marilyn's body in the cottage was too great, some LAPD plainclothes officers decided to relocate her body to the bedroom in the main house. They also came up with a story that Ms. Murray noticed a light emanating from Marilyn's bedroom, and that's when she became alarmed. Donald Wolfe assigns Captain James Hamilton and Billy Woodfield of the LAPD Intelligence Division as being in control, as well as two unnamed detectives who served as Bobby Kennedy's security officers. A police helicopter also landed at a nearby golf course around midnight.

After Dr. Greenson's arrival, he decided to make tracks (after all, it wouldn't look good to have Marilyn's personal psychiatrist present with a corpse on their hands). His departure then leads to another intriguing scenario. Before midnight, a Mercedes tore along Olympic Boulevard in Beverly Hills, going at least 55 miles per hour. Beverly Hills Police Officer Lynn Franklin saw the speeding automobile and threw on his lights. Once pulled over, he discovered the driver to be Peter Lawford, while the other two passengers were Dr. Ralph Greenson and Robert Kennedy. Flashing his attorney general badge, the officer allowed the car to proceed. This incident occurred only a few miles from Marilyn's home. Neighbors also complained later that night (actually the early hours of Sunday morning) that a helicopter landed on the Santa Monica shorefront property of Peter Lawford, blowing sand in their swimming pools. More than likely, this helicopter picked up Kennedy and scurried him out of the city. For supposedly remaining in San Francisco all weekend, Bobby Kennedy and Peter Lawford were certainly at the center of some quite harried activity.

They weren't the only ones. Private eye Fred Otash was contacted and told to enter Marilyn's residence and clean up anything that the killers had missed. In short order, Marilyn's home was rearranged, while the papers and notes in her file cabinets were confiscated. Investigative reporter Tony Sciaca also reported, "The CIA came into Marilyn's house and made it sterile." In addition, Ms. Murray instructed her son-in-law, Norman Jeffries, to fix a broken window while she began loading boxes into the trunk of her car. Matthew Smith later assessed the situation. "All the people who were in and out of the house on Fifth Helena Drive that night had an agenda of one sort or another."

DETECTIVE JACK CLEMMONS

Finally, at 4:25 a.m. Sunday—six hours after Marilyn had been killed—Ms. Murray called Detective Jack Clemmons of the LAPD and reported finding Marilyn Monroe dead. A brief time later, Eunice Murray greeted Clemmons at 12305 Fifth Helena Drive, saying that she'd found Marilyn's body shortly after midnight. Inside the bedroom, he encountered Dr. Ralph Greenson and Hyman Engelberg, who said they'd been there since 12:30 a.m.

Naturally, Clemmons asked why it took them four hours to call (little did he know that she'd been dead another two hours before then). The detective also noticed that rigor mortis began to afflict the corpse, which he believed had been dead since the previous evening. Sensing his suspicions, Greenson blurted, "Marilyn died from an overdose of Nembutals. She committed suicide." Meanwhile, Dr. Engelberg remained despondent and uncommunicative. Clemmons felt both men were lying.

Looking around, Marilyn supposedly gulped down four dozen Nembutal capsules, yet no drinking glass could be seen anywhere. Her bedroom also appeared in perfect order, which is odd because overdose victims usually convulse before death—falling down, vomiting, breaking furniture and leaving fecal remains.

Clemmons didn't buy their ruse. "It looked like the whole thing had been staged. She couldn't have died in that position . . . this is an out-and-out case of murder." He continued, "You know what I think?

I think Marilyn Monroe was murdered and they're covering up this whole damn thing because the attorney general was involved."

His impressions of Eunice Murray were equally less than flattering. Murray tried to float the story that she'd noticed Marilyn's bedroom light on underneath her door sometime past midnight. But Marilyn had just installed brand new carpeting that was so plush she could barely close her door. It would have been impossible for light to escape beneath it.

Even more bizarre, Murray hurriedly did laundry, cleaned-out the refrigerator and vacuumed the floor. Why was she washing Marilyn's bedclothes? To remove any stains that resulted from her being given a fatal enema. Clemmons also noticed that the housekeeper seemed agitated, a mannerism seconded by Sgt. Robert Byron, who felt she was evasive. Byron concluded that Murray had been rehearsed, as if someone told her what to say beforehand.

THE VULTURES DESCEND

Between 5:30 and 6 a.m. Sunday, paramedic Guy Hockett placed Marilyn's corpse onto his gurney. His thoughts at that moment: "Rigor mortis was advanced." By his best estimate, Marilyn had already been dead for approximately six to eight hours, making her time of death anywhere between 9:30 and 11:30 p.m.

By now, the media had gathered outside Marilyn's home, and as paramedics wheeled her body toward an awaiting ambulance, Pat Newcomb once again erupted. "Keep shooting [your cameras], vultures! You bloodsuckers! You vampires! You can't even let her die in peace, can you?"

Others, however, were concerned with more pressing matters. In particular, Peter Lawford placed a frantic call at 6 a.m. to President Kennedy at the White House. Their conversation lasted 20 minutes, and has remained hidden due to "national security" concerns. At Marilyn's home, wiretapping specialist Bernard Spindel listened to a call from San Francisco to Marilyn's private line where a male voice asked, "Is she dead yet?" The identity of this individual remains unknown.

In another part of the city, telephone records were of great concern to Captain James Hamilton, who visited the Brentwood General Telephone Company early Sunday morning. There, he and another "well-dressed man with fancy credentials and badges" confiscated her phone records that contained a history of all outgoing calls. These records were turned over to LAPD Police Chief William Parker, who boasted, "This is my ticket to get Hoover's job once Bobby Kennedy becomes president."

These logs were highly sensitive in that they chronicled Marilyn's calls to not only Bobby days before her murder, but also to the White House and Kennedy lair in Hyannis Port, Massachusetts. For his part, Parker was correct in that the Kennedy brothers wanted to fire Hoover, and these phone records were his insurance policy for the future. The primary problem, of course, revolved around the tons of dirt Hoover held over the Kennedy's heads. He'd been collecting it since JFK served in the Navy during the 1940s, and as a senator in the 1950s. His extra-marital dalliances filled volumes and, as such, the Kennedys were unable to oust the FBI Director.

At the time, however, Parker fully supported Bobby Kennedy. He, along with Captain James Hamilton and DA John van de Kamp, led the cover-up. As Detective Jack Clemmons surmised quite accurately, "No one would dare challenge his [Parker's] orders, such was the authority he commanded."

Here's one of the most ironic twists of all. Marilyn's phone records were Parker's ace-in-the-hole, and he genuinely believed that one day Bobby Kennedy would appoint him FBI director. So, he led the cover-up of Marilyn Monroe's murder by controlling the police department and coroner. But, when Bobby reneged on his offer and hung Parker out to dry, guess what he did when Bobby got murdered in 1968 (a crime subsequently blamed on Sirhan Sirhan)? Parker led the cover-up of Bobby's murder!

At any rate, a few loose ends still had to be tied-up, namely some weak links that could crack and expose the cover-up. In the days following Marilyn's closed funeral (arranged by Joe Dimaggio), Peter Lawford became incommunicado. Eunice Murray had her phone disconnected and disappeared. Pat Newcomb fled to the Kennedy compound, then vanished in Europe for six months. Finally, Dr. Greenson left L.A. for an extended period of time (disturbed by the knowledge that Marilyn's "suicide" was bogus).

Not everyone fell for the ruse. Doubters included: John Miner—present at autopsy; Dr. Thomas Noguchi—coroner; Bob Slatzer—friend; Milo Speriglio—investigator; Detective Jack Clemmons—LAPD; Frank Sinatra—actor; Robert Mitchum—actor; Jeanne Carmen—neighbor; Norman Mailer—author; Sidney Weinberg—chief medical examiner in Suffolk County, New York and noted forensic pathologist, who said that it's extremely rare for women to commit suicide in the nude.

In the media, Ezra Goodman, *Time* magazine's Hollywood reporter, wrote a story linking Marilyn Monroe to the Kennedys. Not only did *Time* refuse to publish it, they destroyed every known copy of the article. Other skeptical reporters included Florabel Muir, Walter Winchell and Dorthy Kilgallen, who gained a great deal of attention after the Kennedy assassination by interviewing Jack Ruby in prison. Declaring that she was hot on the trail of Kennedy's killers and possessed "explosive information," Kilgallen became a murder victim herself on Nov. 8, 1965. The manuscript she'd nearly completed vanished.

Finally, decades later, Geraldo Rivera, Sylvia Chase and Stanhope Gould had finished a blockbuster expose for *20/20* on the Monroe murder, linking it to the Kennedy family. However, the day it was scheduled to air (Oct. 3, 1985), ABC President Roone Arledge pulled the plug on it and refused to broadcast the damning information.

AUTOPSY

The "coroner to the stars," Dr. Thomas Noguchi, concluded that Marilyn had enough barbiturates in her bloodstream to kill three cows. Spin-doctors immediately disseminated a story that Marilyn had swallowed approximately 40-50 Nembutals, yet no—repeat, no—Nembutal capsules were found in her digestive system. Stated differently, no residue or dye from the capsules was discovered in her blood or stomach. In addition, no drinking glass was observed at the death scene, and Marilyn had a mortal fear of choking (making it improbable that she'd swallow four dozen capsules).

Noguchi's report unequivocally stated, "I found absolutely no visual evidence of pills in the stomach or small intestine. No residue. No retractile crystals." He then concluded that the fatal dose of barbiturates was not orally ingested. To support this claim, Noguchi requested kidney, urine and stomach samples from the coroner's office, yet all of them had disappeared. There was also no coroner's inquest or official investigation, while the autopsy reports had been reconstructed, changed, lost and/or altered.

Specifically, bruises appeared on Marilyn's body, yet no mention of this fact appeared in the official report.

The only man with enough power at the L.A. County Coroner's Office to change these autopsy reports was Dr. Theodore Curphey, who worked directly under Police Chief William Parker. A large percentage of Marilyn's personal possessions also vanished from the coroner's office, while one other factor suggested that foul play led to her death. All those who saw Marilyn's corpse described a bluish cast and darkened fingernails, both indicative of cyanosis, or an extremely rapid death. Since she didn't swallow approximately 50 Nembutal capsules, her abruptly fatal demise either resulted from a "hot shot" or fatal enema (or a combination of both).

One other variable from the coroner's office is truly sickening. In an interview with Robert Slatzer, Deputy Coroner's Aide Lionel Grandison dropped this bombshell. "I was told that a lot of viewings of the body by employees, police officials, insurance officials, high officials of our department that viewed the body, and some could very possibly have had sexual acts with the body."

Slatzer then asked, "There possibly was intercourse with Marilyn's body by many people at that particular time?"

Grandison replied, "Yes, there was." In addition, Milo Speriglio writes, "Grandison admitted having firsthand knowledge of certain members of the staff at the coroner's office who were necrophiliacs, who violated Marilyn's body before the autopsy was made." He also noted that quite a number of people in the coroner's office felt that Marilyn had been murdered, and Bobby Kennedy's name was most frequently mentioned.

MAFIA TIES

Now that we've followed this case from the Friday preceding Marilyn's murder to her botched autopsy, what events led to her tragic demise? By all accounts, Marilyn had met John Kennedy as early as 1951, but didn't intimately enter his circle until Frank Sinatra arranged a meeting.

Here's how the story unfolds. Sinatra and Chicago mob boss Sam Giancana were business partners and co-owners of the Cal-Neva Lodge in Lake Tahoe. Sinatra also befriended Sen. John Kennedy, and introduced him to Judith Campbell Exner at the Sands Hotel in Las Vegas. Exner also served another role as Sam Giancana's girlfriend.

So, Exner began an affair with JFK, thereby acting as a liaison between him and Giancana. Then, prior to cementing the Democratic nomination for the 1960 presidential election, JFK and his brother Teddy met with Sinatra and Giancana in Vegas on Feb. 7 to seek their assistance in this matter. A follow-up meeting was arranged by Exner at the Fountainbleu Hotel in Miami to plan how the Mafia could assist Kennedy in defeating Richard Nixon.

The execution of this election-tampering scam required some muscle, so enter Old Man Joe Kennedy, who made his fortune as a bootlegger. Kennedy and Chicago Mayor Richard Daley were also longtime associates, so Daley and Giancana conspired to rig the Chicago polls to ensure a Kennedy victory. Afterward, Giancana reminded Judith Exner, "Listen, honey, if it weren't for me, your boyfriend wouldn't be in the White House."

The Mob, of course, had a vested interest in the Kennedys (or any president, for that matter) because of their lucrative gambling-prostitution-smuggling operations in Cuba. Therefore, Sinatra saw a grand opportunity. Already friends with both John Kennedy and Hollywood star Marilyn Monroe, why not bring these two together? Plus, Marilyn had already dated Giancana lieutenant and big-time mobster Johnny Roselli. Hence, Peter Lawford, Marilyn, and Kennedy were brought together at the Cal-Neva casino, whereupon one thing led to another.

By this stage, we have Joe Kennedy Sr.'s massive Mob ties, while Giancana moll Judith Exner visited the White House nearly two dozen times, spending several weekends there when Jackie was traveling. White House logs also reveal that she phoned the president more than 70 times between 1961 and 1962. A decade later, the Church Committee disclosed that Bobby Kennedy kept a host of underworld characters on his payroll, while he and Jack—along with the CIA—plotted with Giancana and other mobsters to assassinate Cuba's Fidel Castro.

All was rolling along relatively smoothly between JFK and Marilyn, the couple flitting away to playful trysts at Cabo San Lucas, Palm Springs and the Carlyle Hotel. To skirt the press, Marilyn often donned disguises to appear as a random journalist (complete with wigs and horn-rim glasses). Then, all hell broke loose with Marilyn's notorious May 19, 1962 appearance at JFK's Madison Square Garden birthday gala, where she sang the sexiest rendition of *Happy Birthday to You* imaginable. Luxurious (and drunk) in her skin-tight gown, the event caused serious trouble in the White House between Jack and Jackie.

Mrs. Kennedy also came unglued over the many phone calls Marilyn placed to the White House, and their none-too-discreet affair that became common gossip in Hollywood. After the Madison Square Garden fiasco, Jackie threatened to leave her husband and file for divorce. Certain that such a move would sink his presidency, Joe Kennedy once again stepped in and reportedly paid off Jackie with the sum of $1 million if she stayed.

One other factor then entered the equation. Five days after Marilyn sang *Happy Birthday* to him, J. Edgar Hoover met with Kennedy and laid out how Marilyn had also been dating left-leaning screenwriter Jose Bolanos. She'd likewise been in the company of a possible Communist espionage agent named Frederick Vanderbilt Field. Considering Marilyn's loose lips, Hoover stressed that by continuing his affair with her, the president had become a national security danger.

Dramatic changes were immediately made at that juncture, and Marilyn's tryst with JFK after the Madison Square party would prove to be the last time she ever saw him. To prevent any contact, Oval Office switchboard operators were instructed to deny all calls from Marilyn, while her private line to the president was also disconnected.

Furious at being discarded so callously, Marilyn didn't quietly accept the Kennedy verdict. To calm this firestorm, the Kennedy brothers initially sent Peter Lawford to do their dirty work. "Listen, Marilyn," he told the distressed actress, "you're just another one of Jack's [mistresses]." When that tactic didn't work, the president sent Bobby to lay down the gauntlet. There was only one problem—he began an affair with her.

After months of philandering, Bobby and Jack were now both vulnerable to Marilyn. Realizing how easily they could be exploited, the Kennedys tried to leverage Marilyn via backdoor methods. Since Fox Studios bought the options to Bobby's book, *The Enemy Within*, he used his sway with Judge Samuel Rosenman to put the squeeze on Marilyn and force her out of the studio. Rosenman also enjoyed a tight relationship with industrialist Averill Harriman, and along with others in control at Fox—Milton Gould and John Loeb—they could now cut off Marilyn's sole source of income—her acting career.

With a powder keg primed to explode, a meeting orchestrated by Frank Sinatra was arranged at the Sinatra-Giancana owned Cal-Neva Lodge in Lake Tahoe on July 28. There, Giancana played the heavy with Marilyn and threateningly told her not to entertain the press with any lascivious stories about the Mafia, CIA or their relationship with the Kennedys. Some may wonder why Giancana would intervene for the Kennedys, especially since Attorney General Bobby had a vendetta against the Mob. The answer is simple. Despite being at loggerheads with each other, if one of these entities fell in a highly publicized scandal—particularly in their attempts to assassinate Fidel Castro—all of them would fall.

To convince Marilyn, these men resorted to techniques so underhanded that it forever scarred the already fragile actress. According to Donald Wolfe in *The Last Days of Marilyn Monroe*, after drugging the movie star, Marilyn was desecrated beyond comprehension. "When Sinatra returned from Cal-Neva, he brought [Billy] Woodfield a roll of film to be developed. In his darkroom, the photographer was shocked to see that the photos were of an unconscious Marilyn Monroe being sexually abused in the presence of Giancana and Sinatra. Marilyn had been drugged in order for the compromising photos to be taken."

These rape pictures were then used to compromise and ensure her silence. Thinking they'd finally solved their problem, on July 30 Peter Lawford placed an 18-minute call to the White House, telling them that Marilyn would no longer be an issue. Of course, Marilyn didn't succumb to the blackmail, and in a sort of poetic justice, a few of the mobsters got their comeuppance. Right before Giancana was to testify before the Church Committee, somebody murdered him inside his Oak Hill, Illinois home on June 19, 1975. The following year, Johnny Roselli's dead body floated ashore near Miami's Biscayne Bay on Aug. 9, 1976.

DEPOSING THE LEECHES

Convinced that her life had become a shambles, Marilyn engaged in a complete reevaluation of what she'd become. Only a week prior to the rape scene at Cal-Neva, on July 21, she aborted her baby in Mexico City. Uncertain whether it was Bobby's, Jack's or someone else's, Marilyn vowed to rid herself of the toxic elements that sought to destroy her.

Not only did she intend to dump Pat Newcomb and her housekeeper Eunice Murray (whom she considered a spy), Marilyn also wanted to cut the Strasberg family from her will. More importantly, however, she felt compelled to free herself of Dr. Greenson's dramatic influence. Matthew Smith contends that the psychiatrist "became her shadow."

In this role, he took on the duties of a Svengali-style spokesman-manager by negotiating with studios and guaranteeing that she'd show up on time. He also told her what friends she should have, where to live, what movies to make and who to date. Greenson also acted as Frank Sinatra's psychiatrist, and urged Marilyn to hire Eunice Murray as her housekeeper and brother-in-law Mickey Rudin as her attorney.

Visited daily by this doctor who some said tried to mind control her, Marilyn finally (to her credit) attempted to break free. She perceived quite clearly that Greenson and Dr. Engelberg were both associated with the Communist Party, while Murray's husband was a union activist. Not only that, it seemed as if nearly everyone in her inner circle was Jewish: Mickey Rudin—attorney; Dr. Greenson—psychiatrist; Eu-

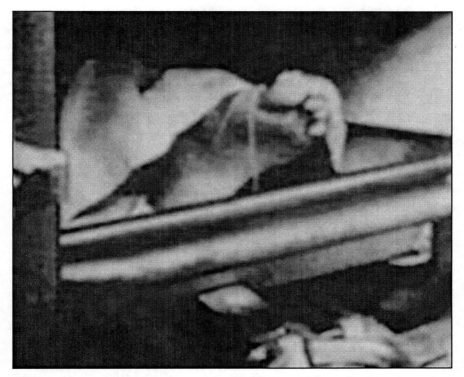

Marilyn Monroe in the morgue: an ignominious end for a charismatic starlet.

nice Murray—housekeeper; Lee Strasberg—acting coach; Hyman Engelberg—doctor; Arthur Jacobs—public relations agent; Arthur Miller —recently divorced husband; Roseman, Gould, and Loeb—Fox Studio owners; and Sam Giancana—Italian Chicago mobster under the thumb of Jewish boss Hyman Larner, who answered to Jewish kingpin Meyer Lansky

Armed with these new convictions, Marilyn determinedly set her sights on eradicating the leeches and vultures from her life. For possibly the first time ever, she now appeared capable of taking control and moving in a positive direction. Matthew Smith, who devoted many pages to Marilyn's home-recorded tapes, provides an overview of where she was heading in the future. "The tapes reveal a Marilyn who is in command of herself and has made positive changes of direction."

Regrettably, this transformation came a little too late.

CHAPTER 2

MYSTERY MAN

WHO IS THE MYSTERY MAN BEHIND *EVIDENCE OF REVISION?*

Since its release in 2006, *Evidence of Revision* has become recognized as the definitive video account of the JFK assassination. Weighing in at over eight hours on five discs, this epic documentary covers not only the events in Dallas on Nov. 22, 1963, but also the Robert Kennedy slaying, the Jonestown mass suicide/massacre, and the horrors of governmental MK-ULTRA mind-control programs. A subsequent production (*Evidence of Revision 6*) examines serious inconsistencies in the Martin Luther King Jr. murder.

Still, despite widespread acclaim, viewers in conspiracy circles, on message boards, and aficionados of this subject, keep asking: Who made *Evidence of Revision?* The boxed-set case gives absolutely no clue as to the producer, nor does any of the footage. Rather, the end credits simply list "Etymon Productions," while elsewhere the audience is informed, "history may be revised even as it is being written."

This mystery compelled me to begin a search one day in June 2006 when a white box arrived in my post office box. Inside was a generic

DVD case with no label, markings or documentation. I was about to discard the packaging when a tiny sliver of paper fell out containing an e-mail address (with no name). A week or so later I watched *Evidence of Revision* and, after being overwhelmed by the material, I decided to contact this enigmatic individual.

ANONYMITY

Shortly thereafter, we began corresponding, and the tale that unfolded was as compelling as his documentary. Going by the pseudonym "Terrence Raymond," I soon discovered that this man in his mid-50s was living in San Diego (he has since moved), and due to a rapidly deteriorating physical condition, expected to die in the very near future. Worse, because of a catastrophic financial situation, he also feared impending homelessness.

With the few remaining dollars left in his possession, Raymond mailed *Evidence of Revision* to 40 different people who ran conspiracy websites, did radio shows or were scholars of the Kennedy assassination. Although he has yet to accept a dime for his efforts, he hoped somebody would notice his work. Little did Raymond know his documentary would become an underground classic. Soon history buffs and those who debunked the enduring cover-up began passing it around like a virus.

To date, Raymond's only interview on this subject took place on WING TV (July 13, 2006). Considering how little publicity has surrounded *Evidence of Revision*, it exploded on the Internet. The sense of intrigue associated with this movie could be part of its cult appeal. When asked why he wanted to remain anonymous, Raymond answered cryptically, "no comment." However, he did add with a chuckle that one online forum speculated that he belonged to some sort of radical political group operating out of the Caribbean.

Beyond his hidden identity, the other most pressing question asked by viewers is: Where did he get all this amazing footage? Raymond explains that in the mid-1970s, he served four years of elite military duty in the Naval Photographic Center in Washington, D.C., where he was employed by the National Archives White House Presidential Motion

Picture Crew. As such, Raymond worked for JFK and Lyndon Johnson's personal location sound recordists.

As President Richard Nixon "crashed and burned" and was forced to resign under the cloud of Watergate, Raymond began his work once Gerald Ford assumed office. He soon received secret clearance status, and was used on classified film projects for the Pentagon, White House and possibly other intelligence agencies. After being transferred to a reconnaissance squadron in the Florida Keys, he was assigned TAD ("Temporary Assigned Duty") as a petty officer to a supply facility that was most likely operated by the CIA.

Being in such close proximity to agency spooks, political scandals and media manipulators, Raymond witnessed firsthand a world that increasingly resembled George Orwell's *1984*, complete with double-think, perpetual war, Newspeak propaganda, behavior modification, genetic control and the alteration of history.

ROBERT KENNEDY AND MK-ULTRA

The technique of using "manufactured consent" to sway public opinion struck a chord with Raymond, harking him back to his youth. Being old enough to recall the Kennedy assassination, he remembers listening to the radio late one evening as a teenager when Robert F. Kennedy was murdered at the Ambassador Hotel. During this broadcast, it was reported that certain people laughed, celebrated and admitted responsibility for the killing. But then, just as quickly, these news items vanished from the media landscape, never to be heard again. Similar to Lee Harvey Oswald, Sirhan Sirhan became the latest lone-nut gunman.

This particular event had a profound impact on the teen because, as a child growing up in Whittier, California, Raymond's mother attended Bible study classes with Richard Nixon's sister in the Nixon household. There, the participants spoke in tongues and eventually lapsed into trances. She also described how the Nixon family kept a "Wailing Wall" inside their home where they cried, prayed and flailed. As a result of these bizarre episodes, Raymond's mother suffered a nervous breakdown, and was placed in a Pasadena hospital where the repeated use of electroshock treatments and sodium pentothal completely erased her memory. These procedures occurred in the mid-1950s at a time when MK-ULTRA experiments were being performed on private citizens without their consent. A decade later, it's likely that Sirhan Sirhan underwent his MK-ULTRA conversion at this same facility. To date, Raymond isn't sure if his mother was definitively targeted, or simply a random subject for these demented doctors.

However, one given remains. After learning that his mother's nervous breakdown was attributable to her bizarre religious experiences at the Nixon household, Raymond's dislike for Nixon and his policies grew into utter disgust. He even remembers being an eight-year-old boy campaigning against Nixon in his grade school classroom during the 1960 election. A decade later, Raymond would be working across the Potomac from the White House as Nixon resigned during the Watergate scandal.

UNDERGROUND SOURCES

Prior to enlisting in the service, Raymond already sensed something was awry in the world. While still in high school, he spent countless hours in the library researching JFK's assassination, especially books by Mark Lane (*Rush to Judgment*), Jim Garrison and several French authors. With his interest piqued by what lurked in the shadows, he began an investigative odyssey that spanned the remainder of his life.

Capitalizing on his experience at the Naval Photographic Center, Raymond embarked upon an obsessive quest to accumulate rare and hard-to-find video footage. To compile a library containing over 3,000 hours of material, Raymond amassed his collection from swap meets, obscure mail order sources, video store used rentals, TV newscasts, documentaries, special underground catalogs and conspiracy bookstores. There were also other like-minded collectors. Raymond also discovered that if you "knew people," it was easier to get material from under-the-counter that wasn't available to the public.

Thirty years later, at death's doorstep, Raymond came to a realization. If he didn't put *Evidence of Revision* together, there existed a high likelihood that this extremely rare material would be flushed down the "memory Hole" for the rest of eternity. "After all," he asked me one day, "how much of the information in this documentary has ever been seen by the American public?" A good deal of the news reportage wasn't officially released by CBS, NBC or ABC. Other clips were only televised once (oftentimes on local stations), then buried.

When it came to documentary products already on the market, much was out of print, didn't contain the information he was seeking, or the price was exorbitant. Raymond recalls one occasion when a CBS employee made it known that he could steal 66 hours of extremely rare footage from network archives. But there was a catch. The man wanted $2,000 per hour to cover the risk involved in misappropriating these tapes. Regrettably, the canisters still remain concealed from public view.

There were other challenges confronting Raymond when beginning this project. He possessed over 200 hours of JFK footage alone, thus compelling him to undergo the laborious process of filtering through this mountain of data. Originally, he intended to make *Evidence of Revision* a 30-hour opus that explained much more than just the John F. Kennedy assassination.

But it soon became clear that such a grand undertaking was unrealistic. Instead, over the course of two years, he pared *Evidence of Revision* down to its current length of approximately eight hours.

MARKED MAN

As one begins watching this documentary, one quickly surmises that the Kennedy assassination was, in essence, inevitable. For starters, the president made a very daring and decisive threat to shatter the CIA into a thousand pieces and scatter it to the wind.

Following the Bay of Pigs fiasco, he fired CIA Director Allen Dulles for drafting Operation Northwoods, a clandestine project which eerily resembled the terrorist attacks which occurred almost exactly 40 years and six months later on Sept. 11, 2001.

For his role in the Bay of Pigs disaster, he also terminated General Charles Cabell, who subsequently never forgave him. A bit too coincidentally, Cabell's brother Earl was the mayor of Dallas, and it was he who helped coordinate the fateful trip to the city in November 1963.

Kennedy also enraged the U.S. military-industrial complex by stressing that the CIA would no longer be in charge of Vietnam—now he would be calling the shots.

At one point, *Evidence of Revision* references an amazing, little-known article written by *New York Times* columnist Arthur Krock that appeared on Oct. 3, 1963. In it, Krock cites how JFK had declared war on the CIA, comparing its growth to a "malignancy." He added that if there ever were a coup against the U.S. government, it would originate with the CIA.

Raymond saw Kennedy as a true "radical" who dramatically wanted to change the course of this country. In his WING TV interview, he asserts that Kennedy was being overtly threatened by the men who eventually killed him, including the CIA, the Mob and core members of the war machine that wanted to perpetuate Vietnam and the Cold War. Prior to visiting Dallas, there were also plausible threats made against the president's life in Chicago and Miami. As Raymond states, "Kennedy was actually trying to do what was right, but we've seen what happens to leaders throughout history who are idealists. Those who are ethical and moral are at a disadvantage because most others don't play by these same rules."

THE UNDESIRABILITY OF PEACE

Beginning with Dwight Eisenhower's 1961 farewell address warning Americans of the military-industrial complex and a "permanent war economy," John Kennedy harbored serious reservations about the Cold War, Vietnam and the continuing Cuban embargo. Whereas J. Edgar Hoover called the Soviet Union an "infectious disease," Kennedy said that he was "anxious to live in harmony with the Russian people." After all, he reasoned, no nation suffered more during WWII than Russia, with 20 million casualties.

In regard to Vietnam, *Evidence of Revision* shows how in October 1963—one month before his murder—President Kennedy signed National Security Memorandum 263, legislation that would effectively pull our country out of Vietnam and bring troops home by 1965. Tragically, four days after his assassination, LBJ signed National Security Action Memorandum 273, which sent *more* troops to Vietnam, beginning a 10-year national catastrophe in Southeast Asia.

Johnson used a manufactured event—the supposed Gulf of Tonkin attack on American ships performing covert operations—to escalate America's involvement even further. But no torpedoes were fired at our ships, and similar to other false flag terrorist events, it was used as justification to intensify our military involvement in the region.

DANGEROUS 'COUNTRY BUMPKIN'

Evidence of Revision vividly paints a portrait of Lyndon Johnson's integral role in the Kennedy assassination. To truly understand this man, the viewer gets a behind-the-scenes peek at how much the vice president despised the Kennedy brothers. Mocked by Jack and Bobby as a buffoon and laughingstock, Johnson developed an inferiority complex that bubbled into seething hatred.

To enact what he saw as justifiable comeuppance, Johnson first instructed the Dallas Police chief to control matters before and after the Nov. 22 shooting.

He then contacted fellow crony and Texas Governor John Connolly to establish the parade route and security details. Johnson also had the power to work in unison with the CIA and J. Edgar Hoover in Dallas, all of whom had a vested interest in seeing the president dead. As a result, Kennedy's limousine came to a virtual stop only moments before gunmen opened fire on him.

Afterward, Johnson made a hurried array of phone calls from Washington to Dallas, telling the district attorney not to look beyond Lee Harvey Oswald as the lone nut killer. LBJ also told chief surgeon Charles Crenshaw that government officials were to be allowed in the operating room after Oswald was shot to take his "deathbed confession." LBJ even took charge of selecting Warren Commission members, including Allen Dulles and Bilderberg member Gerald Ford. Earl Warren later revealed that Johnson told him, "If the truth were told about the assassination, it would lead to WWIII."

One of the most poignant scenes in *Evidence of Revision* originates with Madeleine Brown, LBJ's long-time mistress. According to her,

Johnson, J. Edgar Hoover, Richard Nixon and billionaire H.L. Hunt all met at Clint Merchison's house the night before Kennedy was killed. Merchison deplored the president, and was arguably the most powerful man in Texas at the time. In addition, he ultimately wielded a great deal of influence over Johnson. The following morning, only hours prior to the shooting, the vice president bragged to his lover, "After today, the Kennedys will never embarrass me again." Later, Johnson confessed to Brown that it was Texas oil men and the CIA that killed Kennedy.

Another crucial episode that *Evidence of Revision* brilliantly portrays involves attorney Dan Reynolds, who, on the day of Kennedy's assassination, visited Capitol Hill to present evidence against LBJ regarding corruption, bribery, vote fraud and possibly even murder. Charging that Johnson misused his various political offices, Reynolds brought records, receipts, invoices and other documents to implicate the vice president. These charges were undoubtedly impeachable offenses, and the Kennedys would have most certainly dumped Johnson from the Democratic ticket in 1964. But once Kennedy was shot and LBJ took the oath of office, the entire matter was quickly shelved. Or, if we quote the ancient Latin saying: *Cui bono*—who benefits?

DEFIANT PATSY

Although commonly viewed as a convenient fall guy, *Evidence of Revision* presents compelling film footage taken directly from the 6th floor of the Texas School Book Depository where Lee Harvey Oswald purportedly fired the fatal shots on Nov. 22, 1963. There, shortly after the shooting, investigators found three spent shell cartridges on a window ledge sitting neatly in a row, one-inch apart from each other. The obvious question is: what are the chances that someone would frantically fire three shots, make a hasty getaway, and all three cartridges ejected from his gun would land upright in a line in the exact same place, equidistant apart?

Maybe this ammunition came from the same arsenal that allowed Arlen Specter to form his preposterous "Magic Bullet" theory.

The documentary also presents news clips from dozens of newscasters saying that the weapon used to kill Kennedy was a 7.65 caliber German Mauser rifle that was *found at the scene*. Then, when the cartridges didn't match this particular rifle, broadcasters quickly changed their story—without explanation—saying it was a 6.5 caliber Italian Mannlicher-Carcano mail order rifle. This Orwellian sleight-of-hand is priceless.

Also detailed is direct evidence taken from government documents showing Lee Harvey Oswald's intimate involvement in highly sensitive operations for the CIA and FBI. One example is his agency payroll number, while another clip explains how CIA representative David Atlee Phillips met with Oswald two months before the assassination. The FBI also interrogated Oswald in Dallas only two weeks prior to Kennedy's visit.

Even more incredible are Oswald's actions following the Kennedy murder. First, Don Hewitt, famed *60 Minutes* producer, discusses how Oswald, after leaving his place of employment once Kennedy was shot, actually walked toward Jack Ruby's apartment. Then, sheriff deputy Roger Craig testified that he saw Oswald get into a grey Rambler after a man whistled to him.

Following his arrest, *Evidence of Revision*'s footage presents a frozen moment in time as Lee Harvey Oswald's words are heard firsthand.

Upon being arrested and fully aware that he was a patsy, Oswald declared matter-of-factly (rather than boastfully): "Everybody will know who I am now." Next, sporting a black eye due to his treatment by the Dallas police department, Oswald addressed the cameras, intent on refuting the accusations made against him.

"I didn't shoot anybody, and I have no legal representation," he began. After telling reporters that a "policeman hit me," he continued to answer questions. "Nobody told me what I'm accused of. . . . I've not been charged with killing the President. . . . I emphatically deny these charges. . . . I'm a patsy. . . . I would like certain fundamental rights, like taking a shower."

Finally, only one hour before being scheduled to give a live press conference, Lee Harvey Oswald was dead by club owner Jack Ruby on nationwide television.

SEEDS OF A COVER-UP

To silence their loose cannon fall guy, mobster and Meyer Lansky associate Jack Ruby (born Rubinstein) was selected to fire the fatal shots. *Evidence of Revision* goes one step further, however, by validating that a prior relationship existed between Oswald and Ruby. A number of Ruby's amazing confessions are also included, where he proclaims, "The world will never know the true facts of what happened. . . . It was a complete conspiracy. . . . I'm the only person in the background who knows the whole truth of my circumstances."

Furthermore, Ruby confided that LBJ was behind the Kennedy assassination, while a number of credible witnesses recalled seeing Oswald at Ruby's bar, the Carousel Club. Finally, *Evidence of Revision* asserts that Ruby served as an informant for none other than Richard Nixon in 1947.

In charge of concealing these details from the American public was FBI Director J. Edgar Hoover, who had been compromised for decades because of certain practices that didn't reflect his carefully crafted public image. On the one hand, Hoover indulged his rampant gambling addiction at Clint Merchison's race track, which brought him into contact with organized crime figures such as Lansky, Carlos Marcello, and Santos Trafficante. The ramifications of associating with these notorious underworld figures crippled law enforcement's ability to battle the Syndicate for generations because Hoover wouldn't even admit that the Mafia existed.

An even more damning factor revolved around Hoover's homosexuality and some *in flagrante delicto* snapshots of him performing sex acts with his lover, fellow FBI-man Clyde Tolson. Mob boss Lansky obtained these embarrassing photos, as did CIA counterintelligence chief James Jesus Angleton and Carlos Marcello. Needless to say, Lansky blackmailed Hoover with this devastating information, bragging that he enjoyed "virtual immunity from the FBI." The Mafia's control of Hoover was so powerful that the FBI never even formed an organized crime division.

In addition, Hoover's relationship with the vice president was so close that LBJ called him his "brother and personal friend." This bond grew even stronger due to their mutual hatred of the Kennedy brothers. *Evidence of Revision* clearly illustrates how Hoover's voluminous files detailing John Kennedy's adulterous affairs (Marilyn Monroe, Judith Campbell Exner etc.) was used to blackmail him into selecting LBJ as his runningmate in 1960. If Jack and Bobby didn't bow to his wishes, Hoover threatened to blow the scandal sky high. Following the Kennedy assassination, LBJ put the FBI director in charge of the cover-up. Under this arrangement, all evidence from Dallas was turned over to Hoover, who subsequently attempted to bury anything of relevance.

Rounding out this sordid cast of characters was Richard Nixon, one of the first prominent war hawks following WWII. As Ike's vice presidential selection in 1952, Nixon promoted the "Domino Theory," thus facilitating U.S. military invasions across the globe. Nixon was also one of the first to seek American intervention in Vietnam, at one point even considering the use of tactical nuclear weapons.

In the end, John Kennedy defeated Nixon in the 1960 presidential election, while Kennedy's murder allowed Lyndon Johnson to become commander-in-chief. Then, when LBJ bowed out in 1968 due to an emotional breakdown, Bobby Kennedy became the odds on favorite to win the election. But, when he was slain in L.A., it opened the door for Nixon to stroll into the Oval Office.

Terrence Raymond created *Evidence of Revision* in large part as a reaction to the Kennedy murders. Plus, considering his mother's tragic connection to the Nixon family and MK-ULTRA, it seems ironic that Raymond was employed in Washington, D.C., only a stone's throw away from the White House when Richard Nixon suffered his unceremonious fall during the Watergate crisis. On top of that, many of the Watergate "Plumbers" and planners were members of the exact same cabal that assassinated John Kennedy 10 years earlier. *Evidence of Revision* was born out of this high strangeness, along with the serendipitous links that brought these individuals together to form a tragic conspiracy which still resonates today.

CHAPTER 3

MARY PINCHOT MEYER

MARY PINCHOT MEYER: THE ACID MISTRESS & JFK'S SHADOWY AFFAIR IN CAMELOT

When the *Washington Post* reported on a murdered George-town socialite in October 1964, they deliberately chose not to include the most important details. Mary Pinchot Meyer had been President John F. Kennedy's last great flame. They had done LSD—obtained from 1960s counterculture guru Timothy Leary—in the White House, while previous to this affair she had been married to CIA operative Cord Meyer. The slain woman knew things she wasn't supposed to know, especially about those in D.C.'s elite media, political and intelligence circles. Leary's associate Van Wolfe summarized her death as such. "It's got to be one of the biggest cover-ups in Washington history."

A PRIVILEGED BEGINNING

She was born into one of Pennsylvania's most prominent political families and, at least initially, Mary Pinchot followed in their footsteps.

After attending Vassar, where she became close friends with CIA super-spook James Angleton's future wife, the rising young star began writing for *United Press* and *Mademoiselle*. But with a mindset geared more toward Greenwich Village than Wall Street, she eventually pursued a course that was decidedly more unconventional and non-conformist.

CIA INDOCTRINATION

In 1945, Ms. Pinchot married Cord Meyer, who proved to be one of the most intriguing intelligence figures in American history. At the time, Meyer held memberships in the United World Federalists group and the American Veterans Committee (which was founded by the CIA). In 1947, he met his nemesis Timothy Leary at the AVC, whereupon he began an anti-communist purge of the organization.

By the early 1950s, CIA Director Allen Dulles recruited Meyer into the Company, and over the next two decades, he went from being chief of the International Organizations Division (IOD) that infiltrated leftist groups, to one of the primary masterminds behind Operation CHAOS. A number of different researchers claim Cord Meyer served as Bill Clinton's handler in London during his fledgling years as a CIA asset.

Meyer filled other agency roles, including assistant deputy director of plans (known as the "dirty tricks department"), and was one of the principle operatives for Project Mockingbird, where CIA stories were planted in various media outlets. With millions of black budget dollars at his disposal, some speculate he may have been one of the Watergate "deep throats." Even more interesting, Mary Pinchot Meyer could have also done journalistic assignments for the CIA during the 1950s.

CORD MEYER ON WORLD GOVERNMENT

"Our real choice is not whether we are going to get world government; we are going to get it in a very few years. It is fundamentally the question of world government by consent and empire or world government by voluntary and national consent" (*A Very Private Woman*, Nina Burleigh).

AN INCESTUOUS MEDIA

Mary Pinchot's connection to the media is important because her sister, Toni, was married to Ben Bradlee, executive editor of *The Washington Post*. Prior to this assignment, Bradlee worked for the United States Information Exchange (USIE) in Paris from 1952-53. He was also close friends with Allen Dulles, plus the *Washington Post's* Phil Graham, husband of Katharine Graham.

The USIE disseminated propaganda for the CIA and Frank Wisner's Project Mockingbird, and while Bradlee resided in Europe, he planted stories for Dulles and company. For decades, the *Post* has acted as a hand-puppet for the Bilderberg-CIA cabal, and since Bradlee and Toni Pinchot often dined alone with Jack and Jackie Kennedy at the White House, their media-political worlds bordered on being incestuous. A prime example of this arrangement can be found in Watergate. Ben Bradlee held a long-standing grudge against Richard Nixon, and since the CIA used his newspaper to deflect attention away from their role in the break-in, a convenient "buffer" prevented American citizens from discovering the truth about this landmark event.

CLANDESTINE GENIUS

Quite possibly the most important figure in this menagerie of interconnected characters was the CIA's counterintelligence chief and FBI liaison James Jesus Angleton. Not only were he and his wife, Cicely, close friends with Mary Pinchot, but Angleton's staunchest supporter was Cord Meyer. Angleton's role as the "spook's spook" was so prevalent that most of the information on John F. Kennedy in J. Edgar Hoover's files was derived from him. During the latter part of his life, Angleton admitted to Joan Bross (whose husband was an important CIA member) that he bugged Pinchot's bedroom and telephones. As a result, much of his data concerning Timothy Leary came either directly or clandestinely from Mary Pinchot Meyer.

Angleton's shadowy past extended back to his days in the OSS when stationed in Sicily during WWII. There, he recruited Mafia members for the Allies, thus forging long-standing ties to La Cosa Nostra. After cementing relationships with Corsican drug traffickers, he also used them for other counterintelligence operations. Doug Valentine, author of *The Phoenix Program*, has gone on record as saying, "Angleton ran the CIA's narcotics operations in league with the Federal Bureau of Narcotics until 1971." Equally as important, Michael Collins Piper points out in *Final Judgment* that Angleton served as the primary channel between U.S. and Israeli intelligence, thus creating even deeper ties with organized crime members such as Meyer Lansky.

AFFAIR IN CAMELOT

By 1959, after a series of affairs and personal tragedies, Mary Pinchot Meyer and Cord Meyer divorced. To support her lifestyle as an experimental artist, Pinchot inherited a significant amount of family money after her divorce. Now freer than she'd been in ages, Pinchot entered the most dramatic phase of her life by beginning an affair with the president of the United States.

Pinchot first met John Kennedy during her college days. Then she and Cord became their Georgetown neighbors in the mid-1950s. Her affair—which endured from January 1962 to November 1963—has subsequently been verified by Secret Service agents, who charted more than 40 visits to the White House.

Further, on Feb. 23, 1976 close friend and journalist James Truitt divulged the entire story to *The National Enquirer*. Interestingly, after this story's publication, Truitt's widow revealed that her deceased husband's papers—which chronicled 30 years of government-related secrets—were stolen. She stated that James Angleton had expressed a great desire to obtain them.

Those close to Kennedy and Pinchot said their relationship extended beyond being merely sexual. In *The Georgetown Ladies' Social Club*, C. David Heymann wrote that Pinchot not only sat in on Oval Office meetings with the President and his aides, but also spent the night with Kennedy when Marilyn Monroe committed "suicide." Kennedy even made a trip with his lover to the Pinchot family mansion in 1963.

TURN ON, TUNE IN, DROP OUT

Pinchot's affair with Kennedy involved more than mere adulterous romps. In his autobiography, *Flashbacks*, 1960s countercultural icon Timothy Leary describes how he was sought out by Ms. Meyer. "There was something calculated about Mary, that tough hit you get from people who live in the hard political world. She seemed like the ultimate insider."

What would a Georgetown socialite want from a man who would become the nation's most renowned psychedelic guru? The answer: drugs. During their meetings at Harvard, where they also began an affair, Pinchot told Leary that the CIA had a great interest in LSD for brainwashing and interrogation purposes.

In *Flashbacks*, Leary recounts Pinchot's words. "You don't really understand what's happening in Washington with drugs, do you? The guys who run things—I mean the guys who *really* run things—are very interested in psychology, and drugs in particular. They want to use drugs for warfare, for espionage, for brainwashing, for control." She also described the government's vast COINTELPRO operations that were used to infiltrate various organizations that posed a threat to their power base.

There was more. Pinchot explained how she wanted to run an "LSD session" and learn how to "brainwash" in order to trip with a "very powerful politician" in Washington who would remain nameless. According to Pinchot, she and approximately seven other Georgetown women were plotting to "turn on" the world's political and military leaders with LSD to make them less violent and more peaceful. Since the Cold War was in full swing, this move could avert a global nuclear war.

Was this plan to feed mind-altering drugs to D.C.'s elite simply a cover story, or something imagined? Leary wasn't sure, and since he had cultivated plenty of CIA ties of his own, he eventually gave Pinchot some LSD (which was still legal at the time). Strangely enough, Leary also harbored an intense dislike for Pinchot's ex-husband, which extended back to when both were members of the American Veterans Committee. Meyer had tried to eradicate leftist student organizations, and was now, of course, an integral part of the CIA.

TRIPPING THE WHITE HOUSE FANTASTIC

Now in possession of Leary's LSD, Mary Pinchot continued her affair with President Kennedy. According to her diary, in July 1962 the couple smoked a couple of joints (marijuana cigaretts) in a White House bedroom, then took a mild LSD trip together before making love. JFK also told her that he had previously tried hashish and cocaine.

Due to their LSD use, along with Pinchot's grandiose scheme to make world leaders more benign, was JFK's worldview also being transformed? Is this why he wanted to withdraw troops from Vietnam, sign a nuclear test ban treaty, open communications with the Soviet Union and Fidel Castro, and effectively shift away from the Pax Americana policies of our military-industrial complex? Can a fitting example of Mary's influence be found in Kennedy's commencement address at American University, where his pacifist views were particularly pronounced?

JOHN F. KENNEDY COMMENCEMENT ADDRESS

"First examine our attitude towards peace itself. Too many of us think it is impossible. Too many think it is unreal. But that is a dangerous, defeatist belief. It leads to the conclusion that war is inevitable, that mankind is doomed, that we are gripped by forces we cannot control. We need not accept that view. Our problems are man-made, therefore, they can be solved by man. And man can be as big as he wants. No problem of human destiny is beyond human beings" (American University, June 10, 1963).

OUTED IN PHOENIX

Kennedy and Mary Pinchot managed to keep their affair relatively under wraps until January 1963 when *The Washington Post's* editor, Phil Graham, blew their cover during a drunken speech at the American Newspaper Editors Conference in Phoenix. Graham and his wife, Katharine, were an integral part of the Georgetown social scene where a large portion of Washington's journalists, CIA members, State Department employees, plus Harvard and Princeton alumni, resided. During the 1950s and '60s, these cliques were arguably the real moving force in our nation's capital. Privy to plenty of gossip, as well as being an uncontrollable drunkard, Graham revealed at the Associated Press dinner in 1963 that JFK's new favorite mistress was Mary Pinchot.

After being quickly removed from the podium, Graham was placed in a sanitarium until August 1963. Upon release, he promptly "committed suicide" at his Virginia ranch by blowing his brains out with a shotgun. However, in an article entitled "The High and the Mighty: JFK, Mary Pinchot Meyer, LSD and the CIA," G. J. Krupey tells how he "got a call from a woman who claims that she knew for a fact that it was murder."

TARGET: TEXAS

On Nov. 22, 1963 John F. Kennedy was assassinated in broad daylight as his limousine rolled through downtown Dallas. Countless books have been written about this tragic event, but we'll focus on only one individual—Cord Meyer—who was well aware of his ex-wife's affair with the president due to James Angleton's surveillance. There had also been long-standing animosity between these two men which extended back to the 1950s when Kennedy was a senator. While serving as a journalist, Meyer snubbed JFK and refused to give him an interview—a move that Kennedy never forgot.

Kenn Thomas, editor of *Steamshovel Press*, said that Cord Meyer was definitely involved in the Kennedy assassination as a point man. He cites Howard St. John Hunt, son of E. Howard Hunt, who spoke on April 28, 2007 about his father's deathbed confession. "I think LBJ settled on Meyer as an opportunist (like himself), and a man who had very little left to him in life ever since JFK had taken Cord's wife as one of his mistresses."

MURDER IN GEORGETOWN

One month after the Kennedy assassination, investigative reporter Leo Damore asserts that James Angleton of the CIA had Mary Pinchot placed under 24-hour surveillance. Not only was her phone tapped, her house wired and her mail intercepted, but agents also broke into her residence on several occasions to search her notes and letters. Meanwhile, in a meeting with Timothy Leary, Pinchot frantically presented a possible motive for the Kennedy assassination. "They couldn't control him any more. He was changing too fast. They've covered everything up."

Because of her inside knowledge, Pinchot's name soon appeared in numerous classified government documents which have not been released to this date. Writing for *The New York Post*, Damore addressed the crux issue: "Meyer had access to the highest levels. She was involved in illegal drug activity. What do you think it would do to the beatification of Kennedy if this woman said, 'It wasn't Camelot; it was Caligula's court'?"

On Oct. 12, 1964, while strolling along Georgetown's C&O Canal towpath in the early afternoon (a place, coincidentally, where she used to walk with Jackie Kennedy), Mary Pinchot Meyer was shot at close range in the chest and left temple. Although the crime was pinned on a derelict black man named Raymond Crump, witnesses said the shooter didn't fit Crump's description.

In an interview for *Steamshovel Press*, Deborah Davis, author of a scathing biography on Katharine Graham, said, "It had all the earmarks of a professional assassination." Leo Damore agreed, saying a CIA associate told him that Pinchot's murder was a professional hit. Self-proclaimed CIA contract agent Robert Morrow contends Treasury Deputy Comptroller Marshall Diggs told him that Pinchot was killed because she "knew too much about the Company, the Cuban operations and the president's assassination."

Although police determined that Pinchot's death was related either to a robbery, assault or attempted rape, others knew differently.

Timothy Leary felt that Angleton was behind the hit, while Angleton—using more of his paranoid distraction techniques—told famed journalist Joe Alsop that "the 'real' killer was still at large and, in his opinion, all signs pointed to a Russian mole whose identity Meyer uncovered during visits to the White House." Publisher Myrna Firestone concluded that the CIA played a direct role in the slaying, whereas in a declassified, heavily redacted FBI memo uncovered by Nina Burleigh in *A Very Private Woman*, former CIA Director Richard Helms admitted the agency was involved in the murder. Also named was Angleton.

Finally, although he remained Angleton's most ardent supporter, Cord Meyer's personal assistant, Carol Delaney, said her boss knew that Raymond Crump didn't kill his ex-wife. But still a Company man, there was no possibility of blaming them for it. However, in February 2001—six weeks before his death—when asked who killed Mary Pinchot, Cord Meyer provided his deathbed confession from a D.C. nursing home. "The same sons of bitches that killed John F. Kennedy."

ANOTHER PATSY

When Raymond Crump was finally brought to trial, the Washington courtroom was filled with CIA and FBI agents. Although ultimately found innocent of this crime, Crump was the ideal Manchurian Candidate. Leo Damore provided a fitting overview. "He [Crump] was the perfect patsy, better even than Lee Harvey Oswald. Mary Meyer was killed by a well-trained professional hit man, very likely somebody connected to the CIA. After the assassination [of JFK], Meyer had become a very inconvenient woman, the former mistress of one of the world's most powerful political leaders and the ex-wife of a CIA honcho. The feeling of the agency was that here's somebody who knows too much for her own good. She knows the Warren Commission Report, released shortly before her death, is nothing but a grandiose cover-up. She knows about he Mafia, the Cubans, and the agency, and how any one of them could have conspired to eliminate Kennedy." Although it's not generally in vogue to mention, Mary Pinchot could have also been well aware of JFK's bitter dispute with Israeli Prime Minister David Ben-Gurion.

LITTLE BLACK BOOK

When news first broke that Mary Pinchot had been murdered, Anne Truitt, who was residing in Japan, made an urgent call to Mary's sister, Toni, in Washington. Anne was married to journalist Jim Truitt, who was best friends with Mary's sister. He also broke the story of Mary's affair with JFK to *The National Enquirer* in 1976. Truitt told Toni that Mary possessed a handwritten diary that contained revelations about her affair with Kennedy, and that they better find it before the authorities did. Immediately after placing this call, Anne Truitt also phoned Angleton.

Toni and her husband, Ben Bradlee, raced to Mary's house and upon arrival, found Angleton (nicknamed "the Locksmith") already inside. After frantically searching through the house and an adjacent structure on two different occasions (where they yet again found Angleton prowling around inside), Toni eventually discovered a 6 x 8, 50-page diary that made references to Mary's affair and LSD use with Kennedy in the White House. Ben Bradlee later corroborated this information. Mary Pinchot was indeed a dangerous woman.

Inconceivably, Toni turned the diary over to Angleton, who told them he burned it. But, being that he compiled information rather than destroy it, Angleton kept the diary, made copies, and locked it away in his safe. Years later, he returned it to Toni, but by that time, who knows how many members of the Kennedy clan—including Bobby, Teddy and Jackie—were blackmailed with this data.

GEORGETOWN SOCIAL CIRCLES

Prior to revealing the final piece of this puzzle, it's essential to review the interconnectedness of each character mentioned in this article. First, Mary Pinchot married the CIA's Cord Meyer, who had already developed a grudge against Timothy Leary. Pinchot later had an affair with Leary, and procured drugs from him. She also met JFK while in college, and was neighbors with him in Georgetown. Cord Meyer also held a decade-long resentment against Kennedy. As we now know, Mary Pinchot had an affair with Kennedy, and used psychedelic drugs with him. One of Pinchot's best friends in college was Cicely D'Autremont, who eventually married James Jesus Angleton. Cord Meyer became Angleton's closest ally in the CIA. Within these same circles, Mary's sister Toni married CIA operative Ben Bradlee of *Washington Post* fame. Bradlee later became employed by Phil Graham who, along with his wife Katharine, hosted soirees every weekend where Beltway insiders congregated to gossip, conspire, and eavesdrop. Graham, Kennedy, and Mary Pinchot were all dead within 14 months of each other.

A VAST CONSPIRACY?

When considering the ramifications of a president and his mistress using LSD in the White House, could there be an even darker element to this scenario? Is there any chance that Mary Pinchot was part of a CIA mind-control experiment, with JFK being an MK-ULTRA guinea pig? CIA Director Allen Dulles admitted in 1963 that the agency used sex as bait (i.e. honey pots) during the course of intelligence gathering. Subsequently, G.J. Krupey asked, "What other world leader could they try their theories out on while observing him in closely monitored, intimate situations?"

Consider: On April 13, 1953 the CIA launched MK-ULTRA, the most notorious mind-control program in our nation's history. At this time, Mary Pinchot was already married to operative Cord Meyer, and may have done CIA contract work herself. In the spring of 1962, she sought out Timothy Leary to obtain LSD. In July 1962 she and JFK "tripped on acid" together.

COINTELPRO

Mary Pinchot once told Timothy Leary, "the CIA creates the radical journals and student organizations and runs them with deep-cover agents. Dissident organizations in academia are also controlled." She went on to tell him that the CIA was aware of his LSD experiments, and was glad he was doing its research for them. In 1967, *Ramparts* magazine exposed the CIA's role in creating the National Student Association, which was overseen by Cord Meyer. This program eventually became Operation CHAOS in which anti-war groups were infiltrated. Bill and Hillary Clinton functioned as operatives under CHAOS.

The biggest variable at this point is: who was Timothy Leary? It's already been established that he'd met Cord Meyer in 1947 at the AMV. Some researchers, including Mark Riebling and G.J. Krupey, provide ample evidence that Leary was a CIA agent his entire career.

They point out that while teaching in Oakland from 1954 to 1959, Leary developed a personality test which was utilized by the CIA. His colleague on this project was Frank Barron, who began his association with the CIA in 1953. In 1960, Barron began funding the Harvard Psychedelic Drug Research Center, then recruited Leary from the West Coast. As Riebling shows, Leary admitted that the money for his LSD studies originated from "powerful people in Washington."

TIMOTHY LEARY ON ACID

"The entire LSD movement was sponsored originally by the CIA, to whom I give great credit. I would not be here today if it had not been for the foresight and prestige of the CIA psychologists. So give the CIA credit for being truly an intelligence agency" (*High Times*, February 1978).

One of the CIA's shadow organizations was the Society for Human Ecology, which funneled $25 million into the research of mind-altering drugs at Harvard and other universities. The chairman of the Department of Social Relations at Harvard was CIA agent Henry A. Murray. He served as Leary's mentor during the early 1960s, and likewise developed personality tests for the OSS and CIA.

Riebling further shows how, after he was forced to resign from Harvard, Leary came under the tutelage of William Mellon Hitchcock, who founded a CIA front group called the International Foundation for Internal Freedom. Hitchcock also allowed Leary to use his Millbrook mansion to perform LSD research. One of Leary's associates and acid advocates at this time was Al Hubbard, another figure linked to the CIA, while also an undercover agent for the government and defense industry.

Finally, as the 1960s drew to a close, Leary resided at the Brotherhood of Eternal Love headquarters, which was maintained by Ronald Stark. Similar to the others, Stark had been a CIA operative since 1960. Stark and the Brotherhood also financed many of Leary's travels during this period.

If, indeed, Leary was a CIA asset, and considering Mary Pinchot's marriage to CIA spook Cord Meyer, how should we view her affair with JFK? Did she act as a Mata Hari, a simple thrill-seeking hedonist or a dupe of the CIA? Likewise, was John F. Kennedy an unwitting test subject facilitated by Mary Pinchot? After all, following the Bay of Pigs catastrophe, didn't Kennedy express his hatred of the CIA and threaten to shatter them into a thousand pieces and scatter their remains to the wind? If Mary Pinchot acted as a conduit between Leary and Kennedy, was their use of LSD an attempt to discredit the president?

In his book *Brothers: The Hidden History of the Kennedy Years*, author David Talbot asserts, "the President's unconventional mistress was engaged in a mind control experiment aimed not at the Kremlin, but the White House."

Such practices weren't foreign to the CIA, especially with madmen like George Hunter White at the helm. He was in charge of Operation Midnight Climax where prostitutes dosed unsuspecting johns with LSD to see how they'd react, while he watched from behind a one-way mirror. Could Mary Pinchot and JFK simply be more prestigious subjects of Operation Midnight Climax, with the White House replacing a bordello?

GEORGE HUNTER WHITE ON HIS LSD USE

"I toiled wholeheartedly in the vineyards because it was fun, fun, fun. Where else could a red-blooded American boy lie, kill, cheat, steal, rape and pillage with the sanction and blessing of the All-Highest" (*Acid Dreams*, Martin Lee and Bruce Shlain)?

Mary Pinchot Meyer is a woman who remains cloaked in shadows. She was obviously connected, a quasi-insider who knew the secrets of Camelot. This forbidden knowledge is what got her killed one sunny afternoon in Georgetown, less than a year after JFK was slain in Dallas.

CHAPTER 4

MURDERING MALCOLM X

MURDERING MALCOLM X:
THE MOST DANGEROUS MAN IN AMERICA

O f all the books, articles and documentaries made on the life and murder of Malcolm X, none has pointed to a single pivotal event that may have cemented his execution on Feb. 21, 1965. Granted, Malcolm had been under the FBI's scrutiny since the early 1950s—even while still in prison. Then, after unceremoniously splitting with the Nation of Islam in early 1964, X became an internationalist critic of U.S. policy after a globetrotting pilgrimage to Mecca and beyond. Rallying support from many leaders of impoverished nations, X ultimately sought to bring the United States to trial in the UN for its systematic racism. Obviously, such a stance infuriated the State Department's Cold War cabal, especially since it originated from a former disciple of Elijah Muhammad.

But no researchers have included the significance of some explosive comments X made about Zionism to the *Egyptian Gazette* on Sept. 17, 1964. A short five months later, X's body would be riddled with bullets at Harlem's Audubon Ballroom. Its one thing to criticize Western imperialism, but once the focus is turned toward Israel, that's an entirely different mater.

Although X spoke extensively about this subject, I'll only include five of his remarks:

• "Israeli Zionists religiously believe their Jewish God has chosen them to replace the outdated European colonialism with a new form of colonialism."

• "This "divine" government would enable them to rule all other nations with a rod of iron."

• "Zionists have mastered the science of dollarism, the ability to come posing as a friend and benefactor, bearing gifts and all other forms of economic aid."

• "The number one weapon of 20th century imperialism is Zionist dollarism, and one of the main bases for this weapon is Zionist Israel. The ever-scheming European imperialists wisely placed Israel where she could geographically divide the Arab world. Zionist Israel's occupation of Arab Palestine has forced the Arab world to waste billions of precious dollars on armaments, making it impossible for the newly independent Arab nations to concentrate on strengthening their economies."

• "Did the Zionists have the legal or moral right to invade Arab Palestine, uproot its Arab citizens from their homes and seize all Arab property for themselves just based on the 'religious' claim that their forefathers lived there thousands of years ago?"

As the reader can tell, X's words ring as true nearly half a century later, a fact that surely infuriated Zionist leaders in 1964—a mere 17 years after their phony nation was formed. These modern-day Pharisees were willing to ignore his critiques of American racism or African poverty, but once Israel's antagonistically manipulative (and murderous) role in the Middle East entered the spotlight, the messenger had to be silenced.

NATION OF ISLAM

When speaking of racist Israel, we need to remember that Malcolm X began his public career as a slavish, naïve devotee of the very corrupt Elijah Muhammad. One of the Nation of Islam's primary credos was

Elijah Muhammad addresses followers including Cassius Clay/World Telegram & Sun photo by Stanley Wolfson.

the separatism of blacks from their "slave-owner masters." As such, Malcolm X became a willing hit man in escalating racial tensions between whites and blacks.

In a documentary entitled *El-Haji Malik Eishabazz*, Malcolm X is seen telling a crowd that the white man's closest relative is the dog because they have the same hair, skin and smell. He then informs his supporters that they shouldn't integrate with these "pale faces," and that their goal—opposite of what Martin Luther King preached—was *not* to integrate with whites.

In another speech, X addressed the subject of Abraham Lincoln, who he says "tricked the blacks into thinking they were free." But what he did instead was simply destroy their knowledge of black history.

Now, some may say that Malcolm X's diatribes against the whites changed after his pilgrimage to Mecca in 1964. But this sentiment isn't completely true, because on Feb. 4, 1965—only three weeks before being murdered—he gave a speech in Selma, Alabama where he joined Coretta Scott King. A few months earlier, he met with Martin Luther King—the one and only time—in Washington, D.C. on March 26, 1964. There existed quite a bit of speculation that these two black leaders—despite opposing philosophies—actually wanted to unite their supporters in a quest for equal rights.

But as we can determine from Malcolm X's speech on Feb. 4, 1965—with Coretta Scott King seated at his side—X still proposed a virulent combativeness toward the whites. He explained that there are two kinds of blacks:

> The house Negro, who ate, lived and dressed better than the other slaves. These porch Negroes loved their Massuh.
> The field Negro, who wanted to set the plantation on fire because he had nothing to lose. He prayed that the Massuh died.

Malcolm X concluded that he was one of the field niggers. Subsequently, if he joined forces with Martin Luther King, it would be J. Edgar Hoover's worst nightmare. Their agenda for civil rights had Malcolm rallying blacks up north, while King organized the south. If united as a whole, turbulent 1960s' America could have gone up in flames.

Even after his return from Mecca, Malcolm X's views on embracing the whites remained tepid at best: "I'm for brotherhood for everybody, but I don't believe in forcing brotherhood upon people who don't want it. Let us practice brotherhood among ourselves and then, if others want to practice brotherhood with us, we're for practicing it also. But I don't think we should run around trying to love somebody who doesn't love us."

Interestingly enough, in one of his lectures, researcher Dave Emory proposed that the Nation of Islam's leader, Elijah Muhammad, actually received large amounts of money from none other than Texas oil billionaire and unabashed racist H.L. Hunt. Of course, anyone familiar with the Kennedy assassination knows that Hunt clamored in the shadows of this pivotal event.

In *The Judas Factor*, Karl Evanzz opines that Hunt and Muhammad saw eye to eye on one important point—they both wanted a return of blacks to their native Africa. In this sense, these strange bedfellows are reminiscent of Zionists of the early 1940s working hand-in-hand with Nazis. Emory lays it out very clearly. "There is an historical parallel between the functioning of the Nation of Islam and a wing of the Zionist movement in the 1930s. . . . Prior to Hitler's so-called Final Solution to the Jewish question, the Nazis actively promoted Jewish emigration to Palestine and, in doing so, they found common cause with significant elements of the Zionist movement who actively collaborated with the SS intelligence service. . . . The head of Ahmt4B was Adolf Eichmann." Emory concludes by saying that Elijah Muhammad also cooperated with George Lincoln Rockwell of the American Nazi Party.

Linked by their mutual racism and black nationalist aims, X became Elijah Muhammad's No. 1 disciple upon his release from prison. Filled with passion and charisma, Malcolm X grew the Nation of Islam from 400 to over 10,000 members in the 1950s. During this campaign, X became the most famous black Muslim in America, and was viewed by the establishment as much more threatening than Martin Luther King because of his militancy and threat to the status quo. With heightened suspicions, establishment power brokers watched intently as X became the primary force that mobilized the Black Nationalist Islamic movement. The cornerstone of Elijah Muhammad's teachings was based on the words of W.D. Farad: "Whites are a race of wicked devils."

Terrified of the Nation of Islam's potential, the FBI decided that a wedge must be driven between Malcolm X and Muhammad, especially after an event which took place in Harlem. After the NYPD's men in blue beat a black man, Malcolm X led 2,600 of his disciples to the police station and demanded adequate medical care for the detained man. With tensions at a breaking point, the police eventually agreed to these demands. Then, with a simple wave of his hand, X dispersed this 2,600-strong mob. Upon seeing this display, a police inspector commented, "No man should have that much power."

Over time, animosities grew between Muhammad and X, especially since Nation of Islam leaders were embezzling money and Muhammad illegitimately fathered eight children out of wedlock by six different teenage girls who were his private personal secretaries. Incensed by this hypocrisy, Malcolm X could no longer turn a blind eye to the corruption of Muhammad's ethical cesspool. Due to the adultery, fornication, bastard children, and the way their parishioners were being ripped-off, X promised to do a thorough housecleaning.

Urged on by the FBI's COINTELPRO agents (which I'll address later), Muhammad's own son later admitted that his father feared X's influence, and wanted to oust him from the organization. After X spoke publicly of Muhammad's promiscuity, everything came to a head following JFK's assassination. When asked by a reporter on Dec. 1, 1963 what he thought of this tragic event, Malcolm X said, "The chickens have come home to roost."

A media firestorm ensued, with Elijah Muhammad finding the excuse he needed to suspend Malcolm X. Silenced as a scapegoat, X tried to explain himself. "The hate in white men had not stopped with the killing of defenseless black people, but that hate, allowed to spread unchecked, finally had struck down this country's chief of staff."

He failed to mention that black-on-black violence, rape and ghetto drug dealing far surpassed anything committed by the cops. Still, Nation of Islam officials now viewed him as a dangerous traitor, and the JFK comment became a pretext to dump him. Finally, on March 8, 1964, X officially split with the Nation of Islam, a notion that apparently thrilled the FBI. In reality, however, this move proved to be a mistake for them as now, by separating from Elijah Muhammad, X was given an even bigger stage and larger mission. He became an internationalist that wanted to unite and empower the oppressed worldwide.

As Malcolm X began his quest, darker underpinnings brewed within the Nation of Islam. Deemed a Judas and their chief enemy, Nation of Islam officials admitted on Chicago's *Hotline* program that they wanted to see X dead, and had plans to take him out. Soon, militant Fruit of Islam killing squads tracked Malcolm X's every step, a fact that didn't pass his notice.

At the forefront of this hate campaign was Louis Farrakhan, who said the Nation of Islam would deal with X like they did with any traitor. "There was not a Muslim who loved the Honorable Elijah Muhammad that did not want to kill Malcolm." He also stated, "Such a man as Malcolm is worthy of death" and "the die is cast, and Malcolm shall not escape, especially after such evil, foolish talk about his benefactor."

Not only did Farrakhan publicly call for X's elimination, others reported him as being at the Newark mosque at the time of X's assassination. Those in the know claimed this locale was where X's execution was planned. Years later, in 1993, while addressing a Nation of Islam congregation, Farrakhan directly addressed his involvement in the killing. "If we dealt with him like a nation deals with a traitor, what the hell business is it of yours?" Before his death, Malcolm X realized how his fate dangled in the wind. "Elijah Muhammad gave orders to have me crippled or killed."

COINTELPRO

Even before Malcolm X became a well-known public figure, the FBI began monitoring him in 1953, while still in prison. In a book entitled *History's Greatest Conspiracies*, author H. Paul Jeffers described X as being "a person of intense interest to the FBI and CIA as a possible threat to domestic peace and national security, and foe of organized crime because of his fight against Mafia drug trafficking in black neighborhoods." In *The Assassination of Malcolm X* by George Breitman, Herman Porter and Baxter Smith, they say that X was "the subject of one of the most intensive spy operations ever conducted by the FBI."

To broaden the scope of this analysis, Robert F. Kennedy later admitted that the Department of Justice had black militia groups under surveillance, while Brice Smith wrote on March 31, 2000 in an article called "The Buried Truths of Martin and Malcolm" that X's "activities were of such concern to the government that CIA Director Richard Helms instructed his agents to do everything they could to 'monitor' [his] activities."

The CIA, of course, is only legally permitted to operate on foreign soil. So they entered the picture when X began interacting with foreign leaders before (and after) his split with the Nation of Islam. An Aug. 11, 1964 CIA memo to Richard Helms stated that X was part of an international conspiracy of foreign leaders, and that he was being funded by extremist groups in Africa to foment riots in America. The CIA later admitted these charges were baseless but, nonetheless, Malcolm found himself in the crosshairs, along with other threats such as Fidel Castro, Che Guevera, the Congo's Patrice Lumumba, Iran's Mohammed Mosaddeq and South Vietnam's President Ngo Dinh Diem.

Domestically, President Lyndon Johnson instructed FBI Director J. Edgar Hoover to compile additional data on X, especially after he left the Nation of Islam and became more political. LBJ and Hoover viewed him as a subversive, and thus he fell under the far-reaching umbrella of COINTELPRO. Assistant FBI Director William C. Sullivan, a high-level commander of government covert operations, established this notorious program.

In an FBI document signed by J. Edgar Hoover and later released on March 7, 1974, COINTELPRO aimed to "expose, disrupt, misdirect, discredit, or otherwise neutralize the activities" of certain radicals. To do so, they would "exploit through counter-intelligence techniques the organizational and personal conflicts of the group's leadership."

Specifically in regard to Malcolm X, COINTELPRO documents showed that they wanted to "prevent the rise of a 'messiah' who could unify and electrify the militant black-nationalist movement." Another earlier COINTELPRO document (1958) spoke of "neutralizing Malcolm X" for he seemed a natural as Elijah's heir apparent. To accomplish this goal, the FBI directed paid informers and agent provocateurs to create "fratricidal warfare" (or infighting) among the targeted groups.

The most important infiltrator turned out to be Malcolm X's bodyguard, Gene Roberts, who followed assignments given by the NYPD's "Red Squad" known as BOSSI (Bureau of Special Services and Investigation). BOSSI also became a tangential arm of the FBI and CIA and regularly funneled information to these federal intelligence agencies. Dave Emory claimed in one of his lectures that the FBI's Division Five put pressure on BOSSI to infiltrate the Nation of Islam and X's OAAU. Two of these BOSSI agents were Teddy Theologes and Tony Ulasewicz, the latter becoming Richard Nixon's private detective.

But Gene Roberts's role as bodyguard proved to be even more crucial. As a deep undercover agent in X's newly formed organization, he monitored X's every move, then fed this information back to the NYPD. Roberts's status as an undercover BOSSI detective surfaced in 1970 when he testified as a state witness at the Panther 21 conspiracy trial.

Another highly placed FBI informant was John Ali, who infiltrated the Nation of Islam's national staff and rose to become its treasurer. Some even speculated that after Elijah Muhammad, Ali might have been the most powerful man in this organization. Openly antagonistic toward Malcolm X, Ali frequently turned up in many of the same places to which X traveled. On one occasion, when X's plane landed at Los Angeles Airport, law enforcement officials were notified of Ali's presence, whereupon they rerouted X to a different terminal.

Ali was also seen at a speech given by X only days prior to his assassination, and it's been documented that he was in New York City on the weekend of X's murder. Columnist Jack Newfield even went on record as saying that Ali met with admitted hired gunman Thomas Hayer and brought him into the assassination team only days before the hit. In 2002, James W. Douglass penned *The Murder and Martyrdom of Malcolm X* where he confirms that Ali met with Hayer when the final plans for his assassination were laid.

In all, the FBI's COINTELPRO perfectly exploited the weaknesses of Black Muslim groups by using information to scheme, hurt, discredit, disrupt, neutralize and weaken them until they were no longer a threat. With paid informants such as Roberts and Ali, seeds were planted so that they could exploit other useful idiots to create division. The FBI also circulated critical letters regarding X and sent them to his enemies, or helped get negative newspaper articles written about him.

As a key component of X's assassination, via BOSSI, George Breitman says the NYPD "publicly admitted at the time of Malcolm X's death that they knew an attempt was to be made on his life." Breitman continues in *The Assassination of Malcolm X*, "If the New York police were involved in the assassination, that involvement could not have been on their own initiative, but must have resulted from the decision and direction of the government in Washington, that is, the CIA."

He concludes, "The CIA/BOSSI officials did not try to break up the murder gang. On the contrary, they told their agents to proceed with business as usual, that is, to help the plot develop. The agents provided the weapons and—more importantly—inside information (from BOSSI agents in the OAAU)." In addition, Breitman offers up the probability that they'd allow the killers to escape after the slaying was completed (i.e. no police interference).

PILGRIMAGE

After being banished from the Nation of Islam, X surprisingly transformed into an even more dangerous figure in the establishment's eyes. During his initial 90-day suspension by Elijah Muhammad, X joined Olympic gold medalist Cassius Clay as he prepared for his fight with Sonny Liston. After Clay won the title and changed his name to Muhammad Ali (while also proclaiming his strong Muslim views), he also visited the UN with Malcolm X. The most famous boxer in America (with the biggest mouth) was now aligned with the most dangerous man in America. Moreover, since X had also met with Martin Luther King, the CIA and FBI were horrified that they'd also join forces.

But X didn't seem content to simply focus on America. Freed from the shackles of Elijah Muhammad, he began a whirlwind pilgrimage that spanned the globe. In 1957, he had already met with Indonesian President Achmed Sukarno, whom the CIA sought to remove from office. Now, beginning in 1964, he traveled to Arabia, Ghana, Egypt, Lebanon, Nigeria, Senegal, Morocco, Algeria, Tanzania, Kenya, Uganda, Guinea and Mecca, Saudi Arabia.

Author Bob Feldman writes that the CIA trailed X throughout his African tour in 1964, while George Breitman said the same thing happened during his Mideast jaunt. "A 'truth squad' from the U.S. Information Agency accompanied him wherever he went—slandering him and trying to undo what he was accomplishing." Similarly, James Douglass asserts that intelligence agents from the CIA, Army, Navy and Air Force followed him across Europe.

The reason they so closely monitored X was easy to determine. In the Mideast, he met with King Faisal, head of the oil cartel. U.S. interests were certainly at stake in this regard. He also held conferences with Third World leaders at the UN, and his message rang loud and clear. As a nouveau internationalist and unabashed critic of the CIA and State Department, X denounced U.S. imperialism and the New World Order power structure, while championing the oppressed and exploited masses.

In Africa, he tried to mobilize the poor by putting the U.S. on trial at the UN, condemning it as racist. After pointing out that it would be hypocritical for the U.S. to lecture other nations (considering its own human rights violations), African leaders quoted X at the UN, greatly embarrassing the State Department. Other Asian and African rulers deemed X a visionary spokesman for the UN due to his stance against apartheid, colonialism and the Vietnam War.

But the *coup de grace* came when X directly targeted the cornerstone of America's system. "It is impossible for capitalism to survive, primarily because the system of capitalism needs some blood to suck. Capitalism used to be like an eagle, but now it's more like a vulture."

One other factor entered into this equation. Rather than focusing on the spoon-fed racism of Elijah Muhammad, X somewhat underwent a transformation after visiting Mecca. There, he saw all faiths, races and colors worshipping together—united as one-humanity. Disturbed by the Nation of Islam's overt, hate-filled doctrines, Malcolm X partially altered his views that whites were an inherently inferior, evil race. Plus, he no longer called for an entirely separate black state in Africa. Instead, blacks, whites and everyone else should work together to overthrow their New World Order overlords.

Unity among the poor terrified the elite, as did its mouthpiece. During his UN campaign, a Detroit civil rights attorney said of Malcolm X: "In formulating this policy and hitting the nerve center of America, he also signed his own death warrant."

Likewise, he harbored no illusions concerning his mission. He told famed author and biographer Alex Haley, "You must realize that what I am trying to do is very dangerous because it is a direct threat to the entire international system of racist exploitation."

By becoming so effective among African leaders, especially those who rebelled in the UN after reading his eight-page memo that had a devastating effect on U.S. business interests, Malcolm X knew he lived in the crosshairs. In the documentary *El-Haji Malik Eishabazz*, he reportedly told a number of different people that the CIA would eventually kill him.

The first attempt occurred on July 23, 1964 while eating dinner at the Nile Hilton in Cairo. Constantly followed by CIA agents, X got violently ill that evening, then had to have his stomach pumped. No one else at the table got sick, and X later claimed that he recognized his waiter from previous surveillance encounters.

Then, on Feb. 9, 1965—less than two weeks before his assassination—the French government barred him from entering the country because they thought he'd be murdered on French soil and didn't want to be the scapegoats. In April 1965, journalist Eric Norden said that information given to him by a North African diplomat purported that the French Department of Alien Documentation and Counter-Espionage said the CIA planned to kill X in their country. Not wishing to be a part of this madness, they simply barred Malcolm X's entrance.

FIREBOMBING

Events were now moving fast and furious. Five days later—on Feb. 14, 1965—X's family home in Queens became the target of a firebombing. Bottles of gasoline tapped with fuses (i.e. Molotov cocktails) were thrown through his windows, burning his home to the ground. It took 45 minutes for the NYFD to arrive, and miraculously X's family managed to escape and survive. Adding insult to injury, the police accused Malcolm of torching his own home to generate publicity. Such a ploy was appalling on their part.

In response, X at first blamed the Muslims for bombing him; then he became convinced that this arson was part of a bigger plot beyond the Black Muslims' capabilities. Certain that the police and FBI had infiltrated the Nation of Islam, one can't help but be reminded of X's words concerning radical field Negroes. As X said with fiery passion, when the Massuh's house started to burn, he prayed for a strong wind, and when the Massuh got sick, he'd send the doctor in another direction.

Eventually, evidence surfaced that black Muslims were involved in torching X's home. One man—a Nation of Islam official named Captain Joseph X Gavitts (aka Yusuf Shah)—admitted that he instructed an assistant to wire X's car so that it would explode when starting the engine. Then, in 1995 on his deathbed, he confessed to participating in the firebombing.

AUDUBON BALLROOM

Now homeless, on the day prior to his murder, Malcolm X decided to buy a house in, of all places, a Jewish section of Long Island. Such a move, however, seemed almost futile because X knew death waited. In a letter to Secretary of State Dean Rusk he wrote, "The government has no intention to help or protect my life."

In a speech at the Audubon Ballroom on Feb. 15, 1965—the weekend before his murder—X told audience members, "Don't you think that anything is going down that the police don't know about? The only thing that goes down is what they want to go down." In this same vein, James Douglass quoted X as saying, "I feel in my bones the plots to kill me have already been hatched in high places. The triggermen will only be doing what they were paid to do."

To his biographer Alex Haley, he lamented, "It has always been my belief that I, too, will die by violence. I have done all that I can to be prepared. Each day I live as if I am already dead. I do not expect to live long enough to read this book in its finished form."

Indeed, in his final days, X increasingly laid a foundation to prove that the government was involved in a plot to kill him. Fully aware that black Muslims were a part of this conspiracy, X intended to expose the entire sordid mess at his final speech on Feb. 21, including the names of his would-be assassins. According to James Douglass, on the Tuesday before his murder, he told James Shabazz, "I have been marked for death in the next five days. I have the names of five black Muslims who have been asked to kill me. I will announce them at the Sunday meeting." These names were written on a piece of paper found inside X's jacket the day of his murder.

As X suspected, the plot to kill him did extend beyond the Muslims. A March 3, 1966 FBI report states, "John Ali met with [Thomas] Hayer the night before Malcolm X was killed." As has clearly been established, John Ali served as a deep undercover informant for the FBI, and the plan to murder X ultimately involved three entities: a) the Nation of Islam; b) NYPD via BOSSI; and c) U.S. intelligence agencies. As such, the black Muslims acted as proxies, similar to how the Mafia was hired to snuff Fidel Castro.

Here is how the event went down. John Ali hired Thomas Hayer and four other accomplices who, according to Douglass, "all belonged to the Fruit of Islam, a paramilitary training unit." In fact, there were actually several assassination teams in operation, with a unit out of the Newark mosque finally being the one to pull off the dirty deed. Now, on Feb. 15, 1965—during X's last speech at the Audubon—a disturbance between a few black Muslims erupted in the audience. In hindsight, everyone agrees that this fracas served as a trial run for the real deal a week later. But, as X commented, a situation had now been created where *anyone* could snuff him and Muslims would be the scapegoats.

Increasingly fearful for his own life and his family's safety, X checked into the New York Hilton on Feb. 20. Since the core of X's organization had been infiltrated, his whereabouts quickly became known. That evening, Thomas Hayer and two other black men unsuccessfully tried to reach X at his hotel room.

Thwarted in their efforts, the next day they were found at Harlem's Audubon Ballroom, where X was scheduled to speak. Ironically, every other speaker on the roster cancelled, leaving him to be the sole lecturer. Even more bizarre, X refused to have any extra protection surrounding him, and prohibited security from searching guests entering the door. Did Malcolm X have a death wish, or did he simply accept the inevitable?

As the ballroom filled and X took the stage, a minor disturbance broke out almost exactly like the one a week earlier. As this diversion ensued, hired guns removed their weapons and blasted X in the chest at nearly point-blank range with their shotguns. Unable to protect himself, 10 bullets riddled hiss chest before Thomas Hayer, armed with a .45, shot four more times at Malcom X's prone body.

Malcolm X addresses a crowd in front of the Apollo Theater.

As the killers fled, several members of NYPD's BOSSI unit watched passively from the ballroom's shadows. During the melee, a crowd member shot Thomas Hayer in the leg, which allowed several others in the congregation to capture him. A second man was also caught, while three others got away. If it had been left solely to the NYPD, though, all of them would have escaped.

AFTERMATH

"Apostle of Hate is Dead" —*New York Times* headline

That evening, Feb. 21, famed columnist Jimmy Breslin of *The New York Herald Tribune* wrote, "Police rescue two suspects." But then the next day, the story changed. "Police rescue one suspect." Every paper in New York erased the news of a second suspect being nabbed. Why? Because the second accomplice was either a government agent or one hired by the FBI's John Ali.

Therefore, of the five hired hit men (three shooters and two to create a distraction), four got away and would never spend a day in jail.

At least initially, Thomas Hayer (a foot-soldier patsy) was left to take the entire rap until two others—Norman Butler and Thomas Johnson—were also arrested. But here's the catch. Butler and Johnson weren't even at the Audubon that day because of their status as known Nation of Islam members. It would have been impossible for them to enter the ballroom, for all of X's bodyguards knew them as followers of Elijah Muhammad. In addition, Johnson was home all day, and his neighbor vouched that he'd visited him between 3:30 and 4 p.m. Malcolm X's murder took place at 3:05 p.m.

At his trial, Thomas Hayer confessed that he'd been hired to carry out the assassination of Malcolm X, and that Butler and Johnson had absolutely nothing to do with it. They weren't involved. Although he refused to identify his actual accomplices, Hayer did say that he had no personal motive to murder X. Was Hayer a Nation of Islam member or a devotee of Elijah Muhammad? Circumstantial evidence has been contradictory over the years (depending on each writer's agenda), but one variable is certain—Butler and Johnson were innocent. The other actual killers were allowed to escape by the NYPD.

We know this statement is true because, on Feb. 23, the *Herald Tribune* confirmed that several members of the highly secretive BOSSI team were present at the Audubon during the killing. Plus, on Feb. 22, 1965 *The New York Journal-American* reported: "According to a police spokesman, the department knew in mid-January that an attempt was to be made on Malcolm's life."

Later, at Thomas Hayer's trial, Earl Hutchison wrote in *Revisiting the Malcolm X Assassination* on Feb. 23, 2005 that FBI members closely monitored the proceedings to protect their informants and undercover agents planted in X's organization. Even more egregiously, not only was any mention of a second shooter dropped from every newspaper, it was *never* brought up once at Hayer's trial by his *court-appointed lawyers*. The police arrested two men, but only kept one. The other was released.

Inexplicably, hardly anyone in the black community raised his voice in outrage. Not one black politician attended his funeral, and every black church except one refused to hold religious services. According to Dave Emory, a mysterious fire even broke out at the home of Muhammad Ali on the night of X's murder, yet no one spoke out.

Encouraged by this apathy and cowardice from the black leadership community, the government didn't end their killing spree. On March 13, 1965, Leon 4X Ameer died from an overdose of sleeping pills. Actually, it was first classified as a suicide, then an overdose, and finally death by natural causes. In Bob Feldman's *Who Eliminated Malcolm X*, he notes that Ameer just announced plans to produce tapes and documents of Malcolm proving the government was responsible for his assassination.

On March 1, 1965, Malcolm X's lawyer—Percy Sutton—had his office burglarized, whereupon many of his client's papers were stolen. Another man, Lewis Lomax, initiated an investigation of the murders of Martin Luther King and Malcolm X, which led him to implicate the intelligence community. He also looked into Guy Bannister's role in the JFK assassination. Conveniently enough, after landing a movie deal, the brakes on his car failed and he was killed.

Malcolm X: slain at 39 years of age. A gave injustice took place, yet Martin Luther King didn't vociferously protest. Over the years, neither did Jesse Jackson, Al Sharpton, Louis Farrakhan or Barack Obama. None of them are fit to fill even one inch of the shoes that Malcolm X walked in. X was a true enemy of the New World Order.

CHAPTER 5

KILLING KING

MARTIN LUTHER KING: THE STATE MURDER OF AN AMERICAN RADICAL

According to media sources, James Earl Ray harbored a "pathological hatred of black people, and he couldn't stand Martin Luther King." On Jan. 26, 1975, *Time* magazine quoted author George McMillan (*The Making of an Assassin*), who vouched for Ray's status as an avowed racist, then added that Ray would watch King on TV in prison and erupt with rage. "I'm gonna kill that nigger King!" There's only one problem with this story. Jefferson City prison didn't have cellblock televisions for inmates during his years of incarceration (1963-64).

Another angle to this story is even more interesting. Smear-merchant McMillan married CIA asset Priscilla Johnson who, in 1959, traveled to Moscow and conveniently interviewed none other than expatriate defector Lee Harvey Oswald—the fall guy patsy assassin of John F. Kennedy. American consul John McVickar arranged their meeting while later Johnson shared a residence with Oswald's wife, Marina. Even stranger, when Joseph Stalin's daughter, Svetlana, defected from the Soviet Union, she stayed with Johnson's parents. Priscilla later penned Ms. Stalin's biography.

So, according to the "official story" forwarded by these types of CIA "collaborators," James Earl Ray trailed King from Los Angeles to Memphis, whereupon he checked into a seedy dive. With his bathroom overlooking the Lorraine Motel, avowed racist Ray murdered the reverend, then escaped—but not before dropping a satchel filled with personal belongings so that he could be implicated.

Then, authorities cited the testimony of Mr. Charles Q. Stephens as the cornerstone of their case. But Stephens, a skid row alcoholic, was so inebriated that day he could barely walk. Yet, he purportedly identified Ray. In his affidavit, Stephens "claimed that at about 6 p.m. on April 4, 1968—just after he'd heard a gunshot—he'd seen the 'profile' of a person running down the flophouse hall [of Bessie Brewer's Boarding House]."

In his autobiography, *Who Killed Martin Luther King*, Ray provides the words of Stephens's wife, who contradicted her husband by saying that, without a doubt, Ray *did not* flee from his bathroom at the low-rent motel after King's shooting. In reality, Ray—an unwitting part of this operation—wasn't even inside the motel when the assassination took place. Instead, as an escaped prison fugitive, he heard sirens while waiting in a getaway car and made a hasty exit out of Memphis.

After leaving the United States, Ray was arrested by Scotland Yard agents at London's Heathrow Airport on June 10. The following year, in March (without a trial), James Earl Ray pleaded guilty to murdering King. Three days later, however, he recanted, telling prison officials he wanted a trial because he'd been set up as a pawn.

Why would a man who, according to attorney William Pepper, had "no knowledge of weapons whatsoever," admit guilt? Ray later wrote that threats of legal action would have been leveled against certain family members (his brother and father) if he didn't take the fall. John Larry Ray agreed in his book, *Truth at Last*: "I believe my brother was maneuvered into a fake confession after being framed by a terrifying mix of government and criminal forces."

MIND CONTROL

The manipulation of James Earl Ray's mental faculties began early in life during a stint in the military. Although this incident contradicts Pepper's contention about firearms, as a member of the Army's military police in occupied Germany after WWII (1948), Ray purportedly shot a black soldier named Washington that supposedly assaulted a group of Jewish men. However, the details are so murky and sketchy that no one—including Ray—is even sure what occurred.

In a biography on his brother, John Larry Ray described an array of mind control experiments conducted in Germany by the U.S. Army—a land infamous for Nazi psychiatrists that were smuggled into America via Project Paperclip to begin the CIA. John Ray said they "endeavored to create human robots to be used as killing machines."

This depiction sounds eerily reminiscent of another lone-nut killer. In *The Search for Lee Harvey Oswald*, Robert J. Gordon explains how the CIA placed JFK's "assassin" in an MK-ULTRA brainwashing program. At Japan's Atsugi Naval Air Station (where Oswald served), the agency utilized amphetamines, depressants, sodium pentothal, LSD and mescaline to program their soldiers. In this context, Ray, Oswald and Timothy McVeigh all became assets and patsies of the U.S. military system.

After leaving the Army (again, similar to Oswald), James Earl Ray landed on the CIA's payroll by conducting undercover operations for the federal government where he investigated supposed communists. Later, upon landing in Montreal (1967), Ray claimed to have robbed a pimp to obtain cash. His brother disagrees with this assessment, explaining how the CIA funneled money to him through their organized crime ties. He also admits that the Ray family had a long-standing relationship with the Mob, extending back to their father.

After becoming established in Montreal, not only did Ray meet his eventual handler—a mysterious figure named "Raoul"—but he also underwent a series of reprogramming indoctrinations. In *Truth at Last*, John Larry Ray talks about his book's co-author: "I've been shown CIA documents by investigator Lyndon Barsten that indicate Montreal in 1959 was the home of Subproject 68 of the CIA's MK-ULTRA brainwashing program. Dr. Ewen Cameron ran it at the Allen Memorial Institute of McGill University. Dr. Cameron was an immigrant from England who became a lead CIA mind control expert in Canada. It is in this neighborhood of the Allen Memorial Institute that James decided to hide out back in 1959. Did the CIA order James to go to the Allen Memorial Institute for experimentation? A case could be made that while James was in Germany, the feds repeatedly drugged him with spinal taps of increasingly sophisticated methods and, here he was, more than 10 years after his odd army service in the epicenter of brainwashing in North America."

It must be noted that Dr. Ewen Cameron is quite possibly the most notorious mind-bender in the CIA's MK-ULTRA history.

After hitting Montreal in 1967, Ray made the acquaintance of CIA operative Jules Kimble, a racist with ties to the Ku Klux Klan. Kimble then proceeded to entangle Ray further in this labyrinth by introducing him to another CIA specialist, who gave him the alias "Eric S. Galt." Kimble and Ray were then dispatched to McGill's at Allen Memorial Hospital, where they came under the direct supervision of Dr. Cameron. Ray's brother also divulged that the CIA gathered data on James since 1948. Ray had now been fully primed to become a potential patsy.

PRISON ESCAPE ARTIST

Ray's path to Montreal is even more bizarre. After returning from Germany to the United States, Ray wound up in Missouri State Penitentiary in Jefferson City. On April 23, 1967 after a few bungled escape attempts, he finagled—or was allowed—to "free" himself from this institution. The prison's director, Fred T. Wilkinson, made his mark by coordinating the CIA spy exchange where Russia returned U2 pilot Gary Powers [another case with ties to Lee Harvey Oswald] for a captured Soviet spy. Then, working as an intel op, he replaced Warden Elbert Nash and the prison's chief engineer at Missouri after both "suicided" themselves.

Prior to his ultimate escape, Ray had been placed in Fulton State Hospital # 1 under the auspices of psychiatrist Dr. Donald B. Peterson. Ray's brother describes him as the U.S. Army's chief of psychiatry during the peak of its brainwashing experiments. He also co-wrote a book on hypnosis. Oddly enough, officers discovered Ray carrying a book on hypnosis upon his arrest at Heathrow Airport. In early 1968, akin to Sirhan Sirhan, he began scribbling certain phrases over and over again in notebooks.

At any rate, in the early 1970s, *Freedom* magazine asserted that mind control experiments were being conducted at the Missouri Prison that housed Ray. While under the care of Dr. Peterson, Ray suffered a "nervous breakdown," possibly, his brother claims, from electroshock therapy or the use of LSD-25. Investigator Lyndon Barsten concurs: "The CIA took advantage of [Ray's] unsuccessful escape attempts, and manipulated him into one of many as yet-unidentified brainwashing operations funded by the feds."

Then, amazingly enough, after two failed previous escape attempts, this high-risk detainee with mental problems escaped from the Missouri Prison in July 1967. However, John Ray recounts how Warden Donald Wyrick claimed that he, Director Wilkinson and Warden Harold Swenson allowed Ray to escape so that he could eventually be fingered as Martin Luther King's assassin.

Even more interesting are accusations that Wilkinson switched Ray's fingerprints after the escape so that if a police officer ever did arrest him, they couldn't make a positive identification. Plus, with an alias and completely vulnerable (i.e. fugitives don't report themselves to law enforcement), Ray was at his handler's mercy. Last but not least, John Ray theorizes that none other than CIA Director Richard Helms orchestrated his brother's escape via Fred Wilkinson.

This conjecture will become more plausible later when the motive for King's murder is presented.

'RAOUL'

After traveling to Montreal and assuming the alias of "Eric S. Galt," Ray befriended a shadowy man named "Raoul" at the Neptune Bar in August 1967. The man who arranged this meeting with his ultimate controller was David Gitnacht (aka David Graiver). Researcher Mae Brussell discovered that he had ties to the SITB (Swiss-Israeli Trading

Bank) formed in 1949 by Israel's finance minister, Pinchas Sapir, and the Mossad.

Interestingly, and although it's certainly never been verified, Raoul has been named by numerous investigators as being one of the three "tramps" arrested directly after the JFK assassination. LBJ mistress Madeleine Brown confirmed Raoul's acquaintance with Mr. Jack Ruby (Rubinstein)—Meyer Lansky's mob hit man that killed Lee Harvey Oswald.

Even James Earl Ray brought up a Jewish connection. He claims a man named Randall Erwin Rosenson—a Jewish Defense League (JDL) operative—shadowed Raoul and created the "legend" for himself and his handler that eventually placed him in Memphis at the time of King's murder on April 4, 1968.

This scenario is plausible because Raoul got Ray accustomed to doing illegal and/or risky jobs. After obtaining a passport for him, Ray first smuggled paraphernalia across the U.S.-Canadian border, then later ran guns from Mexico.

In the interim, Raoul made certain that clandestine mind-benders kept their clutches on Ray. His brother tells how, on Nov. 27, 1967, Ray met with Mark O. Freeman, a WWII Army intelligence officer who later worked with the FBI and conducted LSD experiments. Then, on Jan. 4, 1968 Ray entered the orbit of Reverend Xavier von Koss—a Nazi hypnotist smuggled into the U.S. under Project Paperclip who later ran the International Society of Hypnosis. Von Koss also worked with Sirhan Sirhan's hypnotist Rev. Jerry Owen.

ORGANIZED CRIME

In an intriguing article entitled *Mossad Linked to Martin Luther King Assassination*, Michael Collins Piper describes how Raoul became involved in a U.S.-based international arms smuggling operation that also involved Jack Ruby (thus reiterating previous information). The stolen weapons were delivered to Mob boss Carlos Marcello, who then sent them south to Central and South America. The project's supervisor, Colonel John Downie, led the 902nd Military Intelligence Group (inside the Department of Defense). Piper also disclosed that another key figure in this operation was "a senior Mossad agent working in South America who acted as a senior liaison to the U.S. military and CIA." Piper's research leads him to believe this individual was Mossad hit man Michael Harari.

So, we have Raoul tied to U.S. Army gun running (via anti-Cuban, anti-Communist insurgents) and Carlos Marcello, who operated out of New Orleans (where many JFK plotters congregated), as well as the deadly Dixie Mafia (later made famous by Bill and Hillary Clinton).

Piper places an even finer point on this tangled network. Even though arms eventually made their way to Carlos Marcello, Jack Ruby didn't actually work for the Italian Mafia. Instead, kingpin Meyer Lansky of the Jewish Syndicate employed him. Ruby himself bragged that he'd smuggled arms for Israel since the mid-1950s. Even more incriminating, Al Lizanetz—a Bronfman smuggling front man and colleague of Lansky—stated that Ruby's name appeared on the Bronfman payroll.

As Piper uncovered, a direct link can be made between Carlos Marcello and the Israeli Lansky crime syndicate. Plus, since Marcello and military intelligence ran an extensive gun running operation where weapons were stolen from U.S. military bases and armories, John Larry Ray asked a vitally important question about his brother. "Was James working for the Mob? Yes. Was he working for the government? Yes. Raoul, James's notorious Portuguese handler, belonged to the shadow world between U.S. intelligence and the Mob. He came from Joseph Bonanno's territory."

Let's look at the situation in this light. Ray's father and grandfather were both draft-dodgers, with the latter beginning a local racket for Chicago's crime bosses. His father also escaped from prison. The comparisons to Lee Harvey Oswald are striking. Ray had ties to the Chicago mob, while Oswald got entangled with Marcello in New Orleans. Ray served in the Army, Oswald the Marines—and both were co-opted by U.S. intelligence and had contact with federal agents before taking the fall as patsies. Ray himself observed: "When you join the OSS [the CIA's predecessor], it's like joining the Mafia. You never leave."

With this information in mind, many have asked: did the Mafia want Martin Luther King dead? James Earl Ray provides the answer. "It was not the Mafia, but the feds behind the Mafia, who wanted Martin Luther King dead."

Were the feds actually in the Murder, Inc. business? Colonel Fletcher Prouty—a deep intelligence insider who became the inspiration for Mr. X in Oliver Stone's *JFK* film—cites Operation Mongoose, which he called an assassination-incorporated organization. Developed in the early 1960s by Air Force General Edward Lansdale, this secret program ultimately had its highest aspirations in the murder of Cuban leader Fidel Castro.

Sam Giancana described the CIA and Mafia as two sides of the same coin where the government used mobsters for clandestine operations in order to maintain plausible deniability. So, it shouldn't be any surprise that in January 1968 Sam Giancana, Carlo Gambino and Johnny Roselli met with federal agents from the FBI and CIA in Appalachian, New York, to discuss the murder of MLK. After being offered a $1 million contract, Giancana flatly refused. This job was even too hot for him. Giancana's response didn't mean, however, that other mobsters weren't interested.

SURVEILLANCE

Prior to being assassinated, Martin Luther King's house had been burned down, he'd been assaulted, stabbed in the chest, and received uncounted death threats. He knew he'd be killed, and fully realized it would be sooner rather than later. In the documentary *Evidence of Revision*, King is riding on a bus after an event where shooters were positioned in a tree. "They were ready to assassinate me, but they couldn't get a clear shot because I was surrounded," he's seen telling acquaintances.

By 1968, his killers were closing in, but this phenomenon didn't suddenly arise out of nowhere. Attorney William F. Pepper quotes a March 21, 1993 article by a reporter for *The Memphis Commercial Appeal*, Steve Tompkins. "Army intelligence had spied on Dr. King's family for three generations. The article noted that there was an extraordinary fear in official circles about what would happen if Dr. King were allowed to lead masses of American poor into Washington that spring. It stated that Army intelligence was "desperately searching for a way to stop him.'"

Although Army intelligence played a huge role in King's surveillance, Robert F. Kennedy first authorized J. Edgar Hoover's FBI to open a "secret file" on King. Naturally, Hoover pursued this role with a vengeance, thinking King was a Communist and the "most notorious liar in the world." Over time, Hoover became obsessed with the reverend, especially after he criticized his cherished Bureau.

In Pepper's book, *An Act of State*, he relates how December 1963 found FBI officials congregating in Washington, D.C. to discuss how they could "neutralize King as an effective Negro leader." Their solutions included hidden microphones, blackmail, wiretaps from October 1963 to June 1966, burglaries and tapes delivered to his wife Coretta regarding extramarital affairs.

Hoover also used other assets. On April 28, 1993 *The San Francisco Weekly* reported how the ADL (Anti-Defamation League) spied on King because they considered him a "loose cannon." The ADL then passed their findings on to Hoover.

Pepper also discusses John Curington, former chief aide and "bag man" to Texas oilman H.L. Hunt, who had close ties to the FBI and CIA. Hunt maintained a particularly close relationship with Hoover, dating back to the 1950s, thus allowing him a direct line to the FBI's No. 1 man. Curington claimed that Hoover once snarled, "the only way to stop Martin Luther King was to completely silence him."

Hoover and Hunt also harbored close ties with organized crime, especially due to the G-man's gambling addiction. Therefore, Frank Costello became the Mob liaison to Hoover, while Hunt and LBJ were lifelong friends. They even had a crony in Congress—Speaker of the House Sam Rayburn—who as a Texan considered Johnson his protégé. It's not hard to imagine why Congress didn't conduct an investigation into King's murder. They were all in the bag.

In addition, after Bobby Kennedy gave the green light, Hoover's COINTELPRO forces began targeting King in October 1967. Known as the "Black Probe" (with King specifically referred to as "Code Name Zorro"), informants were set-up to infiltrate the civil rights movement.

The man in charge of this program—Cartha DeLoach—had already been tapping King's phones since the 1950s. As COINTELPRO director, his powers were greatly enhanced.

But to reach a degree of observation that adequately suited them, CIA Director Richard Helms and the FBI's Hoover brought in the U.S. Army Military Intelligence Group, or MIG. Due to King's association with Communist Party members (or affiliates) such as Stanley Levinson, Hunter O'dell and Bayard Rustin, Helms unleashed his spooks.

Pepper writes in *An Act of State*, "MIG officers were responsible for eye-to-eye surveillance operations which included audio and visual recordings. . . . Dr. King was a target throughout the last year of his life." Another way to directly burrow inside King's inner circle was via a black agent named Marrell McCollough. Reactivated by the FBI in June 1967, he also belonged to the 111th MIG. After being assigned to the Memphis Police Department, McCollough infiltrated "the Invaders," King's personal bodyguard unit. McCollough later went on to work for the CIA in the 1970s.

ANATOMY OF A SHOOTING

Just because Gambino, Giancana and Roselli didn't accept the FBI-CIA offer to "hit" King didn't mean that other elements of organized crime wouldn't take the contract. To understand the mechanics of the King shooting, we must first turn to Frank Liberto, president of the Liberto Produce Company in Memphis. Liberto's brother had ties to the Marcello crime family, while Liberto himself harbored a seething hatred of Martin Luther King.

William Pepper provides a passage where Orlando, Florida, private eye Buck Buchanan quotes Liberto as saying, "King is a troublemaker, and he should be killed. If he is killed, then he will cause no more trouble." He also told Nathan Whitlock, son of restaurant owner Lavada Addison (and Liberto friend), "I didn't kill the nigger, but I had it done." He further painted James Earl Ray as a "set-up man." Lastly, civil rights leader John McFerren is purported to have directly overheard Liberto screaming into his telephone, "Shoot the son of a bitch on the balcony."

How did he accomplish this task? Liberto engaged in business with a man named Lloyd Jowers, who owned Jim's Bar and Grill (located behind the Lorraine Motel where Rev. King stayed). Jowers was also under contract to Liberto because, according to Pepper, he killed a Mexican man who he discovered in bed with his mistress. To cover his tracks, Liberto disposed of the body, which also meant Jowers now owed Liberto a huge debt.

To collect, Pepper alleges that Liberto paid Jowers $100,000 to orchestrate the murder of King. Under Liberto's control, Jowers soon coordinated planning sessions at his tavern. He also located the shooter, and subsequently received his payment from Liberto before the hit.

Never far from the action, Jowers later acknowledged seeing James Earl Ray with Raoul at Jim's Grill on the afternoon of King's shooting. Even more riveting, Pepper asserts, "on the program [ABC's *Primetime Live*] which aired nationwide on Dec. 16, 1993, Lloyd Jowers cleared James Earl Ray, saying that he did not shoot Dr. King, but that he, Jowers, had hired a shooter after he was approached by Memphis produce man Frank Liberto and paid $100,000 to facilitate the assassination. He also said that he had been visited by a man named Raoul, who delivered a rifle and asked him to hold it until arrangements were finalized." Raoul is also to have been an intermediary between Lt. John Barger (Memphis P.D.), Marrell McCollough (black MIG plant) and Lt. Earl Clark (Memphis P.D. sharpshooter).

But how did the conspirators know where to find King? Enter Marrell McCollough, an FBI and Memphis P.D. undercover agent who had infiltrated King's bodyguard force, the black, militant Invaders. Charles Cabbage, a member of this quasi-security force, heard rumors circulating among Memphis police officers that King would never leave their city alive.

Anyway, late on the afternoon of April 4, 1968 between 5:45 and 5:50 p.m., a housekeeper knocked on the door of the Invaders at the Lorraine Motel and told them that since King's Southern Christian Leadership Conference hadn't paid their bill, they had to leave the premises. In Pepper's book, he states that when asked who gave the motel this order, she said it was Jesse Jackson.

As the Invaders left, Rev. Billy Kyles knocked on King's door and insisted that they had to leave for their appointment. Moreover, Lorraine Motel manager Walter Bailey testified that King reserved a secluded room, but at the last minute he was told to change those plans and instead gave him a balcony room.

Then, as Marrell McCollough moved out of the way toward the north stairwell, shots rang out. The first person to access King after being struck was none other than infiltrator McCollough. As he stood over the slain civil rights leader, he then pointed toward Bessie Brewer's Boarding House, indicating that's where the gunfire originated. This act was a major distraction, for nothing could have been further from the truth.

To further make King vulnerable, enter the head of Memphis's police and fire departments, Frank Holloman, who had directly worked as the inspector in charge of J. Edgar Hoover's office during his 25-year tenure at the FBI. Not only did Holloman transfer two black firemen away from a station adjacent to the Lorraine Motel, he also yanked black detective Ed Redditt from his shift at 2 p.m.—four hours prior to the assassination.

With no impediments to their plan, William Pepper provides the following overview of how he determined the hit took place. Lloyd Jowers claimed that he and Memphis P.D. Lt. Earl Clark entered the bushes behind Jim's Bar and Grill at approximately 5:45 p.m. Pepper quotes him: "Though never emphatic, he [Jowers] indicated that the other man out in the brush area, the actual assassin of Martin Luther King, was Memphis P.D.'s best shot—Lt. Earl Clark." He continued, "Clark, a Jim's Grill regular, had openly boasted that he would kill Dr. King when he came to town."

The shooter, with Jowers kneeling behind him, fired a bullet into Martin Luther King's lower face/jaw. He then handed the gun to Jowers, who raced out of the bushes back into the rear door of the bar he owned. Jowers then transferred the weapon to taxi driver James McCraw, who tossed it over the Memphis-Arkansas Bridge the following morning.

McCollough's misdirection of pointing to the boarding house is a vital distraction. For starters, King's driver—Solomon Jones—and Rev.

James Orange both witnessed a shooter in the bushes. They weren't the only ones to see movement. A Yellow Cab taxi driver clearly identified someone leaping down from a wall near these same bushes after shots were fired. One problem arose, however, according to Pepper. This taxi driver was "pushed from a speeding car on Route 55, on the other side of the Memphis-Arkansas Bridge, late in the evening of April 4."

But what happened to James Earl Ray? According to his brother, while the assassination took place, Ray sat in a getaway car outside the boarding house. He didn't even know a murder would take place that day. Anyway, as Ray waited, Raoul suddenly leaped in and threw a sheet over his head. After speeding away for a few blocks, Raoul then exited the car and fled.

John Ray explains why his brother lied and said he parked at a service station when the hit went down. He didn't want to be accused of aiding and abetting the actual murderers. In addition, investigative journalist William Sartor proposed (shortly before his suspicious death) that the original plan included killing Ray near the Lorraine Motel, but since the proper money hadn't changed hands, it never happened.

William Pepper also located a woman named Olivia Catling, who resided 200 yards from the Lorraine Motel. After hearing gunfire, she described a white man running down an alleyway and jumping in a car [Raoul]. They then proceeded to barrel past Memphis police officers that didn't try in the least to impede their getaway. She added another detail: firemen were shouting to the policemen that shots came from the bushes behind Jim's Bar and Grill, yet their pleas were ignored.

All the while, some of James Earl Ray's personal items were planted on the sidewalk outside Bessie's Boarding House. These conveniently included a rifle (which didn't match the bullet removed from Martin Luther King's body during ballistics testing), and Ray's radio with his prison ID number scratched onto it.

The following morning at 7 a.m., Memphis Public Works Senior Administrator Maynard Stiles received an urgent telephone call from Sam Evans of the Memphis P.D. instructing him to chop down all the thick bushes behind Lloyd Jowers's café. Evans also directed him to place these bushes in a pile to be carted away, and then thoroughly clean the entire area. The cover-up had been completed.

But what if events hadn't transpired as planned? Alas, a contingency plan of sinister proportions existed. William Pepper outlines a second hit squad in *An Act of State*. "The Marcello/Liberto assassination operation provided the government with a plausibly deniable alternative to the use of its own trained professionals who were waiting in the wings and ultimately not required. Organized crime frequently fulfills this need and insulates federal, state and public officials and agencies from responsibility for a variety of illegal acts. The underlying arrangements, even commercial collaboration, such as gun-running and drug dealing joint ventures, which finance the illegal covert operations, rarely come to light."

Specifically, Pepper describes an Operation Detachment Alpha 184 Team consisting of eight members that constituted a secondary hit squad on location in Memphis. Positioned atop the Illinois Central Railroad Building roof (across from the Lorraine), these Special Forces Army intel operatives (as well as their weapons) were contracted from Camp Shelby in Mississippi. Then, when not needed due to their primary gunman performing the job, Sam Evans, head of the Memphis P.D. Tactical Unit, called them off.

They weren't the only ones on hand. Also present, according to Pepper, was the ASA (Army Security Agency) that performed surveillance that day. Further, Memphis P.D. intel officer Eli Arkin claimed that the 111th MIG (Military Intelligence Group) also engaged in its own spy operations. Lastly, a TACT 10 law enforcement squad under Sam Evans's command was also present.

Quite possibly the most bizarre aspect of this multi-faceted operation revolved around Army photographers—identified by Pepper as Reynolds and Norton—who filmed King's murder that afternoon, then handed their evidence over to Col. John Downie, head of the 902nd Military Intelligence Group.

MOTIVE

The impetus for Martin Luther King's assassination can be reduced to three primary factors: racism, militarism and economics.

One of the establishment's most pressing fears concerned Martin Luther King's move from social activism into politics, and quite possibly even becoming a presidential candidate. With over 100 American cities torched in 1967, LBJ began calling King a "nigger preacher" before snarling, "That goddamn nigger preacher's gonna cost me the White House."

Johnson's Texas oilmen friends weren't very enamored with him either, especially H.L. Hunt. Over the years, King family members have publicly stated their belief that the CIA, FBI and Army intelligence were responsible for the reverend's murder. Dexter King went so far as to say that the plot went all the way up to LBJ. Especially interesting is one of H.L. Hunt's associates—OSS Maj. Louis Mortimer Bloomfield—who acted as the Bronfman family's attorney. He also served on the board of Permindex, a CIA-linked organization. In *Final Judgment*, Michael Collins Piper clearly unravels the Bronfman family-Lansky-CIA-Mossad-Permindex connection to John F. Kennedy's assassination. The hit on Kennedy certainly benefited Johnson (making him president), while also immensely benefiting Israel. So, if this clandestine cabal did it once, why not use the same network on King?

The second area of grave concern to the elite was King's vociferous opposition to the Vietnam War. Although Americans as a whole gradually turned against this debacle in Southeast Asia, consider the money at stake for the war machine. Weapons manufacturers and arms dealers made enormous profits, as did chemical companies, construction firms (Brown and Root), oil magnates (H.L. Hunt and Clint Murchison), and banks that generated enormous amounts of interest via loans to the United States.

None of them wanted to see a black Southern preacher take it all away by turning public sentiment against them. But as William Pepper so properly contextualized, "By 1970, Vietnamese babies were being born without eyes, with deformed hearts and stumps instead of legs. Six pounds of toxic chemicals per head of population were dumped on the people of Vietnam." Anti-war resentment began to boil over on college campuses, as well as inside everyday, middle-class American homes.

Below is a sampling of King's powerhouse words, especially from his *Beyond Vietnam: A Time to Break Silence* speech on April 4, 1967—exactly one year to the day before his murder:

- "They watch as we poison their water, as we kill a million acres of their crops. They must weep as the bulldozers roar through areas preparing to destroy their precious trees";
- "So far, we have killed a million of them—mostly children. They wander into the towns and see thousands of children, homeless, without clothes, running in packs on the streets like animals";
- "They see the children selling their sisters to our soldiers, soliciting for their mothers";
- "This is an abominable, evil, unjust war";
- "This is an evil war, and the U.S. is the greatest purveyor of violence in the world today";
- "It's time for America to repent";
- "We need a radical revolution of values";
- "The Vietnamese people proclaimed their own independence in 1945 after a combined French and Japanese occupation. . . . They were led by Ho Chi Minh. Even though they quoted the American Declaration of Independence in their own document of freedom, we refused to recognize them. Instead, we decided to support France in its re-conquest of her former colony";
- "What do they think as we test our latest weapons on them, just as Germans tested out new medicine and new tortures in the concentration camps of Europe?"; and
- "We have destroyed their two most cherished institutions: the family and the village. We have destroyed their land and their crops";

In March 1966 King called the Vietnam War a "social evil," and he was absolutely correct.

While striking at the war machine's soullessness, King also caused fear to rip through the very heart of their decayed empire in Washington, D.C. by calling for a Poor People's Campaign. By transforming his civil rights movement into one that targeted economic exploitation, King called for 500,000 of the nation's poor to establish permanent,

View of a nearby rooming house (on the left) where suspect James Earl Ray was alleged to have fired the fatal shot that killed civil rights leader Dr. Martin Luther King. The bushes in front of the boarding house were ordered cut down and hauled away by a high-ranking member of the Memphis P.D.

evolving tent cities in the nation's capital. In essence, he sought to overrun the Beltway with those who languished in poverty while billions were being squandered in Vietnam (and stuffed into the pockets of those who orchestrated the war). The idea was revolutionary.

Using encampments and civil disobedience, his March of the Poor on D.C. infuriated the elite. Following his Pentagon rally in October 1967, Memphis newsman Steve Tompkins said King was leading a revolution with his challenging new thoughts. On March 18, 1968 King called for a work stoppage in Memphis, and in later speeches demanded a "radical redistribution of economic power" in America.

Economic justice, redistribution of wealth, and black militants that Martin Luther King could not control once they stormed into Washington, D.C. The Army would never allow this preacher man to lead half-a-million poor into their gilded city.

On his final trip to Memphis, they made sure of it.

CHAPTER 6

MANCHURIAN PATSY

SIRHAN SIRHAN:
THE MANCHURIAN PATSY

His assassination is one of the most clear-cut cases of conspiracy and cover-up in American history.

—JOE LEVY
The Little Book of Conspiracies

In the early hours of July 5, 1968—after delivering a speech at the Embassy Ballroom of L.A.'s Ambassador Hotel—presidential candidate Robert F. Kennedy was murdered when three bullets entered his body, while a fourth struck his suit jacket. Immediately, bodyguards seized a jockey-sized Arab named Sirhan Sirhan, who, even while being pummeled by six hulking men, kept pulling the trigger of his now emptied .22 caliber Iver Johnson Cadet revolver.

Despite being labeled an open-and-shut case, peculiarities surfaced from the start that made many question whether Sirhan acted as a lone-nut assassin. Mark Zepezauer in *The CIA's Greatest Hits*, wrote that the

"L.A. Coroner's Report states that RFK was killed by a *point-blank shot from behind.*" In fact, two bullets struck Kennedy in the back, whereas a third lodged in his brain after entering behind Kennedy's right ear. *In the Crosshairs* author Stephen J. Spignesi clearly documents this point, telling of an entrance to the *back* of Kennedy's head, complete with powder burns to his skin.

These facts prove to be troublesome for proponents of the official story because most witnesses place Sirhan at least 3-5 feet *in front of* Kennedy, and never behind him at any time. Not only that, but investigators have located up to thirteen different bullets which were fired in the Ambassador Hotel's pantry. This total creates a new quandary, for Sirhan's gun held only eight rounds. To draw attention away from this inconsistency, Jonathan Vankin and John Whalen describe the LAPD's cover-up in *50 Greatest Conspiracies of All Time.* "Ceiling panels and door jambs where extra bullet holes were sighted and photographed were destroyed."

Of these stray shots which hit walls, the ceiling and random bystanders, another peculiarity arises: The bullets had ballistic markings that were different from those produced by Sirhan's .22 caliber gun. Lisa Pease claims in a fine series of articles: "Criminologist tests only showed conclusively that the victim bullets matched those from a gun that was not Sirhan's."

Since eyewitnesses saw other shooters in the pantry kill zone, and deducing that Sirhan acted under mind-control and/or hypnosis, should his gun also be brought into question? H. Paul Jeffers thinks so. In *History's Greatest Conspiracies*, he theorizes that Sirhan's revolver was simply a starter pistol filled with blanks so that the *actual* killers didn't accidentally get shot. He cites Robert Schlei, who said Sirhan's gun "sounded like a cap pistol," while Richard Lubic concurred. "It sounded like shots from a starter pistol at a track meet." He then goes on to show how Sirhan's model 55-SA is very similar to an Iver Johnson model 56-A, which is simply a starter pistol.

This notion is reinforced in *The Assassination of Robert F. Kennedy.* "Based on the basic physical evidence, Sirhan did not actually shoot Kennedy. In fact, unspent .22 shells were found on Sirhan's person, leading William Turner and John Christian to believe that Sirhan fired no bullets at all—only blanks."

If this scenario is accurate, then Sirhan Sirhan's primary function involved being a mind-controlled decoy to divert attention away from the actual gunmen. Although most members of the LAPD perpetuated the cover-up by intimidating witnesses and destroying evidence, the FBI agent in charge of the investigation, Roger Lajeunesse, said afterward, "the case is still open. I'm not rejecting the Manchurian candidate aspect of it."

Still, why would the killing elite exert so much effort and risk to perform a mind control assassination when hired guns had been doing it for centuries? *The Search for the Manchurian Candidate* author John Marks answers this question. "The purpose of this exercise is to leave a circumstantial trail that will make the authorities think the patsy committed a particular crime."

BRUTISH CESAR

The most commonly recognized extra shooter is Thane Eugene Cesar, a right-wing mob-affiliated security guard with CIA connections to Lockheed. He also told Ted Charach, co-producer of *The Second Gun*, that he'd attended Nazi meetings in the past.

Hired by Ace Guard Service to patrol the pantry, Cesar stood directly behind and to the right of Kennedy when the shooting began, and admitted that he'd drawn his gun at this time. Coincidentally, he held a .22, just like Sirhan did. When Cesar was questioned about this similarity, Lisa Pease writes in *The RFK Plot Part II: Rubik's Cube* that Cesar said he sold this gun before the assassination. Yet, a sales receipt contradicts his assertion, proving that he sold it after the Kennedy murder. Cesar likewise lied about his employment record. In *Conspiranoia*, Devon Jackson relates how Cesar claimed to have worked for Ace six months prior to the assassination. But, his hiring came in May 1968, with his first day on the job being May 31—less than a week before the shooting.

Proof of Cesar's role may have been found in the film of 15-year-old high school student Scott Enyart, who snapped three rolls of film during the shooting. Within moments, however, two LAPD officers confiscated these pictures and sealed them in files for 20 years. To retrieve his footage, Enyart filed a lawsuit and won. As a result, his photos were located in a Sacramento office. Did these pictures show Thane Cesar shooting Bobby Kennedy? We'll never know, because when being delivered to Enyart, the agent in charge said his briefcase (containing the prints) was stolen from a rent-a-car at the airport. Just like that, the pictures disappeared forevermore.

A couple of other anomalies persist. As the phenomenal conspiracy writer Jim Keith asks in *Mind Control, World Control*, who were the two men that approached kitchen personnel at the Ambassador Hotel the day prior to Kennedy's assassination and tried to get waiter's uniforms? More importantly, why did head of security Bill Barry decide, supposedly at the last minute, to change Kennedy's exit direction after delivering his speech? This one crucial moment completely altered Kennedy's fate. Had they followed the original route, the candidate would have never been led into the lion's den (i.e. the pantry), where Sirhan (the decoy), Cesar and others awaited him, primed for murder.

POLKA-DOT DRESS

Quite possibly the most puzzling enigma concerning the Kennedy assassination was a young, polka-dot dress-wearing woman who raced from the Ambassador Hotel squealing delightedly, "We've shot him! We've shot him! We shot Sen. Kennedy." Accompanying this female was a tall young man, who ran by her side. Although researchers have been trying to identify this couple for decades, the son of a maitre d', Thomas Vincent Dipierro, is certain that this same woman accompanied Sirhan prior to the shooting.

Fortunately, Carl Wernerhoff's article, *The Assassination of Robert F. Kennedy*, could finally be the long-awaited missing link. According to him, after graduating college, a 23-year-old woman named Kathy Ainsworth joined the White Knights of the KKK. An ardent segregationist with radical views, she soon willingly became involved in violent acts with her partner, Thomas Tarrants, many of them directed against Jews. On Sept. 18, 1967 they bombed a synagogue in Jackson, Mississippi.

Consistent with Wernerhoff's analysis, Tarrants's skills as a marksman were excellent. Also a racist with extreme political views, Wernerhoff contends that Tarrants was at least peripherally involved in the assassination of Martin Luther King. Kathy Ainsworth's mother acknowledges that her daughter and Tarrants were in Memphis the day King was shot.

Wernerhoff goes on to say that Ainsworth became Sirhan's handler, while Tarrants, Michael Wayne (Sirhan's double), Thane Cesar, Gabor Kadar and a traitor within RFK's camp (Frank Mankiewicz) were all involved in the Kennedy murder. How did these two get caught up in the world of paid assassinations? Wernerhoff describes an arm of the FBI's COINTELPRO known as the White Hate Program, which ran from 1964-1971. Here, the KKK and right wing vigilantes were actually *given* money and information to take out left-wing targets.

So, Ainsworth and Tarrants were recruited into the Martin Luther King and RFK hits by right wing extremist elements of our own government. But then, when the mysterious "woman in the polka dot dress" (Kathy Ainsworth) became such a hot-button issue, a "clean-up operation" became necessary. Since Jewish targets were often selected by this duo, the Anti-Defamation League (ADL) turned the tables by bribing two KKK informants (Allen Wayne Roberts and Raymond Roberts) to lure Ainsworth and Tarrants into a murder trap.

Specifically, the couple's next target was Jewish businessman and ADL leader Meyer Davidson, whose Meridian, Miss. house they were told to dynamite. What they didn't know was that Davidson and his family were moved into a hotel before the bombing, and that FBI agents hid in the bushes, waiting to ambush them. A Bonnie and Clyde firefight ensued, and on the evening of June 30, 1968, Kathy Ainsworth died, while Tarrants was severely wounded by more than 70 bullets. Many Klansmen attended her funeral.

What, in effect, do we have here? Ainsworth and Tarrants were used as hired gunmen under COINTELPRO to take out leftist targets, then elements of the right wing FBI and ADL silenced them. The Meridian bombing therefore created an opportunity to eliminate the "polka dot dress woman" before she had a chance to spill the beans.

Wernerhoff also claims that J. Edgar Hoover closely monitored the Meridian set-up, with his agents keeping him abreast of the developments. It's no secret that Hoover despised Bobby Kennedy. Did the orders to kill Ainsworth come from the FBI director before she could expose their plot, or Sirhan Sirhan could identify her? No one can be certain, but if the ADL worked in unison with the FBI by putting up the money for Ainsworth and Tarrants, such a scenario is certainly possible. In addition, the late William Pierce, a well-known anti-Semite, proposed that the ADL's involvement in killing Ainsworth was its way of telling the KKK not to mess with the Jews anymore.

OCCULTUS SERENDIPITOUS

Is a Jewish angle actually feasible? If we look to the "official" explanation as to why Sirhan supposedly killed RFK, he decided, "Bobby Kennedy was no good because he was helping the Jews." He may have been correct. In May 1968 Kennedy announced that he intended to send 50 new jet bombers to Israel.

Similar to JFK's murder, there were certainly other mitigating factors. H. Paul Jeffers expounds on this notion. "There were good reasons to have Robert Kennedy eliminated. He wanted to end the Vietnam War. He wanted to get to the bottom of his brother's assassination. He wanted to break the back of the Teamster's Union. He wanted to end the wild adventures of the CIA."

Like others before him who died at the hand of government hit men, did Bobby also hear the reaper's call? Lisa Pease quotes him shortly before his death telling friends, "I play Russian roulette every time I get up in the morning. But I just don't care. There's nothing I could do about it anyway. This isn't really such a happy existence, is it?"

In light of these foreboding thoughts, Kennedy's *chutzpah* remained, especially toward the power elite. Pease included this gem directed to America's kingmakers. "David Rockefeller isn't the government. We Kennedys eat Rockefellers for breakfast." Many would question the wisdom of such a statement, because none of the Rockefellers got slain by thugs. But look at the tragic lives of Jack, Bobby, Teddy and John Jr. (to name just a few).

What's most compelling about this story are some of the events leading up to the shooting. Other than assassination aficionados, how many people know that on the night before dying, Bobby Kennedy dined with Roman Polanski, Sharon Tate and *Manchurian Candidate* director John Frankenheimer? The Manson-sex-mind control variables drip with too much coincidence.

On the other hand, it's reported that Sirhan attended parties at the Polanski/Tate house, knew members of the Process group, and qualified as being a card-carrying Rosicrucian. Sirhan also learned self-hypnosis from the Rosicrucians, visited their Pasadena chapter on May 28, 1968 (a little more than a month before the shooting), while Rosicrucian material was found in his apartment and car after Kennedy's murder (including Manly P. Hall's *Healing: The Divine Art*). Sirhan also frequented Hall's L.A. library, which served as a treasure trove of occult material. So, yet again we see a Polanski-Manson-occult-Process-Rosicrucian link to an infamous crime. (See chapter 7 of this book.)

MIND CONTROL

At 10:30 p.m. on June 4, 1968, Mrs. Mary Grohs—a Western Union Teletype operator—said that Sirhan "stared fixedly" at a Teletype machine inside the Ambassador Hotel. Later, in the moments following RFK's assassination, onlookers described him as a "puppet" and thought Sirhan was mind-controlled. Others determined that he appeared to be in a trance.

In *Mind Control, World Control*, late researcher Jim Keith quotes two different sources who confirm Sirhan's state of mind. Charles McQuiston, a former high-ranking U.S. intelligence officer, declared, "I'm convinced that Sirhan wasn't aware of what he was doing. He was in a hypnotic trance when he pulled the trigger . . . someone else was involved in the assassination. Sirhan was programmed through hypnosis to kill RFK. What we have here is a real life Manchurian candidate."

Dr. John W. Heisse Jr., president of the International Society of Stress Analysis, concurs. "I believe Sirhan was brainwashed under hypnosis by the constant repetition of words like 'you are nobody. You're nothing. The American Dream is gone'." At that stage, somebody implanted an idea—kill RFK,—and under hypnosis the brainwashed Sirhan accepted it.

UCLA psychiatrist Dr. Bernard Diamond, who treated Sirhan following the murder, said he went under hypnosis so rapidly that he found it difficult to keep him conscious. Such a proclivity suggests that he'd undergone previous hypnosis. Diamond took this notion to the extreme by making him climb the bars of his cell like an orangutan during one session.

At another meeting, the following conversation took place between Diamond and Sirhan:

Diamond—"Is that crazy writing?"

Sirhan—"Yes, yes, yes."

Diamond—"Are you crazy?"

Sirhan—"No, no."

Diamond—"Well, why are you writing crazy?"

Sirhan—"Practice, practice, practice."

Diamond—"Practice for what?"

Sirhan—"Mind control, mind control, mind control."

Sirhan didn't recall shooting Kennedy, nor did he have any conscious memory of writing in notebooks prior to the killing. What police investigators found were the apparent ramblings of a madman. "RFK must die. . . . RFK must be killed. Robert F. Kennedy must be assassinated." These memory blackouts facilitated a type of automatic writing where Sirhan wrote entries such as, "God help me . . . please help me. Salvo Di, Di, Salvo Die, S Salvo."

The words "Di"/ "Salvo" are especially telling because they refer to the famed (and framed) Boston Strangler (allegedly Albert DeSalvo), who we'll reencounter in a few moments. For the time being, however, we need to address one of the CIA's most notorious and inhumane programs—MK-ULTRA. A 1954 CIA document shows that via these experiments, they wanted "to perform an act, *involuntarily*, of *attempted assassination* against a prominent politician." On Feb. 9, 1978, Nicholas Horrock of *The New York Times* wrote a headline declaring "CIA Documents Tell of 1954 Project to Create Involuntary Assassins."

Sirhan Sirhan's notebook. Some of the scribblings include the words Illuminati (written three times), Northern Valley, sukroot, Al HILAL, Saffire and Triune. Symbols included the star of David (three times), two triangles and a four-leaf clover shape. The inclomplete phrase "Do we look like foreigners to you who are not able or unable. . . ." On other pages Sirhan wrote "de salvo," a possible reference to the purported Boston Strangler who was also alleged to have been a victim of mind control.

The mastermind of MK-ULTRA was Jewish military psychiatrist Sidney Gottlieb, while other movers and shakers included Allen Dulles, Richard Helms, the Rockefeller Foundation and Nazi doctors smuggled in via Project Paperclip. It should also be noted that CIA Director Richard Helms held a special animosity for RFK, as did FBI Director J. Edgar Hoover, as we have discussed earlier.

For the sake of accuracy, Richard Condon based his novel *The Manchurian Candidate* on the CIA's Project Artichoke, which then later developed into MK-ULTRA. Artichoke, in simplest terms, sought to program assassins through the use of hypnosis, which then dovetailed into MK-ULTRA. Lisa Pease described their *modus operandi* in *Sirhan Says "I Am Innocent"*: "The CIA was avidly and amorally experimenting on both witting and unwitting subjects with drugs, electric shock, hypnotism, electrode implantation and other techniques in search of ways to completely control the actions of humans." Years later, Richard Helms took it upon himself to destroy the majority of these mind control files.

Entire volumes have been written on this subject, but let's fast-forward to Sirhan. Again, Jim Keith recounts how the LAPD said Sirhan could tell time to the precise minute without the use of a clock. Such a feat indicates that he'd undergone an extended series of hypnotic episodes, or was in fact a mind-control subject.

Naturally, most will ask at this point: who precisely hypnotized Sirhan and turned him into a Manchurian candidate? An answer can be found in his automatic writings and the phrase "Di-Salvo." It seems Dr. William Bryan Jr.—a hypnosis expert involved in CIA mind control experiments—not only had the alleged Boston Strangler Albert De-Salvo as a patient, but also Sirhan Sirhan. That's how these references wound up in his notebooks. Commenting on this subject, independent researcher and George Orwell authority Jackie Jura wrote, "Anything mentioned in the presence of a subject under hypnosis is automatically etched into the subject's mind, especially if it comes from the hypnotist." Jura also adds that Bryan was used by the LAPD to perform hypnosis on patients. We all know, too, that Sirhan lived in the L.A. area, and Kennedy was murdered in downtown L.A.

But who exactly is William Joseph Bryan? As founder of the American Institute of Hypnosis, he claimed to be a technical consultant for the cinematic version of *The Manchurian Candidate*, and boasted of not only hypnotizing Sirhan, but to working on other CIA and top secret projects (e.g., Candy Jones—nee Jessica Wilcox). In addition, directly following the Kennedy murder, Bryan spoke with Ray Briem of *KABC* radio in L.A. and said that Sirhan Sirhan had acted under hypnosis.

If Sirhan did undergo intense mind control, it had to happen somewhere. The big question is: where? Well, it seems that not only did Bryan delve into the realm of extreme hypnosis, but he also fancied himself a fundamentalist preacher (and a sex-crazed one at that). In this role, he associated with Rev. Xavier von Koss in L.A. (head of the International Society of Hypnosis), who hypnotized James Earl Ray.

Now, let's retrace our steps for a moment. It's said that Thomas Tarrants and Kathy Ainsworth (polka-dot dress girl) were participants in the Martin Luther King assassination.

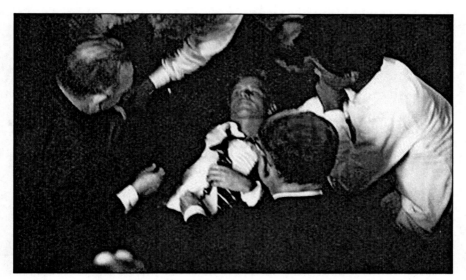

Robert F. Kennedy being tended to after being hit by three bullets, including one to the head. He died 26 hours after being shot.

Who got blamed for this crime and played the fall guy? James Earl Ray, the hypnotized subject of von Koss.

Another fundamentalist preacher who ran in these circles was Jerry Owen, also known as "the Walking Bible" due to his ability to quote passages from the Old and New Testaments. In trouble with the law for years, Owen was an associate of William Joseph Bryan, and also trained horses at Wild Bill's Stables in Santa Ana, California.

In an article by Allen Branson, we learn that:

• Sirhan Sirhan earned a living working with horses;

• Bill Powers, who owned Wild Bill's Stables, said that he'd seen Jerry Owen with Sirhan several times, and that he'd heard Owen mention Sirhan's name;

• On the night of RFK's assassination, Owen visited the LAPD and claimed that he picked up Sirhan hitchhiking;

• Owen said Sirhan wanted to buy a horse, so they agreed to meet—of all places—behind the Ambassador Hotel at 11 p.m.—the precise place Kennedy was shot. (Imagine, doesn't it sound extremely peculiar that a horse sale would be made in downtown L.A. behind a renowned hotel in the middle of the night?); and

• While driving Sirhan around during their hitchhiking jaunt, they stopped at one point so that Sirhan could speak with a woman in a *polka dot dress*.

Owen insisted that the night of his hitchhiking adventure was the first and only time he'd ever met Sirhan. But eyewitnesses saw these two together in the days leading up to the murder. Moreover, Sirhan disappeared for three entire months in 1967. Where did he go? According to former LAPD police officer Mike Ruppert, "Sirhan Sirhan was hypno-programmed using hypnosis, drugs and torture by, among others, the Rev. Jerry Owen and CIA mind-control specialist William Bryan. They hypno-programmed Sirhan at a stable where he [Owen] worked months before the shooting."

Who were the "others" to which Ruppert referred? Although not necessarily directly involved, expert hypnotist Milton Kline said that he could create a patsy in three months, and an actual assassin in six months. I'm not saying he had anything to do with the Sirhan case, but his comments are intriguing.

Another interesting figure in the annals of MK-ULTRA history is Dr. George Estabrooks—a Harvard-trained psychologist, CIA and FBI consultant, and military hypnotist. He was also extremely close to J. Edgar Hoover, and corresponded with him from 1936-1962. In his book, *Bluebird: Deliberate Creation of Multiple Personality by Psychiatrists*, Colin A. Ross, M.D. says, "Dr. Estabrooks is the only psychiatrist or psychologist to have claimed that he built Manchurian candidates."

In *The Perfect Assassin*, Jerry Leonard attributes two quotes to Estabrooks:

1.) "The key to creating an effective assassin rests in splitting a man's personality, or creating multi-personalities, with the aid of hypnotism. This is not science fiction. This has been and is being done. I have done it."

2.) "Is hypnosis dangerous? It can be. Under certain circumstances, it is dangerous to the extreme. It has even been known to lead to murder. Given the right combination of hypnotist and subject, hypnosis can be a lethal weapon."

Estabrooks also suggested that doctors should be "planted" in hospitals to hypnotize specific patients and, according to Dr. Armen Victorian in *Mind Controllers*, "certain types of information given under hypnotic influence cannot be retrieved unless a key element is given (word, picture etc.)." Could this be the reason Sirhan stared so fixedly at the Ambassador Hotel Teletype machine moments before the assassination? Was this device his trigger to send him reeling into a hypnotic trance?

Last but not least, notorious mind-bender Dr. Louis Jolyon West also examined Sirhan Sirhan after his arrest. What makes this point especially pertinent is, West was a CIA contract agent who examined none other than Jack Ruby during his prison stay. Of course, Ruby (Rubinstein) shot his associate, patsy Lee Harvey Oswald, after the JFK assassination. Deeply averse to his role as a fall guy, Ruby protested that he was part of a right-wing conspiracy to kill JFK. Shortly thereafter, he died of "cancer." Jolly West was also summoned to meet with Timothy McVeigh as part of an "Oklahoma City response team." Many claim that McVeigh also unwittingly participated in a much larger conspiracy, and that doctors subjected him to mind control prior to being executed. Sirhan Sirhan was in good company in this regard.

CHAPTER 7

CHARLES MANSON

SHEEP-DIPPING CHARLES MANSON

"I am what you've made me. The mad dog killer fiend leper is a reflection of your society." —CHARLES MANSON

—*Geraldo: Live From Death Row*

I s Charles Manson actually a savage, psychopathic killer, or did he simply *play* one on TV to further the agenda of a hidden cabal that effectively used him to put a dagger through the heart of America's 1960s counter-culture? After all, Manson is the only man sitting on death row not convicted of murder. Rather, jurors found him guilty of *conspiracy* to commit murder. Therefore, the most pressing question should be: who conceived this *conspiracy* to initiate the Tate-Labianca slayings, and what purpose did it serve?

Researcher extraordinaire Mae Brussell postulated in an interview on Oct. 13, 1971 with Gloria Baron of KLRB Radio that the same team that assassinated JFK, RFK and Martin Luther King also orchestrated the Manson killings. Agreeing with this premise, Carol Greene wrote in *Test-Tube Murders: The Case of Charles Manson*, "The Summer of Love was not spontaneous, but an exhaustively planned behavior-modification experiment to subvert the 1960s youth movement, with the Family as its end product."

Naturally, such an assessment flies in the face of everything we've learned about Manson via television *programming*. But what if a hidden military-industrial cabal felt so strongly that the anti-war rock 'n' roll hippie movement was "hurting business" to such an extent that they had to be knocked down a few notches?

Enter Charles Manson—the ultimate hypnotic bogeyman demonized by the mainstream media in each and every American's living room. After laying his spooky rap on the masses, longhairs were no longer peaceful and loving. Instead, they'd steal your sons and daughters, pump them full of mind-altering drugs, then send them out on mass-murder sprees. Charlie became a vehicle through which the propagandists spread their message.

If this hypothesis is correct, who held the wires upon which Manson dangled like a voodoo doll marionette? The first widespread article on Manson came from publisher Patrick Frawley, who coincidentally enough was a large financial supporter of Richard Nixon. Penned by a man named Ed Butler, it also happens that this same writer worked with, of all people, Lee Harvey Oswald in New Orleans prior to the Kennedy assassination. Entitled *Did Hate Kill Tate*, Butler blamed the killings on hippies and Communist Black Panthers, who he said were intent on spreading terror. Hmmm, again the word *terror* . . . similar to the 9-11 *war on terror*. Mae Brussell also mentioned how certain symbols were used—i.e. the hood over certain victims' heads represented the KKK, while the rope around Sharon Tate's neck represented a slave-day lynching.

That initial impetus, or stimuli, led to the infamous *Life* magazine cover where Charles Manson reached full-blown bogeyman status with his eyes . . . those creepy eyes . . . glaring out from every corner newsstand. His Love and Terror Cult could get *your* children next door, or else he'd dispatch a slew of hitchhiker killers to burst into your home at night. Even our president—Richard "I Am Not a Criminal" Nixon—assured us of Manson's guilt.

The media magicians behind this ploy used Edward Bernays' *Propaganda* tactics to their fullest. Let's face it: weren't these the same ones that covered up the killers who ambushed JFK in Dallas and blew his brains out? Then, LBJ and his cronies spent billions ramping up the disastrous war machine in Vietnam. Do you think they'd let a few long-haired rock 'n' roll musicians like John Lennon stop their progress in the Asian jungles?

The counter-culture represented a real-life threat, making the Tate-Labianca killings a *political massacre.* Brussell called this technique a "strategy of tension," which falls right in line with the power elite's use of Hegelian dialectics:

Thesis: The onset of a violent war in Vietnam.

Antithesis: A youthful, Camelot president who wanted to bring our troops home.

Synthesis: Violently traumatize the nation via a bloody assassination, then rapidly escalate the war.

Thesis: Rake in billions of war profits while the country increasingly opposes military involvement in Vietnam.

Antithesis: A youth movement championed by the Beatles and other rock musicians led large numbers in saying "stop the war," "give peace a chance," and "make love not war."

Synthesis: Turn a longhaired cult musician's "Family" into psychopathic killers—all based upon the Beatles' *Helter Skelter.* The result: more war, law and order—and fewer civil rights.

Those in control sought to discredit their primary opponents to the war, specifically John Lennon, so why not prop up an antithetical witch doctor named Charles Manson who perpetrated a deliberate plan of increased violence. The death of 1960s counter-culture can be attributed to the following factors: JFK assassination; Malcolm X assassination; Martin Luther King assassination; widespread race riots, including Watts; RFK assassination; Chicago '68 Democratic National Convention riots; LSD made illegal; Helter Skelter mass murder; deaths of Neal Cassady and Jack Kerouac; Altamont; the overdose deaths (or murders) of Brian Jones, Jimi Hendrix, Janis Joplin and Jim Morrison; and Kent State.

Meanwhile, tens of thousands of American soldiers were being slaughtered, contaminated with Agent Orange and addled by hard drugs in Southeast Asia, not to mention the "little yellow people" whose lives and homes didn't seem to matter one iota. In all honesty, name one thing any of the Vietnamese ever personally did to us or to the men who (albeit reluctantly) killed them. Yet the carpet bombings, poisonings and carnage continued until 1975—easily becoming one of the most shameful chapters in American history.

Yet, here emerged on the scene a charismatic little ex-con named Man-Son, whose purpose revolved around discrediting the entire hippie movement. After Helter Skelter went down, Charlie then carved a bloody swastika in his forehead, further causing society to despise him and be reminded of that *horrible* Holocaust. Generating immediate sympathy for the Jews, Manson deliberately (and calculatingly) equated himself with Adolf Hitler. But none of these actions were random. Under the umbrella of the FBI's COINTELPRO and Operation Chaos, Manson filled the role of agent provocateur—one of many to infiltrate the counter-culture and lead to its eventual demise.

SHEEP-DIPPING

In the words of Salvador Astucia, who included two sections on Charles Manson in his fantastic article on the murder John Lennon, he defines sheep-dipping as "an intelligence process in which a person's image is changed for a desired effect. If someone is going to be the fall guy for a murder, they must be tricked into doing incriminating things that will later be used against them."

Lee Harvey Oswald's duping by various intelligence agencies is legendary (his trip to Russia, handing out pro-Castro leaflets in New Orleans), while Timothy McVeigh's role as an infiltrator of far-right militia groups led to him being a patsy for the OKC bombing. Even the purported 9-11 Islamic terrorists had an extensive *legend* created around them by Mossad art-student spies. Of course, all of these parties were handled on a need-to-know basis. In Charlie's case his controllers dressed him in bell-bottom jeans, a frayed leather coat, and slung a guitar around his neck. With hair growing past his shoulders while laying a hippie/prison rap, he fit right in with all the others at Haight-Ashbury in San Francisco.

In reality, Charlie never considered himself a hippy. He grew up with 1950s beatniks, then especially became schooled by some of the best conmen and mind-benders in federal prison. Mae Brussell likened Charlie to a soldier sent to kill in Vietnam, or a Mafia hit man. He had a job to do, and soon he mingled with Hollywood stars while rubbing elbows with some of the country's most recognized musicians.

Again, Mae Brussell provides an invaluable overview: "In this strange world of covert overthrow of the governments and clandestine armies and secret operations, the problem we're facing is that you're working with two realities: what we assume is the real way to function and move, and then a system of what we call power—exchange of power, economic power; power over people by controlling their lives. In order to do that, you disguise certain persons and send them into roles to influence. They become actors on a stage and they influence our minds in a way that is not real, but affect a reality that will touch us later."

Manson realized that manipulation games were being played with him, but not entirely. A fitting story comes from Adam Gorightly in *Shadow Over Santa Susana* where Charlie is propped up like a little guru in his desert hideout, preparing his followers for a coming apocalyptic race war. But then, after his arrest, he remarks caustically, "I want to know who was peeing on my leash." In hindsight, Manson's handlers gave him a great deal of leeway, but once his purpose was served and the Helter Skelter killings materialized, they clamped down on him with a vengeance (just like those who preceded him).

One must wonder, however, how this minute petty thief—victimized in a cesspool of pedophilia at Father Flanagan's Boys Town and other reformatories—wound up in such a precarious position. Some researchers purport that MK-ULTRA monitoring began during his youth in West Virginia. Such claims could be dismissed as absurd if it weren't for one strange anomaly. Manson's mother befriended the mother of Sara Jane Moore in West Virginia, making Charlie a childhood pal of a woman who attempted to assassinate President Gerald Ford on Sept. 22, 1975. Later, Moore admitted to being an FBI informant. Stranger yet, Charlie's number one gal—Squeaky Fromme—also unsuccessfully tried to shoot President Ford, thereby putting Vice President Nelson Rockefeller in charge of the White House. Now ask yourself: what are the odds that any one person would know two individuals who'd become wannabe presidential assassins—all happening within 17 days of each other?

Whatever the case, it's certain that those who operated MK-ULTRA mind-control programs kept their feelers out for potential recruits. The overall goal of this nefarious experiment was to create programmed assassins, such as Sirhan Sirhan. Being that religious cults laid a perfect foundation and became breeding grounds for such activities, could the Family have been nothing more than a convenient group mind-control experiment?

It's also documented that MK-ULTRA programs were in existence at Vacaville State Prison during the 1970s and 1980s—a penitentiary that Manson resided in during that era. Hundreds of prisoners were subjected to an array of bizarre tests, so who's to say that Manson couldn't have been an earlier victim prior to his release from Terminal Island on March 21, 1967 (the spring equinox)?

This possibility isn't so outlandish if we accept that Manson befriended one of the most famous gangsters of all-time—Frank Costello. Acting as an apprentice to this Mafioso legend, what if Costello recognized in Manson all the qualities needed for a charismatic, mind-control guru that could be set loose to discredit left-wing radicals? Why would Costello choose to do such a thing? Answer: because his closest associate was none other than Jewish kingpin mobster Meyer Lansky.

To appreciate this point's importance, we need to remember that global politics is nothing more than a vast organized crime syndicate. With that being said, it's also been proven time and again that governments and intelligence agencies work hand-in-hand with established criminals. Since Lansky reigned at the top of this underworld, he was also directly connected to the JFK assassination. In addition, Jack Ruby worked for Lansky, who maintained vast holdings in Cuba. Lansky's name repeatedly shows up in relation to various government operations, not to mention that he was also an ardent Zionist—a point that will become important later.

INFORMANT?

If Manson was "noticed" by in-the-know wardens, prison psychiatrists or Frank Costello as being a possible patsy in the future, an arrangement would have certainly been made at some point.

"Look, Charlie, you've spent the majority of your life in jail. You're a loser for the umpteenth time. If we set you free, you're going to wind up back here again in the federal pen. So, how would you like to play a game with us? We'll give you all the women, drugs and freedom imaginable. All we ask in return is to corral a bunch of flower children into a commune and lay your freaky pimp-rap on them. How's that sound?"

Charlie, being a streetwise con, certainly viewed them with suspicion, but eventually jumped at the chance. To someone that knew nothing but rape in juvenile detention centers, slamming doors, alarms and tiny cells with iron bars, the chance to play cowboy and indians with the Feds seemed a sweet deal.

With the wheels tentatively set in motion, Charlie became one of many potential subjects. I say "many" because the mind-benders never put all their eggs in one basket. Contingency plans always exist, as can be seen by Adam Gorightly's book on Kerry Thornley, who functioned as a possible alternative patsy to Lee Harvey Oswald if need be.

A pertinent question at this stage is: was Manson mind-controlled, or simply a naïve opportunist? Probably both.

Cisco Wheeler, who co-authored a book with Fritz Springmeier called *The Illuminati Formula to Create an Undetectable Total Mind Control Slave*, purports that Manson fell into the MK-ULTRA Monarch program, and that he received his initial programming at a secret military base near China Lake off Route 66, 45 minutes northwest of Barker Ranch.

It's also known that Manson's parole officer in San Francisco (where he migrated after being released from prison) had strong ties to the CIA, as did others who ran "clinics" in Haight-Ashbury. Another notorious figure on the scene was Dr. Jolly West, one of the most infamous of intel mind-benders. West ran a safe house in San Francisco where he'd hypnotize subjects and give them post-hypnotic suggestions prior to being administered LSD. Then, once they started tripping, the individual could be pushed in whatever direction the doctors desired.

This technique sounds eerily like what Manson did during his many LSD group sessions with the Family.

After amassing the core members of his cult in San Francisco, Manson and gang relocated to the L.A. area, where an entirely new set of insanity ensued. However, one notion must be interjected. Did part of Manson's deal include becoming an informant for the LAPD? Again, such a thought seems preposterous on the surface, but let's examine it a little more closely.

First, it's been established that Manson grew up with Sara Jane Moore—an admitted FBI informant and would-be presidential assassin. According to Maury Terry in *The Ultimate Evil*, Manson also had a significant dinner date in 1967 with Abigail Folger and Shorty Shea. Folger, of course, became one of those slaughtered at the Tate Residence on Aug. 8, 1969. She also periodically gave money not only to Manson, but also funded occult filmmaker and Aleister Crowley devotee, Kenneth Anger.

On the other hand, anyone that's read Vincent Bugliosi's fairy-tale *Helter Skelter* knows that ranch-hand Shorty Shea was allegedly killed and decapitated at the Spahn Rahn, then buried at an undisclosed location. But Salvador Astucia theorized that Shea acted instead as an FBI informant, then told the kids at Spahn Ranch to stay away from Charlie or they'd end up in prison. Obviously, Shea's revelations would have ruined the entire Manson scheme, so the powers-that-be had him killed to preserve their plan (by Manson or otherwise).

The concept of FBI-CIA-LAPD involvement in the Manson cover-up becomes more real when we consider one crucial element—Manson repeatedly and unabashedly violated his federal parole on a repeated basis. There existed clear evidence of rampant drug and alcohol use, theft, plus Manson was arrested two times before the Tate killings for statutory rape of underage girls. Yet no police actions were taken, and not once did he serve time in prison during his hiatus.

Further, Gorightly quotes former L.A. Deputy Sheriff Preston Guillory, who stated, "A few weeks prior to the Spahn Ranch raid, we were told that we weren't to arrest Manson or any of his followers. Somebody very high up was controlling everything that was going on and was seeing to it that we didn't bust Manson."

These words are extremely powerful, but fitting. After the Tate-Labianca slayings, it seemed as if the LAPD took every step possible to cover-up the crimes and *not* solve the case. Investigators were deliberately stymied, and it wasn't until Susan Atkins snitched in prison that legal proceedings took place. It's even been reported that Lawrence Schiller gave Atkins $150,000 to say Charlie masterminded the entire affair. Schiller is the same man who stoked the fires of Gary Gilmore's execution in 1977.

Once his trial began, the public heard one of the most fantastic legal theories in American history. Vincent Bugliosi—who later penned an epic tome supporting the Warren Report's conclusion of Lee Harvey Oswald's guilt as a lone-nut assassin—proposed that the Family's killing spree was rooted in Manson's apocalyptic vision of a coming race war, all generated by messages he received from Beatles songs, especially *Helter Skelter*. Charlie then "brainwashed" and "programmed" his followers to kill for him.

In reality, "Sexy Sadie" Susan Atkins and Little Paul Watkins (at one time Manson's right-hand man) were the first to decipher and interpret supposed messages emanating from the Fab Four. We must remember in the psychedelic-soaked '60s, *everybody* thought the Beatles were communicating with them (e.g., "Paul is dead" rumors). For the public to fall for such a convoluted notion as *Helter Skelter* is laughable. Even its engineer—Bugliosi—stated that Charlie's "mind control" closely resembled tactics used by the U.S. military.

PIMPING THE PATSY

Let's face it: Charles Manson emerged from Terminal Island Penitentiary a well-versed jailhouse pimp-conman-philosopher who studied Scientology and Dianetics, hypnotism, psychology, religion, magic, astral projection, freemasonry and Rosicrucianism. When new prisoners entered the system that had something on the ball, he'd sit at their feet and soak up knowledge. Manson also learned how to play the guitar from Alvin "Old Creepy" Karpis, a vaunted member of Ma and Doc Barker's gang. Karpis also taught Charlie how to use Masonic hand signals (which he flashed at the judge during his trial).

By the time of his release, insiders realized that Charlie had a natural inclination to fill the role of messiah cult leader. In his book *Death Cults*, Adam Gorightly even notes that Manson met with a stage hypnotist on the Sunset Strip who later opened the Hollywood Hypnotism Center. In all, however, Manson understood that the entire matter was a put-on. "When I start believing I might really possess all the powers attributed to me and I try to work a whammy on my prison guard—he or she shuts the prison door in my face. Back to reality. I realize I'm only what I've always been, a half-assed nothing."

Still, the unaware and famous seemed to fall for this well-crafted ruse. Briefly, Charlie served as a "religious consultant" for Universal Studios during the production of a Jesus movie. He also hob-knobbed with elites from the music business, including Neil Young, Dennis Wilson of the Beach Boys and Terry Melcher. Young said that plenty of rock 'n' rollers knew Charlie; and even though he didn't make it *per se* as a superstar, Manson reached the upper echelon in terms of who recorded him (e.g., Terry Melcher, son of Doris Day).

In this regard, we have to examine Terry Melcher's role. According to prosecutor Bugliosi, Manson had his Family members target Roman Polanski's residence as revenge against Melcher because he refused to sign a recording contract. But again, Bugliosi's version is deliberately incorrect. First, Manson fully realized that Terry Melcher had moved out of his property at Cielo Drive months earlier. Secondly, Manson told Nuel Emmons that he actually *liked* Melcher because he gave him money, credit cards, his car, and at least the chance to record in his studio. So, revenge against him wasn't a motive.

Now, why would Terry Melcher—America's version of Beatles manager Brian Epstein—take such a keen interest in a lifelong con and product of the penal system? Salvador Astucia speculates that as a music insider, Melcher had interests in Manson other than music. Rather, Melcher served as a conduit, forging ties to people like Dennis Wilson.

Other peculiarities existed. Mae Brussell wonders why Manson met with Beverly Hills attorney George Shibley prior to his release from Terminal Island. Then, after setting his sights on San Francisco, Manson cruised around in a bus, had access to credit cards for gas, and had to support dozens of men and women in his Family, yet he never had a job. As months passed, children were added to the mix, plus all the other bills associated with keeping these people alive. Bugliosi dismissed this concern by saying that Charlie's gals dumpster-dived for food. But try to imagine how many trashcans needed to be hit on a *daily basis* to keep 30 people alive. Where did the money come from?

THE OCCULT

Since we're discussing the Family, another perspective should be considered. Although Bugliosi characterized Charlie's scene as being one of stoned-out brain-dead hypnotic zombies, the reality is far different. Tex Watson and Sadie Atkins were authentic bad seeds—and it was these two who performed most of the Tate-Labianca killings. Atkins, along with Bobby "Cupid" Beausoleil, belonged to Anton Lavey's Church of Satan, with Atkins playing a topless vampire in one of his productions. Beausoleil also lived with experimental filmmaker Kenneth Anger, while starring in his movie *Lucifer Rising*.

These ties to the occult are important because, often, intelligence agencies disguise their programs in the form of Satanism or witchcraft. In *Death Cults*, Adam Gorightly suggests that Anton Lavey, the Church of Satan founder in San Francisco, belonged to the MK-ULTRA fraternity, and that Sharon Tate's murder was in reality an occult ritual.

Here is where circumstances get very heavy. After leaving the Bay Area, Manson and his Family traveled south to the L.A. area, whereupon they eventually became acquainted with a group called the Spiral Staircase. This meeting served as a transition point for the Family, because instead of simply spending their time in pursuit of hedonistic pleasure, they now associated with people deeply into the occult. Included were witches, sadomasochists, practitioners of mind control, and those who drank blood during animal sacrifices. (Do any of these descriptions sound like the Helter Skelter slayings?)

From there, Manson branched-out to other potentially government-affiliated organizations, such as Timothy Leary's Himalayan Academy and the Esalen Institute. More importantly, at the Spiral Staircase, Manson met Robert DeGrimston and Mary Ann MacLean, ex-Scientologists who founded the Process Church of the Final Judgment. Although I won't delve into their lengthy history here, the Process presented a philosophy that ultimately paralleled that which Charles Manson preached to his Family.

Their symbiotic relationship has been proven on a number of different fronts. First, while still living in San Francisco, Manson and his girls resided at 636 Cole Street, whereas DeGrimston's address was 407 Cole—only two blocks away. The Process also tried to form a union with Lavey's Church of Satan. Reportedly, and this is quite bizarre, Manson once met with the Process leaders at Roman Polanski's residence. Taken one step further, "Son of Sam" patsy David Berkowitz has revealed that Manson actually belonged to the Process Church, and that he was working "on orders" from them when orchestrating the Tate-Labianca murders. Then, after his arrest, Manson spouted-off quite extensively about his relationship with the Process Church until one of their members visited him in prison and told him to clam up. It seems Charlie was supposed to remain a lone-nut killer with no affiliation to any external dark forces.

Yet, Manson came in direct contact with and was influenced by Scientology, the Church of Satan, OTO (Ordo Templi Orientis) and DeGrimston's Process Church. The significance of these associations cannot be overstated, as Adam Gorightly compares Manson to a "game board pawn in a reign of terror, orchestrated by a vast underground network consisting of members of the intelligence community, rogue or otherwise, in league with satanically influenced cults and secret societies, who deal in drugs, prostitution and pornography, using mind control and ritual murder as a method of their madness."

These are potent words, and probably closer than anyone has ever gotten to encapsulating the Helter Skelter phenomenon.

DRUGS

Manson, Atkins and Bobby Beausoleil were all independently lured into the occult before ever coming together as Manson Family members. We also need to reexamine Tex "I'm Here to Do the Devil's Work"

Watson, who Bugliosi portrayed as a naïve Texas teen and football star that unwittingly got ensnared by the wily Charles Manson. In reality, Watson migrated from Texas after high school, then started dealing drugs in L.A. By all accounts, his efforts were less than stellar, and along the way he burned plenty of dangerous people (bikers, Black Panthers etc.) and subsequently made lots of enemies. Plus, Watson also ran around with a rock 'n' roll crowd, with Manson meeting him through his affiliation with Beach Boy Dennis Wilson.

As a result, Tex by no means epitomized the country bumpkin boy-next-door figure that had innocently fallen prey to the monster, Charles Manson. There are also allegations made by Mae Brussell that he met 30 to 40 times with an attorney in L.A. named Mr. DeLoach. If her claim is true, why would Watson confer with a lawyer prior to his encounter with Manson?

Similar to scores of other groups that were targeted by the government's COINTELPRO operations—including anti-war groups, the Panthers, and later militia groups prior to the 1995 OKC bombing—it appears the Family was also infiltrated by informants. Bikers such as Danny DeCarlo are mentioned, as well as other lesser-known members. In addition, Little Paul Watkins provided crucial "race war-Beatles-Book of Revelation" testimony to the D.A. But, could Tex Watson and Susan Atkins have been mind-controlled assets of a clandestine intelligence agency?

Salvador Astucia answers this question very adroitly: "I am not claiming that either Atkins or Watkins consciously worked with the FBI; I am saying that the FBI essentially conducted extensive mind control processing on them, then pointed them in Manson's direction and steered them into the group."

Remember: Atkins and Watson did the vast majority of killing at the Tate-Labianca residences. Manson didn't kill anyone at either place. Atkins had been through Anton Lavey's madhouse, while Watson plunged deeply into drugs, even frying his brains once on belladonna. Further, it's known that not only did Charlie always take much smaller amounts of LSD than his cohorts, he also fed his Family other "mind control" types of drugs, such as STP, MDA and psilocybin. Jonestown researcher John Judge even went so far as to say that Manson was bestowed with a military MK-ULTRA version of LSD used at the infamous Wright-Patterson Air Force Base called psilocybin EA1729.

Here's where things get full-blown insane. In *The Ultimate Evil*, Terry Maury proposed that two days after the Tate murders, Manson was seen driving a black Mercedes belonging to a "big LSD dealer." He also characterized him as a "former Israeli who had strong ties with the intelligence community." It ends up that the person described by Maury was none other than Ronald Stark, and although not actually an Israeli, he did *pose* as one at times.

In an earlier chapter about Mary Pinchot Meyer and JFK, I clearly established Ronald Stark's direct ties to the CIA. It's now known that he also played a profound role in regard to the MK-ULTRA program. Here is a quick overview. Stark first appeared on the "hippie" scene in 1969 with loads of acid that he used as an enticement. He then formed The Brotherhood of Eternal Love and manufactured a type of LSD called Orange Sunshine.

Shortly thereafter, Timothy Leary resided with The Brotherhood while Stark funneled money to a place called the Esalen Institute. Not so coincidentally, Abigail Folger (slain victim of the Folger coffee family) attended seminars at this locale. Robert DeGrimston gave lectures, while Charles Manson also frequented Esalen. But here's the real catch. Stark's Orange Sunshine acid produced extreme violence, negativity and thoughts of death. Tex Watson said they dropped Orange Sunshine the night before the Tate massacres, while others claim this was the same acid used at the Rolling Stones' Altamont concert where all hell broke loose and the Hell's Angels beat a man to death after he pulled a gun and aimed it at Mick Jagger. There's also every possibility that Charles Manson associated with Stark, and may have dealt Orange Sunshine.

The picture that is now emerging is far different than the one portrayed by media sources where the Family consisted of some innocent peace and love flower children wearing beads. Once Satanism, bad drugs and covert intelligence agencies enter the picture, the scenario got much hazier. Consider, for instance, the make-up of Charlie's encampments. Upon their initial raids, police referred to the various locales as "military-style communes." They were correct. There were guard shacks, lookout points, walky-talkies and telescopes and military style telephones. Their dune buggies had machine-gun turrets mounted on them. Those on patrol carried guns and swords.

These supposed "flower children" were living in a boot camp; and Charlie—by arrangement with his government handlers—was their longhaired guru drill sergeant. It was only later (once an agenda needed to be served) that the media called their crash pads a "hippie commune." In actuality, however, these were, as author Dave McGowan called them, paramilitary compounds. Charlie had a mission, and that mission ultimately led to one goal—kill, kill, kill.

HOLLYWOOD BABYLON

To begin this section, it's already been established that Charles Manson didn't direct his killers to 10066 Cielo Drive as revenge against music producer Terry Melcher. He knew Melcher had moved out, and, in fact, Manson had actually visited this residence prior to the fateful night of Aug. 8, 1969.

So, if revenge against Melcher is ruled out, why did Tex, Sadie and gang gravitate toward Sharon Tate's home? On one level, Joel Norris, author of the book *Serial Killers*, has stated that Charles Manson was not only a drug dealer, but also a contract killer involved in organized crime and a murder-for-hire ring. After the slayings were committed, Manson unequivocally said that the victims deserved to die because they were involved in kiddy porn. In prison hierarchies, child molesters are seen as the worst kind of criminal.

Such a statement is very provocative, but is it true? Let's examine each of the victims to gauge the accuracy of Norris's assessment. For starters, in 1977 Roman Polanski entered a guilty plea for the statutory rape of 13-year-old Samantha Gailey. *Easy Rider* actor and 1960s wild man Dennis Hopper has gone on record as saying that sadistic movies with Hollywood stars were filmed at the Tate residence.

It's also rumored that Polanski and Sharon Tate collected "fame porn" and wife-swapping films, and may have also produced them. In addition, the LAPD seized undisclosed porn videos from the Tate household after the murders.

Although Roman Polanski was overseas when the massacre occurred, his wife wasn't so fortunate. In an article entitled *Celluloid Heroes: The Tangled Web of Charlie Manson*, Dave McGowan posits that Sharon Tate was introduced to witchcraft on the set of Polanski's *Fearless Vampire Killers* by Alexander Saunders, also known as "King of the Witches." Others claim she made racy stag films with Steve McQueen, as well as other less-than-virtuous figures.

Also killed alongside Sharon Tate was Jay Sebring, her former lover and hairdresser to the stars, who once acted in a movie with Mansonite Bobby Beausoleil. Sebring's tastes also delved into the risqué, as he and Voytek Frykowski are said to have engaged in live S&M movies that became very extreme. Another story has him luring some of Manson's girls into one of his S&M flicks, then abusing them with whips and chains.

Lastly, it seems Leno and Rosemary Labianca weren't quite squeaky clean either. In McGowan's *Celluloid Heroes*, we find Leno immersed in the underworld, owing upwards of $250,000 in gambling debts. His situation was so dire that Leno's phone lines were reportedly tapped to keep track of his whereabouts. In addition, multiple sources have them being drug traffickers of crystal meth. But if the truth is told, nearly the entire crowd that was slain dealt in narcotics, including Frykowski, Abigail Folger, Jay Sebring, the Labiancas, and possibly even Sharon Tate who may have dealt hallucinogens.

Eventually, the Family's path intersected with these figures at the Tate and Labianca residences, producing one of the most gruesome multiple murder scenes in American history. Mae Brussell didn't view the killings as something random or amateurish, but more as a military ambush. Her reasoning is clear. First, somebody shimmied up the telephone poles at Sharon Tate's house and had the foresight to cut the wires so there'd be no contact with the outside world. Then, while multiple people were violently slaughtered, nobody heard a sound. Dogs didn't bark, the caretaker didn't hear gunshots, and nobody noticed a getaway car. Considering how many jobs the CIA has botched during their history, these hits were remarkably clean. It's even debated that

Manson himself ventured to the Tate residence afterward to tidy up the scene, in addition to wiping away all fingerprints. A drug-crazed homicidal lunatic, or someone very in-tune with what his mission entailed, like a hired contract killer.

ROSEMARY'S BABY

Since all that's been written thus far is accurate, we need to ask: why were the Labianca and Polanski residences targeted? Well, obviously *somebody* needed to be the victims, so the Labiancas were an easier choice. If these wet jobs (i.e., covert assassinations performed by government operatives) were contracted out to a rogue, underworld arm of an intelligence service, then the Labiancas may have been nothing more than payback for vast gambling debts. They were in way too deep, and as a result got offed.

But why did they select a nine-month pregnant Sharon Tate? Salvador Astucia provides a compelling hypothesis. In 1968, Roman Polanski directed one of the hottest movies of the year—a cinematic version of Ira Levin's *Rosemary's Baby*. In this film Polanski—who is Jewish—depicted the Jews living in New York's Dakota Apartments as satanic witches.

Reinforcing an age-old stereotype that Jews are of the devil, he took it a step further by showing them as practicing a Talmudic form of witchcraft. He also depicted the actors as reinforcing Jewish stereotypes with their large noses, names (Saperstein), and using poor table manners.

But his worst move revolved around the Jewish practice of *blood libel* where a Gentile baby is sacrificed for Jews in a black magic ritual. To reinforce this occult element, Polanski hired occult showman Anton Lavey as his technical director, then had him play Satan when Rosemary (Mia Farrow) was impregnated with his demon seed.

The Jewish elite were furious at Polanski for airing their dirty laundry and telling their darkest secrets (i.e., that they're devil worshipping witches who practice ritual murder and other occult rites). To them, Roman Polanski had committed the ultimate crime with *Rosemary's Baby*. So, as revenge, they told their gun-for-hire—Charles Manson—to target Polanski's wife while he was away in the UK. After all, if Polanski wanted to depict blood libel in a movie and finger the Jews, then these high-powered Jews would give him the *real thing* by slaughtering his wife and unborn baby. The gory message couldn't be clearer: how's that for blood libel, Polanski? Then, a few years later, Polanski was forced to flee the country due to his dalliance with an underage teenage girl.

CONCLUSION

If Charles Manson ultimately filled the role of patsy, why hasn't he spilled the beans and ratted out his superiors? To answer that question, let's look at it this way. It's 1967, and 33-year-old Manson has spent two-thirds of his life in some type of reformatory or prison. At one point, it's noticed that he's charismatic, amoral and brilliant (Neil Young called him "living poetry").

So, a cabal of intelligence mind-benders confront him prior to his release and say, "Listen, Charlie, you're a lifetime con in federal prison, and it's a pretty safe bet that once you're free, it'll only be a matter of time until you're back. Now, we have this idea. Why don't you work with us? We'll give you all the women, drugs, guns, cars and freedom that you want. You'll finally get to LIVE by being our little undercover guitar-playing hippie guru."

They lay out the scenario—on a need-to-know basis, of course—then conclude, "Now, Charlie, if you say no, do you know how easy it'll be for us to trump up some charges against you in a few months? You'll be back in federal prison as a lifer, and that's all you'll ever know."

As a streetwise con, Charlie agreed, and two years later "Helter Skelter was comin' down fast" according to the Beatles. Manson ultimately realized that he'd been Lee Harvey Oswalded.

So why didn't he then speak out? There are two possible reasons. First, he may have done so on any number of occasions, and the media simply edited it out.

Or, if he did spill the beans, what would the spin-doctors say? "Oh, that's crazy old Charlie flying off the handle again. He's insane with all his mumbo jumbo." More than likely, however, upon being arrested, his handlers laid it out all too clearly. "Okay, Charlie, yeah, you played the fall guy. But here's the deal. You're heading back to

A Process Church ceremony in the 1960s. Some Process members were allegedly people who had left L. Ron Hubbard's Church of Scientology and the Process Church was accused of Satanic leanings as they preached a duality of Jesus and Satan.

federal prison. Do you want to be thrown out in the general population where you'll be beaten, brutalized, raped, set on fire and probably killed? Or, we'll make you our superstar bogeyman that we can trot out every once in awhile to scare the hell out of middle-class America. We'll give you a celebrity cell, interviews with Geraldo Rivera, a guitar and, in all honesty, you can live a pretty good life, relatively speaking. So, whatta ya say?"

Alas, the ultimate bogeyman emerges in the likeness of Charles Manson.

CHAPTER 8

KENT STATE BLOODBATH

THE MASSACRE OF STUDENTS IN OHIO

"Right here!"
"Get set!"
"Fire!"

Contradicting prevailing conventional wisdom, on May 1, 2007 a reel-to-reel tape lasting 20 seconds (recorded by Kent State student Terry Strubbe) found the light of day, proving that at 12:24 p.m. on May 4, 1970, officers of the Ohio National Guard issued a *verbal command* to their troops, directing them to shoot at unarmed students who posed absolutely no threat to them.

For four days, tensions had been high on the Ohio campus. Prior to the shooting, Strubbe placed a microphone outside his dorm room window, at first catching the banter of anti-war protesters. Then, according to activist Alan Canfora in *U.S. Government Conspiracy at Kent State*, "there was a verbal order to fire and a dozen Troop G killers stopped, turned, began to shoot [their deadly M-1 rifles] and continued to fire 67 times into our crowd of unarmed students."

The firing squad proved, according to Bob Fitrakas and Harvey

Wasserman's May 6, 2007 article, "The Lethal Media Silence on Kent State's Smoking Guns": "What 'conspiracy theorists' have argued since 1970—that there was a direct military order leading to the unprovoked assassination of unarmed students. Freedom of Information Act documents showed collusion between Ohio's Gov. James A. Rhodes and the FBI that aimed to terrorize anti-war demonstrators and their protests that were raging throughout the nation."

VIETNAM

On April 30, 1970, Richard Nixon outraged the country by announcing that combat troops were being sent into Cambodia. For a candidate that promised to end the catastrophic Vietnam War in 1968, escalating and expanding this fiasco became a pill too bitter to swallow. Nixon's "peace with honor" would soon turn U.S. campuses into a raging battlefield.

SDS (Students for a Democratic Society) member Canfora paints a vivid picture: "It is difficult to overstate the political and cultural impact of the killing of four Kent State students and wounding nine more on May 4, 1970. The nation's campuses were on fire over Richard Nixon's illegal invasion of Cambodia. Scores of universities were ripped apart by mass demonstrations and student strikes."

Eventually, 58,256 American soldiers were needlessly killed in the Southeast Asian jungles, while hundreds of thousands returned home wounded, paralyzed, drug-addicted, addled by Agent Orange (and other chemicals) or traumatized by post-traumatic stress disorder. In the meantime, our war machine generals and CFR elitists approved the slaughter of a million Vietnamese—poisoning their land, destroying villages, separating families, while CIA mercenaries exported heroin by the ton from Golden Triangle locales such as Burma, Laos and Thailand.

The Vietnam War is a national atrocity—a shameful, disastrous chapter in our history—and those who commanded it should be damned to hell for eternity. These men were "War Pigs"—psychopathic monsters who spread a cancerous sickness across the world.

This tiny campus outside Cleveland could not tolerate the killing fields any longer. In a July 10, 2005 article entitled "Was a Government Conspiracy Responsible for the Kent State Massacre," Greg A. Schwartz described how students were readied: "Leaders of the Kent State University SDS [were] one of the most well-organized and militant groups"—so much so that the U.S. House of Representatives Committee on Internal Security investigated its activities in June 1969.

MAY 1

A day following Nixon's Cambodia announcement, incensed activists held a rally where they conducted last rites for the U.S. Constitution, claiming that the president had killed it. Students then arranged a mock funeral and buried the fallen document.

That evening, crowds gathered and lit bonfires in the streets of Kent. With anti-war sentiment running high, the youth spray-painted buildings with graffiti, threw beer bottles at police cars, looted two stores and smashed the windows of "establishment" venues such as the gas, electric and phone companies.

Realizing that SDS forces were participating in the riots, Kent's mayor declared a state of emergency and closed the taverns, while local police officers tear-gassed students and arrested 14 others. Not to be outdone, the SDS took over a part of the Kent State campus. Alarmed, Ohio Gov. Rhodes called in the National Guard.

MAY 2

Saturday opened with rumors that outside militants and agitators such as the Weather Underground were coming to town. Sensing serious trouble, Mayor Leroy Satrom announced that his police forces were not equipped to handle a major disruption, and therefore welcomed the Ohio National Guard. Behind the scenes, Governor Rhodes met with National Guard General Sylvester Del Corso—an insanely hawkish warmonger who often condemned student protesters in his speeches.

A powder keg readied itself to blow, especially after Kent Chief of Police Ray Thompson declared to *The Cleveland Press*, "Armageddon was at hand."

That afternoon, Kent State Police Detective Tom Kelley provided a stark indication that something was brewing. Seeing an NBC news crew preparing to leave campus, he confided, "Don't pack your cameras, we're going to have a fire tonight." He admitted to this disclosure on Aug. 8, 1973 by telling *The Akron Beacon Journal* that, yes, he tipped NBC cameramen Fred Debrine, Jorge Gomez and Joe Butano that a fire would be set—even providing an exact time: 8 p.m.

Clairvoyant or conspiratorial, a fire did indeed ensue. Viewing the campus ROTC building as a symbol of military aggression, approximately 2,000 students marched through the university, then gathered around the ROTC. But the congregation, despite numerous attempts, couldn't get the building to erupt in a full-scale blaze.

While others broke windows, only a few actual arsonists tried to torch the ROTC. For 45 minutes, the KSU police stood by passively and made no effort to intervene. Even after the Kent fire department arrived and students cut their hoses and jumped on firefighters, police oddly did nothing. KSU Safety Director Chester Williams clearly acknowledged, "When the ROTC Building was set on fire, we were observing, not trying to stop the crowd from starting the fire."

Frustrated by their lack of success, the students dispersed and walked downtown, torching a shed and destroying a fence and telephone booth along the way. After no arrests were made and the ROTC Building stood intact, Kent's fire department left the scene.

Then, something strange occurred. Once all the students departed, the ROTC Building suddenly shot up in flames. The only individuals still present on the scene were Kent State police officers. When the students surrounded it, very little damage resulted to the ROTC. Now, flames fully engulfed it. Alan Canfora vocalized the suspicions of many. "There's reason to believe that the fire was re-started *after* the building was controlled by law enforcement personnel after the students were chased away."

Could it be that an element within the KSU police deliberately torched the ROTC to set the stage for an eventual assault on student protesters? In the documentary *Kent State: The Day the War Came Home*, it's revealed that campus police logs contained a mysterious gap from

8 p.m. to 9:45 p.m.—the exact time when flames consumed the ROTC. Similar to the Watergate tapes, no one could hear the police dispatchers, or what transpired during this time.

MAY 3

Sunday, with embers still smoldering, the military took over KSU by erecting 150 pup tents and rolling in with armed National Guardsmen in Jeeps. "Throwing fuel on the fire," Gov. Rhodes held a press conference on campus, vowing to use "every force necessary" and "eradicate the problem, not treat the symptoms." With a gubernatorial primary only two days away (and losing in the polls), Rhodes ratcheted up the rhetoric to appear strong. A martial law occupation had been established, complete with 12,000 leaflets posted on campus: All gatherings were barred.

Undaunted, a group congregated at the Commons, only to be intercepted by Guardsmen. Using their constitutional right to assembly, the students staged a sit-in and demanded to speak with KSU's president. In response, the Guard tear-gassed the students and jabbed them with bayonets. Taken aback by the confrontation, students chanted and threw rocks as helicopters with searchlights hovered overhead. Still stabbing students with their bayonets, the Guard pushed the crowd back toward their dorms—all the while throwing rocks at their windows. Fifty-one arrests were made.

Gov. Rhodes's words rang forth with ominous urgency: "We are up against the strongest, well-trained militant revolutionary group that has ever assembled in America. They're worse than brownshirts and the Communist element and the nightriders and the vigilantes. They are the worst type of people that we harbor in America. They intend to destroy higher education in America."

At this point in the press conference, a reporter asked Gen. Del Corso how long his men intended to stay at KSU. Rhodes interrupted by responding, "Until we get rid of them." Echoing this stance, Kent Police Chief Ray Thompson sneered, "I'll be right behind the National Guard to give our full support—anything that is necessary." Lastly, Ohio Highway Patrol Chief Robert Chiarmonte stated that if students started "sniping," [they could] expect his men to return fire.

In all, two different law enforcement agencies promised to shoot at students *before any gunfire ever took place*. Were they conditioning media sources—or planting a seed—that the youth of KSU were dangerous elements, and they would simply react accordingly?

In downtown Kent, students sang John Lennon's *Give Peace a Chance* while Guardsmen continued to stab them with bayonets.

MAY 4

By Monday morning, classes resumed as the military continued to occupy the Kent State campus. At 11 a.m., students gathered at the Victory Bell [a small bell donated by the Erie Railroad and placed on the commons by Taylor Hall in 1950] while Guardsmen assembled near the torched ROTC Building. When a handful of kids proceeded to chant and yell, armed Guardsmen vacated their vehicles and formed a line, telling the students to disperse.

When they refused, Guardsmen fired tear gas canisters into the crowd. Almost playfully, students returned the gesture by tossing rocks and the tear gas cans. Equally as childish, Guardsmen then picked up the rocks and cans and threw them back. Unable to disperse their adversaries, the Guard mobilized and marched to a pagoda at the crest of a hill. From there, inexplicably, they proceeded down the hill to a football practice field. This move proved to be a tactical error, for they were now trapped on three sides by the hill and a chain link fence.

Desperate, and somewhat alarmed by their ineptitude, a commander lied as he yelled through a bullhorn, "Students of Kent State, we have you surrounded!" In fact, it was they who were figuratively trapped. Meanwhile, students continued to throw bottles, bricks and rocks. The Guard felt compelled to throw them back.

The situation—at least on one level—appeared absurd, for classes had resumed as usual that morning. In another sense, however, National Guardsmen stood among the students—M-1 rifles, shotguns and .45 caliber pistols in hand. To make matters worse, these same men were hungry, agitated and fatigued from only three hours sleep the previous evening. In addition, they'd spent the preceding week on duty at a truckers' strike. Sleep deprivation, high stress levels and potential chaos had them on a dangerous edge.

Still circled by students, the Guard again fired tear gas toward the crowd, only to see the wind blow it away. Advancing, they discharged more tear gas as students threw rocks, yelled, and swore at them. At a loss, the Guard retreated to their original position at the pagoda.

PROVOCATEUR

Unbeknownst to most everyone else on campus, only one other person at Kent State (except police and National Guardsmen) carried a gun. That man—Terry Norman—not only concealed a .38 pistol, but also a camera and gas mask. Why was he equipped with such paraphernalia? In Greg Schwartz's previously mentioned article, he describes the infiltrator: "Norman came to be known as an undercover informant for both campus police and the Akron office of the FBI [and] may have acted as an *agent provocateur* on the day of May 4 and possibly on the night of May 2."

While taking pictures on the morning of May 4, Norman traded fisticuffs with a student, then pistol-whipped him. The previous evening, he showed off a .357 Magnum to NBC newsmen. Following this altercation, KSU police confiscated his weapon.

But Norman hadn't finished his antics. When Guardsmen marched to the football practice field, Norman stood between them and the students, then threw rocks at the kids to incite them. Clearly provocative, he next approached the Guard and became surrounded by them. The fateful shooting now approached, only minutes away.

Although proven to be a government asset, Schwartz writes, "FBI Director Hoover went so far as to lie about the Bureau's relationship with Norman." Further blurring the truth, 13 statements from the KSU police on Norman vanished, only to reappear later in edited form.

SHOOTING

In the meantime, Guardsmen continued their retreat toward the pagoda, students scattering as the troops slowly ascended up Blanket Hill. Although Alan Canfora, the primary agitator, waved a black flag and strolled toward the Guardsmen, most students felt the skirmish had ended and started returning to classes or their dorms. Absolutely, positively no shots rang out from the KSU student body, and the Guard was not in jeopardy of attack. A few kids still lobbed rocks, but otherwise the confrontation had ended.

Seemingly for no reason, an unidentified troop member fired a shot into the air, which caused approximately 10 soldiers from Troop G to kneel and assume a firing position, their guns leveled at Alan Canfora and a few other vociferous protesters.

With the Guard—wearing tear gas masks—crouched in a kneeling position, their pointed weapons obviously signified that the standoff *had not* ended. Canfora recounts the lead-up: "On two occasions before the shooting, for no logical reason, the ONG (Ohio National Guard) troops stopped and aimed their powerful M1 rifles at unarmed student protesters. While the ONG was assembled on the practice football field, minutes *before* they marched up the hill and fired. Colonel Charles Fassinger told his men to prepare to fire when they reached the hilltop if the students were viewed as a threat."

Kent State journalism professor Charles Brill continues the story: "They were organized. It was not scattered. They all waited, and they all pointed their rifles at the same time. It looked like a firing squad."

At that stage, Guardsmen huddled in a circle and called an impromptu meeting. Is this where the final conspiracy was hatched? Or, did the men inextricably find themselves in a situation that had spiraled perilously out of control? Whatever the case, a decision had been reached.

Atop Blanket Hill, when the huddle broke, one of the students popped them the bird. At that point—on the command "fire"—the men of Troop G—formed in a tight line—wheeled around, leveled their rifles and began shooting. In a matter of 13 seconds they fired a total of 67 shots. Hundreds of students dove for cover on the ground, while others were struck. Only after an order of "cease fire" was issued did the Guardsmen stop pulling their triggers. As they stood at the crest of Blanket Hill near the Taylor Building and pagoda, four students lay dead—Sandra Scheuer, Allison Krause,

William Schroeder and Jeffrey Miller.

During the melee, three soldiers—Morris, Pierce and McGee—had removed the *sewn-on* nametags from their uniforms. Years later, as reported by Greg Schwartz, one of the participants told Alan Canfora, "He was part of Troop G during the ghetto riots in the Hough and Glenville areas of Cleveland in 1965-66. The same guys that shot you guys at Kent State were the ones that shot the people in Cleveland. They were experienced killers."

And yes, a command most certainly arose to commence with the bloodshed. In William Gordon's *Four Dead in Ohio*, Harry William Montgomery—a Vietnam vet well acquainted with combat situations—"testified that [Sgt. Myron] Pryor tapped three or four Guardsmen in front of him on the back or hind side. Then almost simultaneously, the men that were directly in front of him—seemingly he had communicated with, them—turned and began firing."

Gordon also describes how Guardsman James Pierce viewed the demonstrators "not as people, but savage animals." G Troop Sgt. Lawrence Shafer admitted to bayoneting a disabled Vietnam veteran.

These men turned together—in unison, eight at once in a concerted fashion—and fired 67 shots at unarmed students. Gordon cites researcher Peter Davies. "How can we possibly accept that eight Guardsmen, within the same second, all suddenly decided, as individuals, that their lives were in danger and spun around together in a coordinated unit and commenced shooting?"

REPORTS

Immediately following the slaughter, Gordon dissected the array of lies strewn by official sources. First, Gen. Del Corso claimed that students opened fire at his Guardsmen. He soon retracted that statement, for his troops were the ones that shot at unarmed civilians. Secondly, his squad faced no imminent threat whatsoever. Only two Guardsmen were mildly injured by thrown rocks all day. Lastly, students did not surround the Guard or endanger their lives. Not one photo depicts students any nearer than 30 yards from the shooters. And don't forget—not one student possessed a gun, while every

Guardsman carried a weapon.

Conversely, the killers turned simultaneously and started spraying bullets indiscriminately into the crowd. The students posed no threat, and they were all unarmed. The shooters did not proceed into action due to self-defense. No angry mobs were assaulting them.

Rather, what everyone witnessed can be construed as a sick, murderous abuse of power.

The closest slain student—Jeffrey Miller—stood 250 feet away from his slayers. All the rest were even farther in the distance—330 to 375 feet away. The madmen exhibited such bloodlust that their commanding officers had to frantically and physically restrain them, or else they would have kept shooting. Yet the lies continued. Canfora provides two examples of their cowardice. "One officer stooped and pretended to find a pistol on Jeff [Miller's] dead body. The same ONG officer claimed he found brass knuckles on another student protester. The officer later admitted he planted these items in an attempt to blame the students as 'violent.'"

Ultimately, 300 FBI agents and the Department of Justice investigated the Kent State massacre, including interviews with hundreds of witnesses who watched firsthand in broad daylight as our military opened fire on American citizens.

They concluded that the shootings were "unnecessary, unwarranted and totally inexcusable." Gordon adds a further incrimination: "The Justice Department summary of the FBI Report states that none of the fatalities was in a position to pose even a remote danger to the National Guard at the time of the firing."

Sgt. Matthew McManus (a direct participant) is in full agreement. "The shootings could have been prevented with proper leadership. If that general [Canterbury] had his head out of his ass, he never would have put us in this situation."

To date, not one of the shooters has ever faced any criminal prosecution.

RICHARD NIXON

"Tin soldiers and Nixon's coming." —NEIL YOUNG, *Ohio*

"He was a cheap crook and a merciless war criminal who bombed more people to death in Laos and Cambodia than the U.S. Army lost in all of World War II, and he denied it to the day of his death. When students at Kent State University in Ohio protested the bombing, he connived to have them attacked and slain by troops from the National Guard."
—HUNTER S. THOMPSON, 1994

The gonzo journalist's comments are truer than most people realize, especially after the Watergate tapes were released and we hear Nixon telling his dirty tricks operatives to hire knuckle-breakers, and then pummel those in the peace movement. "They'll get what they deserve," he snaps.

Others in his administration shared Nixon's sentiments. Similar to Ohio's Gov. Rhodes, who promised to "eradicate the problem," Vice President Spiro Agnew called those who opposed their Vietnam policy "brown shirts." Likewise, William Gordon quotes J. Edgar Hoover telling his aide, Egil Krogh: "The students invited the shootings and got what they deserved."

But Nixon held a special disdain for the students at KSU. Greg Schwartz lists the reasons:

- "In October 1968, Nixon gave a campaign speech at the University of Akron, which was attended by members of Kent State's SDS, who repeatedly attempted to disrupt Nixon's speech by chanting slogans against him;

- " 'Nixon also encountered a group of approximately 150 hecklers that began their jeering as soon as he approached the lectern and did not quiet down until Nixon left the stage,' read the Oct. 15, 1968 edition of *The Daily Kent Stater*"; and

- Nixon's inauguration parade in Washington, D.C. on Jan. 20, 1969 was also attended by members of Kent State's SDS. The Jan. 21, 1969 *Daily Kent Stater* led with a headline that read, "Hecklers Mar

Nixon's Day," and reported that three Kent State SDS members were among those arrested.

As a result, with groups such as the SDS, Weather Underground, Black Panthers, Yippies and John Lennon's association with Jerry Rubin and Abbie Hoffman, did Nixon finally decide to make an example of one campus in particular to quell dissent?

In this context, Gordon writes, "Journalist Seymour Hersh revealed that Nixon told [H.R.] Haldeman to get Teamster thugs to beat up on protesters." He continues, "One of the theories was that Nixon gave one of these crazy orders in a fit of anger, 'Knock off some students' or something to that effect, and somebody like [Charles] Colson took it seriously and put into motion a series of events which culminated in the shootings."

But this assessment is too benign because it's now known that Nixon spoke directly with Gov. Rhodes two times in the days just prior to the Kent State slaughter. *Gallery* magazine ran a story a few years later where it quoted a low-level intelligence operative that said during these clandestine talks with Rhodes, the president issued a command: "Make a goddamn good example of someone at Kent State."

After the massacre, Rhodes denied ever partaking in these talks. Then, according to Greg Schwartz, "Rhodes admitted that he did have two private conversations with the White House in the week preceding May 4, 1970." Alan Canfora wondered, "If there was no conspiracy, then why did Rhodes feel the need to lie about the calls in 1970?"

Fitrakas and Wasserman add another element to the picture. "Rhodes was the perfect messenger. Bumbling and mediocre, with a long history of underworld involvement, Rhodes was a devoted admirer of Nixon and of FBI Director J. Edgar Hoover. Public records reveal that Rhodes was a virtual stooge for the FBI because of the agency's files tying Rhodes directly to organized crime." [Note: J. Edgar Hoover also had a long-standing involvement with the Mob due to his gambling addiction, in addition to risqué photos of him in various compromising homosexual acts as we discussed earlier.—Ed.]

So, considering Nixon's hatred of the Kent State SDS, and Rhodes's subservience, Kent State became prime target No. 1 to kill students and

The events of May 4, 1970 have been extensively detailed since that day and there still remain many unresolved inconsistencies surrounding the activities of the Guardsmen, the U.S. government, students and agents provocateurs.

end campus rebellion. In addition, behind in the polls, Rhodes needed to look strong in the GOP primaries on May 5. On top of that, Rhodes enjoyed a special closeness with the two top National Guard commanders at Kent State—Robert Canterbury and Sylvester Del Corso. The chain of command from Nixon to Rhodes to his generals has now been firmly established.

Finally, to close this case, William Gordon describes how, in November 1970, Chief Domestic Advisor John Ehrlichman hand-delivered a presidential memo to Attorney General John Mitchell, telling him to cease and desist in the Justice Department's investigation of Kent State. Other than a skirmish in Jackson, Miss., student protests on American campuses had been effectively eradicated. Four students slain at Kent State constituted the deadly remedy.

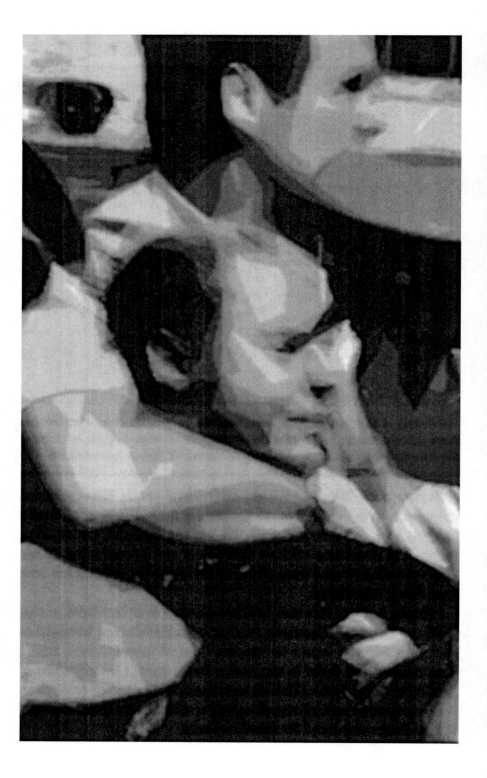

CHAPTER 9

ARTHUR BREMER

ARTHUR BREMER . . .
TAXI DRIVER ANTI-HERO

Robert Deniro as alienated and misguided Travis Bickle in Martin Scorsese's *Taxi Driver* still stands as one of the most stark and haunting characters ever to appear on the silver screen. Popping pills, drinking, attending porno flicks, swooning over Cybill Shepherd, drawn to underage prostitute Jodi Foster, and stalking a presidential candidate all culminate in an ultra-violent finale that leaves dead bodies and blood strewn across New York City's mean streets.

Few people realize that this movie was loosely based on the life of loner wannabe assassin Arthur Bremer, a 21-year-old drifter who supposedly kept a diary, failed in his tryst with a 15-year-old girl (Joan Pemrich) and then shaved his head prior to the shooting of George Wallace in 1972 (all traits portrayed by Travis Bickle).

Weirder yet, Jodi Foster's "Iris" character—the 12-year-old hooker—became an obsession to another thwarted gunman, John Hinckley, who attempted to murder Ronald Reagan in early 1981. Art has a strange way of imitating life, which then leads to life imitating art in a sort of vicious and irreversible cycle.

Returning to Bremer and his cinematic protégé, one of the most riveting scenes in *Taxi Driver* is when Bickle shaves his head into a Mohawk. Bremer said he performed this act for his teenage girlfriend "to show her that inside I felt as empty as my shaved head." Similarly clueless as to what constituted normal social relationships, Bickle tries impressing Shepherd on a date by taking her to a raunchy Times Square XXX theater. She storms out, disgusted. Likewise, Bremer showed Pemrich porno pictures and talked dirty to her. She called him "goofy" and "weird," then subsequently dumped him. Scorned, Bremer dealt with his rejection by stalking the high-school girl and constantly calling on the telephone (just like Travis).

Desperately lonely and alienated, Bremer purchased a gun (as did Bickle—many of them), and then set out to become famous by knocking off a high-profile politician. Bickle did the same, but after almost being arrested by a Secret Service member, he took his frustrations out on Iris's pimp (played by Harvey Keitel), riddling him and others with gunfire before holding a mock blood-spattered pistol to his own head as the gory, traumatizing scene ends.

1972 ELECTION

In Birmingham they love the governor / Now we all did what we could do / Watergate does not bother me / Does your conscience bother you? / Tell the truth.

—LYNYRD SKYNYRD, *Sweet Home Alabama*

Alabama's Gov. George Wallace made a notorious name for himself by declaring in his 1963 inauguration speech, "It is very appropriate that from this cradle of the Confederacy . . . in the name of the greatest people that have ever trod this Earth, I draw a line in the dust and toss the gauntlet before the feet of tyranny, and I say segregation now, segregation tomorrow, segregation forever."

In light of, and even despite this baggage, George Wallace's American Independent party had Richard Nixon terrified that he'd lose the

1972 election to George McGovern. *Newsweek* magazine analyzed the situation: "Not since Theodore Roosevelt's Bull Moose Party emerged in 1912 has a third party so seriously challenged the two-party system."

The entrenched D.C. establishment as a whole was even more troubled by Wallace's populist rhetoric that exposed the fallacy of their "democratic system." "There's not a dime's worth of difference between the Democrat and Republican parties. If I'm elected, one of the first things I'm going to do is tax the Rockefeller Foundation."

Nixon, of course, had long been a Rockefeller boy. Further, to his dismay, Wallace seriously threatened to steal an entire bloc of conservative Southern voters from him. According to controversial Chicago researcher Sherman Skolnick, Wallace garnered approximately 21% of the vote in many polls. With these types of numbers, independent film producer Aguay Banar asserted, "There was no way that Richard Nixon was ever going to be re-elected with Wallace in the campaign."

Wallace actually won six states during the Democratic primaries, and pulled every single county in Florida. If he split the right wing in Dixie, McGovern had a realistic chance of becoming president.

Desperate, Nixon strategist Harry Dent said, "Wallace was the man Nixon feared most." *Silent Coup* author Len Colodny concurred: "Of all the people who wanted Wallace dead, Nixon was on top of the list."

During the 1968 election, Wallace received 10 million votes on his American Party Ticket. For Nixon to win a second term, Wallace needed to be eliminated so that he could secure the Southern vote. To fight his nemesis, Nixon actually financed Wallace's gubernatorial opponent, Albert Brewer, during the 1970 Alabama election by dipping into a clandestine $2 million slush fund. Wallace still won, so Nixon next unleashed the IRS on the governor and his brother. It didn't work.

George Wallace, fully aware of Nixon and his dirty tricks team, realized the dangers surrounding him. Christopher Ketcham writes in *Bigger Than Watergate: The Cover-Up That Succeeded*, "On May 3—just under two weeks before he was shot—Wallace had confided to a journalist that he had a feeling 'somebody's going to get me one of these days.'" He told this same reporter from *The Detroit News*, "I can just see a little guy out there that nobody's paying any attention to. He reaches into his pocket and out comes the little gun, like that Sirhan guy that got Robert Kennedy."

Years later, Wallace privately confided to newsmen that he suspected the White House Plumbers were involved in his shooting, while *United Press International* reported, "He hoped the Watergate hearings would turn up the man who paid the money to have him shot."

RICHARD NIXON'S JEWISH PROBLEM

Another factor that sent Nixon into spasms of justified paranoia revolved around his suspicions of Jewish media control, and Jewish power in general. Fearing that the Jewish press would smear him, Nixon often expounded on this problem.

In a Feb. 21, 1973 phone conversation with evangelist Billy Graham (who dropped a number of anti-Semitic remarks himself), Nixon theorized about the Jews' self-destructive nature: "Anti-Semitism is stronger than we think. You know, it's unfortunate. But this has happened to the Jews. It happened in Spain, it happened in Germany. Now it's going to happen in America if these people don't start behaving. It may be they have a death wish. You know that's been the problem with our Jewish friends for centuries."

During an earlier conversation with Graham, who spoke of the Jews controlling America's media, Nixon responded, "The Jews are an irreligious, atheistic, immoral bunch of bastards." To aide H.R. Haldeman, he referred to them as the "satanic Jews."

What follow are a few excerpts of Nixon's attitudes as he explained them to Haldeman.

• July 3, 1971: "I want to look at any sensitive areas around where Jews are involved, Bob. See, the Jews are all through the government. And we have got to get in those areas; we've got to get a man in charge who is not Jewish to patrol the Jews."

• July 5, 1971: "Jewish families are close, but there's this strange malignancy that seems to creep among them—radicalism."

And then this transcript of a conversation between Nixon and Haldeman:

Nixon: "Very interesting thing. So few of those who engage in espionage are Negroes."

Haldeman: "Not intellectual enough, not smart enough . . . not smart enough to be spies."

Nixon: "The Jews—the Jews are born spies. You notice how many of them are up to their necks?"

Haldeman: "A basic deviousness."

FOLLOW THE MONEY

If we're to believe official sources, Arthur Bremer shot Gov. George Wallace five times at close range on May 15, 1972 in Laurel, Md. What caught the attention of many researchers is the fact that his 1971 income tax return claimed $1,611 in total earnings as a bus boy. The *New York Times* inflated this figure to $3,016, but Lisa Pease points out in *Bremer and Wallace: It's Déjà Vu All Over Again* that their figures don't add up.

Yet, despite his meager income, Bremer's timeline indicates someone living very large, and well beyond his means. On Feb. 16, 1972 Bremer abandoned his employment as a janitor in Milwaukee. On March 1, he appeared at a Wallace rally at the Pfister Hotel in his hometown. On March 23, he showed up again at a Wallace event at Milwaukee's Red Carpet Airport Inn. By April 4, Bremer celebrated at a victory rally inside the Milwaukee Holiday Inn ballroom.

In the interim, Bremer purchased an AMC Rambler for $800, then hopped an airplane to New York City on April 6, where he checked into the Waldorf Astoria, bought the services of a masseuse (leaving a $30 tip), rented a limousine, and chartered a helicopter to tour the city. He then flew home. Later, some cover-up artists tried to rationalize Bremer's spending by saying he lived in his car. Yet Bremer snapped to a newsman, "Why would I be living in my car when I stayed at the Waldorf Astoria Hotel?"

His spending didn't stop there. The unemployed bus boy-janitor also bought a pair of binoculars, multiple cameras, a CB radio-scanner (with law enforcement bands), a tape recorder and three guns—including a Browning 9 mm semiautomatic pistol.

April 10 found Bremer in Ottawa, Canada, where he lodged at the

Lord Elgin Hotel and followed Richard Nixon during a state visit. On April 10 he drove from Canada to New Carrollton, Md., where he spent three days.

Following a return to Milwaukee—still without a job or any source of income—Bremer traveled to Michigan for a week from May 7-13. There, he mirrored Wallace at rallies in Lansing, Cadillac, Jackson and Kalamazoo. Then, on May 14 Bremer crossed the country back again to Maryland.

Hot on Wallace's trail, the assassin attended a rally on May 15 in Wheaton, then followed the candidate to Laurel, Md. where he allegedly fired the fatal shots. However, wearing black sunglasses and dressed in garish red-white-and-blue clothing, Bremer had been by no means inconspicuous.

Lisa Pease delivers this damning information: "CBS cameraman Laurens Pierce made a now famous film of the attempt on Wallace's life. What's odd is that this was the third time Pierce had caught Bremer on tape. Pierce had seen Bremer twice before shooting day—once at an earlier rally in Wheaton, Md., and once before [in Michigan]." Bremer had also been arrested in Milwaukee for carrying a concealed weapon, yet he mingled freely at rallies despite being specifically targeted by Wallace Secret Service agents as being suspicious.

SHOOTING

Another huge inconsistency arises when viewing the shots delivered from Bremer's .38 caliber revolver, which left Wallace paralyzed from the waist down. Bremer supposedly fired five bullets, yet according to Christopher Ketcham, "Wallace alone was wounded in nine different places, while three other victims—a Secret Service agent [Nicholas Zarvos], a campaign worker [Dorothy Thompson] and an Alabama State Trooper [Capt. Eldred Cothard]—were each wounded once."

A total of 12 wounds don't match five bullets fired from Bremer, who stood in front of Wallace and allegedly shot at close range into his abdomen. Again, Ketcham explains, "Altogether 12 separate wounds were inflicted on that fateful day by a lone gunman firing a .38 caliber revolver that held only five bullets—magic bullets, one might assume. Yet this wound count presumably includes entry and exit wounds, rendering the scenario entirely possible, though improbable. *The New York Times*, however, made note of the fact that 'four persons had suffered at least seven separate initial entry wounds from a maximum of five shots.'" Ketcham then delivers a huge blow: "Several of the bullets recovered could not be matched to Bremer's .38 caliber weapon."

Lisa Pease adds this information:

• "Doctors who treated Wallace said he was hit by a minimum of four bullets, and possibly five. Yet three other victims were hit by bullets";

• "*The New York Times* reported that there was 'broad speculation on how four persons had suffered at least seven separate wounds from a maximum of five shots'";

• "None of the [law enforcement] officers or agents had discharged their weapons";

• The inspection of wound photos from a May 17, 1972 edition of *The Washington Post* led her to note: "Bullets would have had to enter Wallace from three directions—his right side, his front, and from behind his left shoulder. How could one man, firing straight ahead, do that?";

• "The bullet [trajectories] do not trace a single firing position, and instead require the shooter to be both behind and somewhat above Wallace";

• "There were policemen on the roof of the shopping center, looking for snipers. Did they miss one? Did they include one?";

• "Bremer's fingerprints were not found on the gun recovered at the scene. In the CBS film, Bremer is clearly shown holding a gun without gloves. How is it that he failed to leave fingerprints?";

• "The gun could not be matched to the victim bullets";

• "Robert Frazer [of the FBI] admitted that Bremer had been given paraffin casts, but tested negative for nitrates, as had Lee Harvey Oswald in similar tests nine years earlier";

• "The gun itself was not wrestled from Bremer's hand, but was found on the pavement by Secret Service agent Robert A. Innamorati";

- "During the trial, Bremer was placed in the audience portion of the courtroom. Several witnesses could not identify him in the crowd as having been the gunman they claimed to have seen or tackled"; and
- "The Maryland police originally issued a bulletin regarding a second suspect in the shooting."

DIARY OF A MADMAN?

Purveyors of the official story contend that Arthur Bremer so hated George Wallace that he attempted to kill him. But as Timothy W. Maier wrote in a Dec. 14, 1998 article, "New Chapters in the Assassin's Diary," Bremer was actually "a one-time Wallace supporter who owned his own Confederate flag." Baltimore attorney Benjamin Lipsitz supported this claim after reading his diary: "I thought Bremer rather admired Wallace."

Media spin-masters also convinced the public that Bremer's act was a desperate attempt to gain fame. Yet after his arrest, he refused nearly every interview requested of him. Also, Bremer scrawled in his diary that he sought [spelling error intact]: "To do SOMETHING BOLD AND DRAMATIC, FORCEFULL and DYNAMIC, A STATEMENT of my manhood for the world to see."

But here's the catch. Did Arthur Bremer actually even write this diary and, if so, had it been tampered with after the fact? For instance, what are we to make of this passage: "Now I start my diary of my personal plot to kill by pistol either Richard Nixon or George Wallace." If Wallace indeed were the target, why is Nixon's name also mentioned? Or, is this inclusion an overt red herring to make it appear as if Nixon were also in the crosshairs, when in reality nothing could be further from the truth?

Or, could the diary itself be a complete distraction? Ketcham writes, "Wallace himself came to believe that the diary, with its bizarre mixture of sophistication and stupidity (complete with spelling errors so egregious they seem almost purposeful) was in fact a forgery. Its tone, he noted to reporters, was 'contrived,' as though it were deliberately written to throw off inquiry into a possible conspiracy." Maier holds the same doubts. "The fighting little judge [Wallace] never believed Bremer's diary was anything but a ruse."

Even his courtroom opposition harbored suspicions. Timothy Maier supposed, "What bothers him [Prosecutor Arthur Marshall] is Nixon's obsession with the case, particularly [the government's] failure to turn over Bremer's original diary, which the FBI had provided to the White House. Or, as Marshall always prefaces it: '*If* you believe Bremer wrote the diary.'"

The plot deepens. On the PBS expose *An American Experience—Portrait of an Assassin: Arthur Bremer*, they bring a world-famous novelist into the picture. "Gore Vidal wrote a long essay about Arthur Bremer's 'diary' that seemed to him to have evidence of forgery, too literate, [yet with] deliberate misspellings."

But who could have been behind such a spectacular con job? Lisa Pease provides the answer: "Gore Vidal, in *The New York Review of Books*, wrote a long essay in which he postulated that Watergate figure, expert forger and longtime Kennedy assassination suspect Everett Howard Hunt had penned Bremer's infamous diary."

Hunt was a published author and novelist, and admitted that dirty tricks operator Charles Colson requested his presence in Milwaukee to inspect Bremer's apartment. Vidal's article, "The Art and Arts of E. Howard Hunt," doesn't seem quite so outlandish now. Consider this from Christopher Ketcham: "One wonders if Nixon's payoffs to the blackmailing E. Howard Hunt (as much as $180,000 in cash at a time) served not merely to cover up the break-in at the Watergate Hotel—but to cover up a Hunt-Bremer-Wallace connection to Chuck Colson and the White House."

THE PLUMBERS AND DIRTY TRICKS OPERATORS

When one considers the intel operatives of this period, a definite literary bent existed. Cord Meyer (head of the CIA's Covert Action Staff for the Directorate of Plans, and also former husband of JFK mistress Mary Pinchot Meyer) was a novelist, as was White House Plumber (and JFK "tramp") E. Howard Hunt. Similarly, CIA counterintelligence chief and spook extraordinaire James Jesus Angleton adored poetry, while the entire Watergate case became public knowledge via the written accounts of Pulitzer Prize winners Carl Bernstein and Bob Woodward. Speaking of which, Woodward received anonymous "Deep Throat" tips regarding Nixon's "plumbers" and Arthur Bremer well before he ever started chasing the Watergate case.

In this light, is it possible that Bremer's forged diary via E. Howard Hunt existed as nothing more than a red herring? By inserting Nixon's name as the original target—when he never was at all—did the dirty tricks operatives simply want the public to believe Bremer targeted Nixon, when their only victim was Wallace all along? In this sense, Hunt's prowess as a forgery expert becomes invaluable in using Bremer's diary as a propaganda vehicle.

To implement this plan, enter the FBI and Mark Felt, a man who existed as at least one of the undercover Deep Throats. Following Wallace's hit, historian Dan Carter (who authored *The Politics of Rage*) states that Felt hastily phoned Charles Colson, who then proceeded to contact Nixon. After contemplating their next course of action, Colson and Felt spoke a half-dozen more times, whereupon Colson called Hunt and authorized a break-in of Bremer's Milwaukee apartment.

In the meantime, Secret Service Chief James Rowley also commanded his men to likewise enter Bremer's premises. Thus, within only a few hours, FBI and Secret Service agents were both simultaneously prowling inside Bremer's abode.

In addition, Colson also tipped reporters form *The Detroit News* and *Washington Post* that there may be "a story" inside Bremer's unlocked home. Of course, the prowlers were motivated by two primary factors—to remove any evidence linking the attempted murder to Nixon, and to plant information linking Bremer to McGovern.

During an interview, Sherman Skolnick summarizes: "E. Howard Hunt, Frank Sturgis and others were involved in the break-in at the Watergate. And there's reason to believe that the White House sent E. Howard Hunt to Arthur Bremer's apartment in Milwaukee." Aguay Banar answered, "on orders from Charles Colson."

As Nixon's favorite dirty tricks operative and Watergate planner, Timothy Maier claims that Colson "publicly has admitted to ordering the Bremer break-in." Then, upon Nixon's encouragement to continue their dirty work, Colson assured his boss that Bremer would "be a left-winger by the time we got through with him."

The rabbit hole gets even deeper. Christopher Ketcham relates this incredible tale: "According to Wallace biographer Dan T. Carter, Martha [Mitchell, wife of the U.S. Attorney General] told Wallace that John Mitchell, unnerved by what he believed to be a 'Colson-Bremer connection,' had repeatedly wondered aloud to his wife: 'What was Charles Colson doing talking with Arthur Bremer four days before he shot George Wallace?'"

This information is crucial, especially when Prosecutor Arthur Marshall held his own plaguing doubts: "We had concern that someone else was involved. The question I always had is how the Secret Service found out who he was as quickly as they did. They were in his apartment within an hour."

Maier continues this line of reasoning: "Nixon stepped in to control the Bremer investigation shortly after the shots were fired, according to [Deputy State Attorney Vincent] Femia. At the hospital, an FBI agent hung up a phone, turned to Femia and barked: 'That was the president. We're taking over.'"

He elaborates further. "*The New York Times* reported Watergate hush-money operative Hunt testified in a Senate Watergate hearing that White House aide Charles Colson, upon hearing news of the shooting, immediately ordered him to 'bribe the janitor' or pick Bremer's lock to find out what type of literature Bremer read."

Moreover, "The FBI hauled both Hunt and Colson in for secret questioning in 1974. Both acknowledged that a conversation about Bremer's apartment took place." Maier then further implicates the president: "Nixon ordered the FBI to take charge and get the Secret Service out of the case. FBI Director [Patrick] Gray provided Nixon with daily briefings on the case. [Files] show the president personally ordered all materials seized inside Bremer's apartment be taken not to FBI headquarters, but to the White House. Nixon was concerned Bremer might be tied to the White House Plumbers."

This clandestine unit plays an even more integral role if Aguay Banar is correct: "Bremer was in the City of Ottawa when Nixon was visiting Pierre Trudeau, Canadian prime minister. Bremer and Frank Sturgis [another one of the supposed "tramps" at the JFK assassination] stayed at the Lord Elgin Hotel in Ottawa. They stayed in the same section of the hotel. Frank Sturgis was the control officer of Arthur Bremer on the road. It was he who was passing on money and information to Bremer. Sturgis and Bremer stayed at the same section of the Lord Elgin Hotel that the Secret Service detail of Richard Nixon was staying in."

This analysis is expanded upon by Lisa Pease: "According to [reporter] Sybil Leek and [investigative attorney] Bert Sugar, while Bremer was at the Lord Elgin Hotel in Ottawa, he met with Dennis Cossini. Famed conspiracy researcher Mae Brussell and Alan Stang identified Cossini as a CIA operative. Cossini was found dead from a massive heroin overdose in July 1972, just two months after the Wallace shooting. Cossini had no history of drug use."

Maier supports the existence of this hidden network: "In his book, *The Taking of America*, Richard E. Sprague argued that Donald Segretti and Dennis Cossini supplied money to Bremer before he attempted to assassinate George Wallace. Others have claimed that Bernard L. Baker, one of the Watergate burglars, was used to pass money to Bremer."

Another infamous member of the Plumbers also makes an appearance: G. Gordon Liddy. Maier writes, "A *CBS News* crew provided the FBI with a film clip depicting a man resembling Liddy who CBS alleged 'led Wallace into Bremer's line of fire.' Could this mystery man be the same person who chased down a photographer and paid $10,000 for pictures unseen and undeveloped that were strictly of the crowd?" Christopher Ketcham adds this remarkable detail. "George Wallace told the FBI that he believed Liddy was standing directly behind Arthur Bremer."

In this vein, Wallace minced no words when telling reporters after having been crippled. "I think my attempted assassination was part of a conspiracy."

Who did he feel directed the job? Aguay Banar fills in the blank. "One of the questions I asked the governor in writing was, 'Was there a conspiracy behind the shooting of your person?' He said, 'Yes, definitely a conspiracy.' And then he looked up on the page to where a previous question had been asked regarding Richard Nixon. And with the stub of his cigar he poked at the name of Richard Nixon. He said, 'Conspiracy! Conspiracy!' And he poked at the name of Richard Nixon on the page."

MIND CONTROL

As is so prevalent in cases such as these, did mind-benders meddle with Arthur Bremer's brain? Ketcham quotes previous sources: "Authors Freed, Leek, Sugar and others have suggested that Bremer had a control agent who was running him in the Wallace assassination project. The writers have also speculated that Bremer was a programmed assassin, mind-controlled by CIA handlers using psychedelic brainwashing techniques—massive doses of LSD and BZ coupled with hypnosis—perfected in government Cold War programs such as MK-ULTRA and Operation Artichoke."

To reinforce this premise, consider the similarities to Robert Kennedy patsy Sirhan Sirhan. First, Bremer fashioned a sickly smile during the shooting, remaining calm, detached and trance-like as pandemonium erupted around him. Secondly, in the months prior to Wallace's assassination, Bremer checked out two books from the Milwaukee Public Library: *Sirhan* by Aziz Shihab and *RFK Must Die* by Robert Blair Kaiser.

Lisa Pease offers another chilling element to the puzzle: "Even more curious is Bremer's half-sister relationship with the Rev. Jerry Owen, who figured prominently in the RFK case." It should be noted that Owen worked directly with Sirhan's CIA hypnotist, William Jennings Bryan. His secretary told researchers that immediately after Wallace's attempted murder, Bryan received an emergency phone call notifying him.

In addition, L.A. County Supervisor Baxter Ward penned a letter outlining his interaction with Rev. Owen (as told by Lisa Pease): "Owen volunteered that he was personal friends with the sister of Arthur Bremer. Owen stated that Gale Bremer was employed by his brother here in Los Angeles for several years, and had then left Los Angeles for Florida because she was constantly harassed by the FBI."

This incestuous cabal of psychiatrists seems to keep revolving in the same Murder, Inc. circles.

CHAPTER 10

SQUEAKY & NELSON

THE LYNETTE 'SQUEAKY' FROMME & NELSON ROCKEFELLER CONNECTION

What does the release of Lynette "Squeaky" Fromme—one of Charles Manson's most ardent devotees—from the Carswell Federal Medical Center in Fort Worth, Texas on Aug. 14, 2009 have to do with a Rockefeller in the White House? What follows is one of the most intriguing stories in recent American political history.

THE GIRLS WHO COULDN'T SHOOT STRAIGHT

On Sept. 5, 1975 Squeaky Fromme tried to assassinate President Gerald Ford in Sacramento, California. Although her gun possessed ammunition, there wasn't a bullet in the chamber because she'd removed it earlier. Seventeen days later, on Sept. 22, Sara Jane Moore also made an attempt on Ford's life in front of the Saint Francis Hotel in San Francisco. Coincidentally, Moore had been arrested the day before this incident took place for carrying a concealed .44 caliber revolver and 113 rounds of ammunition.

How could this woman that police released a day earlier get so close to the president? By her own admission, Moore acted as an FBI inform-ant while also working for the ATF and SFPD. Further, as an "SLA-wannabe" [Symbionese Liberation Army] with a long history of involvement in radical Bay area activism, Moore managed to become a bookkeeper for William Hearst, then functioned as an intermediary be-tween him and the SLA during the famous Patricia Hearst kidnapping.

Here's where it gets even stranger. According to eclectic researcher Adam Gorightly, author of the definitive Manson book, *The Shadow Over Santa Susana*, Moore's mother and Manson's mother knew each other in Charleston, West Virginia, while Charlie and Sara Jane were briefly childhood friends. On the other hand, Squeaky Fromme is fre-quently depicted as Manson's most loyal follower.

What are the odds that two women directly connected to America's spookiest criminal would both attempt to kill the president within two weeks of each other, by chance? On top of that, Moore escaped from the Alderson, West Virginia penitentiary in 1979, while Fromme es-caped from the very same prison on Dec. 23, 1987. Neither woman could adequately explain why they tried to slay the president. "I never got a satisfactory answer from her [Moore] as to why she did it," attor-ney James F. Hewitt commented after the trial.

SHADOW VICE PRESIDENT

Because of his brief tenure as president, most people tend to forget that if Ford had been assassinated, his vice president—former New York Gov. Nelson Rockefeller—would have become the commander-in-chief without ever receiving a single vote from the American public. This cal-culated plot began when Richard Nixon's original vice president, Spiro Agnew, resigned after pleading no contest to tax evasion. As a replace-ment, Nixon selected two-time Bilderberg attendee (1964, 1966), CFR insider and Warren Commission member Gerald Ford.

The next step in this process involved Richard Nixon's fall from grace via Watergate. Famed researcher Gary Allen wrote on this subject in *The Rockefeller File*: "As we unravel the twisting threads of this strange saga, we find that each try to ultimately topple Nixon from the

Nelson Rockefeller gives an obscene hand gesture to a critic.

throne can be traced to Rockefeller."

Specifically, the two biggest conspirators inside the White House were Henry Kissinger and Gen. Alexander Haig, both Rockefeller protégés. Radio talk-show host Keith Hansen cites an interesting angle on his website: "The justification for Kissinger's actions may have been [Nixon's] overt dislike for Israel and his penchant for saying so. Then, again, [Nixon] calling Kissinger 'Jew boy' probably didn't help, either."

In *The Rockefeller File*, Allen augments this point: "It is now known that Henry Kissinger was responsible for creating the Plumbers squad in the first place, while the 'instant general,' Alexander Haig, made sure that the most incriminating evidence on the tapes was given in advance to the men investigating his boss."

Rather quickly, Nixon found himself cornered, and resigned under a cloud of controversy on Aug. 8, 1974, thereby making Gerald Ford president. On Aug. 20, 1974 Ford named Nelson Rockefeller his vice president designate. Reflecting upon this nomination, Rockefeller quipped, "When you think of what I had, what else was there to aspire to?"

At this stage, the White House's central power-base consisted of Gerald Ford, Henry Kissinger (Bilderberg, CFR, Trilateral Commission), and Nelson Rockefeller. In an article entitled "All the President's Men," Aaron Tomek observed, "Gary Allen says that Nelson Rockefeller had key Nixon men on his side, including [chief of staff] Alexander Haig and Henry Kissinger. He says that they wanted to put a Rockefeller in the White House, and it was the whole purpose for crafting the elaborate scandal [Watergate] that would take Nixon out and put Ford in. Ford would be easily taken out by many possible means, including assassination." On Dec. 19, 1974, Rockefeller was officially appointed vice president.

THE JFK ASSASSINATION

Richard Nixon realized with perfect clarity that a sitting president could be eliminated. He was in Dallas on Nov. 22, 1963. Moreover, the Rockefeller clan felt no love lost for John Kennedy, especially since they (and the CIA) blamed him for the Bay of Pigs fiasco. The Rockefellers held a significant amount of stock in United Fruit and other sugar plantations in Cuba, which Fidel Castro nationalized upon rising to power. The Rockefellers also held great disdain for Kennedy's perceived monetary changes at the Federal Reserve. To protect themselves against this powerful family, New York State Sen. Walter Mahoney revealed that JFK sent federal agents to Albany to dig up dirt on Nelson Rockefeller. Attorney General Robert Kennedy ran the operation.

Needless to say, Kennedy's presidency ended abruptly, and the single most crucial element in the cover-up of his assassination revolved around a concept known as "the Magic Bullet Theory." The Warren Commission—stacked with Rockefeller and CFR cronies—used this ludicrous notion to pin the blame solely on "lone-nut shooter" Lee Harvey Oswald. The single-bullet theory arose from attorney Arlen Specter, who was requested as chief counsel for the Warren Commission by none other than Gerald Ford.

Interestingly enough, the man who selected Oswald to be the patsy was CIA Counterintelligence Chief James Jesus Angleton. He also acted as a self-appointed "primary researcher" (i.e. gatekeeper) for the Warren Commission, thus preventing any damning information to make it before the panel. Years later, various researchers have speculated that once Richard Nixon turned on Israel, Angleton surreptitiously instigated the Watergate scandal. Then, when Nixon requested his help in covering up the deliberately botched break-in, Angleton refused to lend any assistance, thus guaranteeing his downfall.

PROJECT PAPERCLIP AND MK-ULTRA

In a February 2005 article for *Nexus* magazine entitled "Princes of Plunder," David Guyatt writes that when the Rockefeller family became involved in Project Paperclip and the Nazi ratlines to smuggle gold, currency and scientists out of Germany after WWII, they had three significant assistants: Allen Dulles (future CIA Director), George Herbert Walker (George Bush Sr.'s grandfather) and James Jesus Angleton, who was awarded his later intelligence position.

A decade later, during Dwight Eisenhower's presidency, Nelson Rockefeller became undersecretary of Health, and in this role certainly became apprised of the CIA's nefarious MK-ULTRA programs (as did CIA directors Allen Dulles and Richard Helms). This point is vitally important because I've previously asserted that Charles Manson willfully participated in a covert operation to discredit the peace-and-love generation (on a need-to-know basis, of course). He played his part perfectly (ultimately as a fall guy), with his Family members carrying out the grotesquely traumatizing Tate-Labianca murders in August 1969.

Where did Manson get his start in this horrifying odyssey? After being released from Terminal Island Prison in 1967, he gravitated to San Francisco's Haight-Ashbury district, a focal point for extensive mind-control experimentation at the time. This CIA hot bed is also the place where Sara Jane Moore embarked upon her journey into radical left-wing politics (aka SLA mind-control). Similarly, Manson united with Squeaky Fromme in San Francisco. Adam Gorightly called Moore and Fromme "MK-ULTRA dupes" and, half-a-decade later, both women would try to assassinate Gerald Ford, making Nelson Rockefeller president. This saga has now come full-circle.

Behind-the-scenes, the Rockefeller family has been involved in eugenics, mind control and other black sciences since the early 1900s. These sinister endeavors almost put one of their own in the White House circa September 1975. Fortunately, neither of the female "triggers" was adept enough with handguns to make this Rockefeller dream come true.

ADDENDUM: THE BUSH-CROWLEY CONNECTION

Could former president George W. Bush actually be a spawn of the 20th century's most notorious Satanist? Considering the rampant evils perpetrated by his administration, including 9-11, the Patriot Act, the U.S. invasion of Iraq, Afghanistan heroin trafficking and the deliberate bankrupting of America's economy, nothing can be ruled out.

The key to this intriguing mystery rests with Bush's grandmother, a woman named Pauline Pierce, who gave birth to Barbara Bush on June 8, 1925. The timeline that follows is vitally important because Pauline Robinson married publishing magnate Marvin Pierce in 1919, then had two children with him by 1921. Pauline, however, wasn't a doting stay-at-home mother. Rather, similar to the carefree flappers of her time, she possessed a pronounced wild streak that made her anything but conventional.

In early 1924, overcome with wanderlust, Pauline Pierce left her husband and two children and traveled to Paris, where she stayed with free-spirited adventuress Nellie O'Hara. Here is where the story gets especially interesting. O'Hara was involved with a still-married American expatriate writer named Frank Harris, who penned the titillating *My Life and Loves*, which chronicled his sexual excesses and debauchery. This book was so scandalous that it was banned in several countries.

But Harris wasn't the most controversial figure living with Pauline Pierce and Nellie O'Hara. Their other roommate was famed cabalist Aleister Crowley, known alternatively as "the Great Beast 666" and "the Wickedest Man in the World" (as he was dubbed by British newspapers). An avowed practitioner of "sexual magick" that touted bisexuality, prostitutes and orgies, Crowley held membership in occult societies such as the Golden Dawn and OTO (Ordo Templi Orientis) as well.

Crowley was also a Freemason, and is credited with the reemergence of modern day witchcraft and the New Age movement.

Due to the notoriety associated with his rampant drug use and carnal indulgences, along with a well-publicized death that occurred during one of his magical sex rites, famed dictator Benito Mussolini eventually deported Crowley from Italy in 1924.

Exiled, Crowley journeyed to Paris where he took up residence with Nellie O'Hara, Frank Harris and Pauline Pierce. Yes, George W. Bush's grandmother may have actually lived with "the Great Beast," Aleister Crowley. Not only that, Pierce reportedly became a high-level initiate in Crowley's OTO. This point should not be taken lightly, because George Bush Sr., Prescott Bush and George W. Bush were members of the clandestine Skull and Bones fraternity at Yale University. So, what we're seeing is the Bush Family's multi-generational involvement in one of this nation's most cryptic secret societies.

Another added element of intrigue arises from Aleister Crowley's long-standing association with British Intelligence, particularly as an operative for MI6. In fact, a recently published book, *Secret Agent 666*, recounts how Crowley performed many duties for this spy agency. Likewise, George Bush the Elder was director of its American counterpart, the CIA, during the early 1970s. Researchers have even linked Crowley with American Intelligence during WWI and II.

Returning to Pauline Pierce, by October 1924 she returned to her husband in the U.S. The only problem was, Mrs. Pierce was pregnant, and on June 8, 1925, she delivered Barbara Bush. Now, if we do the math, Pauline would have conceived this child in September 1924—when she was living with Crowley—a full month before arriving back in America. Not only did Marvin Pierce never visit his wife in France, but the facial similarities between Barbara Bush and Mr. Crowley are striking.

This tale gets even more bizarre. In 1949, after rumors swirled that she was engaged in an adulterous affair with Gen. Dwight D. Eisenhower, Pauline Pierce died after her husband Marvin crashed their car into a wall on Sept. 23 in Harrison County, New York. Behind the scenes at that time, it was none other than Prescott Bush who urged Eisenhower to run for the presidency, which he success-fully attained in 1952.

Granted, this information is purely circumstantial and admittedly quite spectacular and conspiratorial, but remember that Prescott Bush—George W. Bush'ss grandfather—laundered money for the Nazis during WWII, and pleaded no contest to trading with the enemy in 1943 (see chapter 40 of *The New World Order Exposed* for more details).

Likewise, George Bush the Elder has been linked to the JFK assas-sination, masterminding the October Surprise in 1980 and coordinat-ing massive amounts of Iran-Contra guns and drug running from the vice president's office during Ronald Reagan's presidency. Finally, it was under George W. Bush's watch that the state-sponsored terrorism of 9-11 took place.

Was Barbara Bush a *Rosemary's Baby* of sorts to the notorious sex fiend and mystical womanizer Aleister Crowley? Akin to the mysterious lineage of Bill Clinton's real father that was documented in *Hillary (and Bill): The Sex Volume*, medical records have long been destroyed or sup-pressed. In their absence, the key point to focus on is what the Bush family has been involved in: running money for Hitler during WWII; the murder of a president; Skull and Bones; secret deals with the Irani-ans who held American hostages, importing billions of dollars worth of cocaine into the U.S. throughout the 1980s; decades of CIA sub-terfuge; war profiteering; and ultimately 9-11.

The vast majority of traditional families don't partake in such crim-inal activities, but those in league with the forces of darkness do. Many people consider Barbara Bush an innocent, grandmotherly figure, but in reality she's a monstrously domineering woman who reeks with ar-rogance. When asked by Diane Sawyer in 2003 about the impending war in Iraq, the former first lady replied coldly, "Why should we hear about body bags and deaths? It's not relevant. So why should I waste my beautiful mind on something like that?"

Equally as callous were her views on the thousands of homeless people stranded in New Orleans after Hurricane Katrina. Barbara Bush commented, "So many of the people in the arena here were underpriv-ileged anyway, so this (chuckle) is working very well for them." Con-

ALEISTER CROWLEY   **BARBARA BUSH**
Is it possible Crowley is Barbara's real father?

sidering all that's been covered in this article, these words were spoken with the true heartlessness of someone who just might be Aleister Crowley's daughter. Who is Barbara Bush?

CHAPTER 11

SON OF SAM

SON OF SAM SPEAKS FROM THE SEWERS

"Y'all got to start thinking on a different level, like the CIA does. Now we're through the looking glass here. White is black; and black is white."
—JIM GARRISON monologue, Oliver Stone's *JFK*

"The Cryptocracy is not a myth. It seeks to transform humanity through an alchemical processing of the mass consciousness or Group Mind."
—CRAIG HEIMBICHNER, *Blood on the Altar*

The Son of Sam—David Berkowitz—slithered into the world via a young Jewish woman, Betty Falco, who was impregnated out of wedlock by a Jewish man who never claimed him, Joseph Klineman. Unable to raise the child on her own, Falco allowed a Jewish couple—Nathan and Pearl Berkowitz—to adopt him. Recalling his youth, Berkowitz later commented, "I always had a fetish for murder and death."

Later, as an adult, Berkowitz joined the U.S. Army, where he used hallucinogens (while others say he underwent drug experimentation conducted by his superiors in the military). The confused man next flirted with membership in a fundamentalist cult prior to employment at the U.S. Postal Service in Yonkers, New York.

By age 24 during America's bicentennial in 1976, Berkowitz became our nation's most notorious criminal. Known initially as the .44 Caliber Killer due to his penchant for a Bulldog .44 revolver, the Son of Sam reign of terror extended 13 months from July 29, 1976 to Berkowitz's arrest on Aug. 10, 1977.

During this campaign where six victims were murdered, one blinded, one paralyzed, and seven more wounded, New York City Mayor Abe Beame announced, "We have a savage killer on the loose." Similarly, in *The Encyclopedia of Serial Killers*, Michael Newton summarized the fear. "For 13 months, New York would be a city under siege."

To combat the mysterious night stalker who lurked through New York's shadowy streets, the NYPD established Operation Omega, a 200-man squadron slated specifically to nullify the Son of Sam. Eventually, a parking ticket placed on Berkowitz's Ford Galaxie during the Moskowitz/Violante shooting led to his capture. In *Satanic Killings*, Frank Moorhouse describes what officers discovered: "In his apartment, all police found was a lone mattress, a bare light bulb and a littering of empty cartons and bottles. On the walls were scrawled the stuff of Berkowitz's interior fantasy world: *'In this hole lives the Wicked King. Kill for my master. I turn children into killers'.*"

Echoing the Zodiac Killers' taunts to media sources and policemen, handwriting expert Charles Hamilton actually claimed that the notes sent to famed journalist Jimmy Breslin weren't written by Berkowitz. Similarly, other researchers theorized that a secret journal containing notes on more than 300 arsons was fabricated and blamed on Berkowitz, a virgin loner patsy pushed forward to take the blame for those controlling him.

LETTERS FROM HELL

According to the legend of Sam, Berkowitz claimed that a 6,000-year-old man or demon sent messages via Berkowitz's neighbor's dog, commanding him to kill. As such, an entire demented mythology arose from letters that were sent to Jimmy Breslin at *The New York Daily News* and Capt. Joseph Borelli. It's even accurate to say that these correspondences from the gutter contributed more to New York's terror than did the actual shootings.

Michael A. Hoffman sets the stage in *Secret Societies and Psychological Warfare*: "At the site of the April 17, 1977 Son of Sam murders, the gunman left an envelope at the crime scene addressed to Police Detective Joseph Borelli. The packet contained a letter filled with occult symbolism and mocking hints of identity, reminiscent of the anonymous Rosicrucian manifestos circulated in the 17th century."

Below are excerpts from the letters that traumatized New Yorkers for month after nightmare-filled month:

TO JOSEPH BORELLI

"I am deeply hurt by your calling me a wemon [sic] hater. I am not. But I am a monster. I am the 'Son of Sam.' I am a little brat.

"I am the monster—'Beelzebub'—the Chubby Behemoth.

"I love to hunt. Prowling the streets looking for fair game—tasty meat.

"When Father Sam gets drunk he gets mean. He beats his family. Sometimes he ties me up to the back of the house. Other times he locks me in the garage. Sam loves to drink blood.

"'Go out and kill' commands Father Sam.

"Behind our house some rest. Mostly young—raped and slaughtered—their blood drained—just bones now.

"Papa Sam keeps me locked in the attic, too . . . I feel like an outsider. I am on a different wavelength than everybody else—programmed to kill."

TO JIMMY BRESLIN

"Hello from the gutters of N.Y.C. which are filled with dog manure, vomit, stale wine, urine and blood. Hello from the sewers of N.Y.C. which swallow up these delicacies when they are washed away by the sweeper trucks.

"Hello from the cracks in the sidewalks of N.Y.C. and from the ants that dwell in the cracks and feed on the dried blood of the dead that seep into these cracks.

"Here are some names to help you along. 'The Duke of Death.' 'The Wicked King Wicker' . . . John Wheaties—Rapist and Suffocator of Young Girls. . . ."

THE CARR FAMILY

To reiterate, in a *Time-Life* book entitled *True Crime*, Berkowitz told cops, "[He] was carrying out the wishes of a 6,000-year-old demon named Sam, who passed his instructions through the unlikely medium of a black Labrador retriever." But who is this mysterious "Sam"? Harold Schechter and David Everitt provide an answer in *The A to Z Encyclopedia of Serial Killers*. "Berkowitz explained the meaning of his bizarre moniker. 'Sam' turned out to be the name of a neighbor, Sam Carr, who—in Berkowitz's profoundly warped mind—was actually [possessed by] a 'high demon' who transmitted his orders to kill through his pet dog, a black Labrador."

It appears that during the .44 Killers' rampage, Berkowitz engaged in a personal battle with his neighbor—60ish Sam Carr. At first, Berkowitz sent an anonymous letter to Carr complaining about his barking dog. Unsatisfied with the lack of results, Berkowitz exploded a Molotov cocktail in Carr's driveway on May 13, 1976, then actually shot and wounded the black Lab on April 27, 1977.

These were obviously the reactions of an unbalanced individual. So, why did the letter-writer make such direct references to Carr, as well as other family members? One of Sam Carr's sons, John, was nick-named "Wheat," as in John Wheaties—rapist and suffocator of young girls. In addition, the cult he belonged to purportedly killed German shepherds on Wicker Street in Yonkers. Michael Carr—brother number 2—belonged to the Church of Scientology. Berkowitz also claimed that Michael held membership in "the Children"—a cult group involved in satanic worship, snuff films, sex rituals, child prostitution and murder.

New York Daily News assistant managing editor Richard Pienciak takes the story from here: "[Berkowitz] claimed that there was a cult;

that he'd been the group's hit man; that 10 members were still alive and had served as lookouts for his shootings; that the two dead sons of Sam Carr, Michael and John, had been part of the group; and that they had all used hallucinogenic drugs together."

In fact, Berkowitz alleged that he'd only committed the first two Son of Sam murders, and that at least half a dozen more, to varying degrees, had murdered and/or wounded the others. Two of the participants named by Berkowitz were John and Michael Carr. Could this possible involvement explain their untimely deaths shortly following Berkowitz's arrest? Newton explains: "Suspect John Carr fled New York in February 1978 and 'committed suicide' under mysterious circumstances two days later. Brother Michael Carr died in a single-car [DUI] crash in October 1979."

John Carr's case is particularly interesting. Born in Yonkers on Oct. 12 [coinciding with Aleister Crowley's birthday], he used LSD, dabbled in the occult, and entered a mental institution after being diagnosed as a "paranoid schizophrenic." He also commuted back and forth between Yonkers and Minot Air Force Base in North Dakota. There, at this government military installation, Carr purportedly placed a shotgun to his head and pulled the trigger.

But that's not all. The numbers "666" were carved into Carr's hand, while the cryptic letters "SSNYC" were scrawled on a wall in the victim's blood. The message was deciphered to mean "Son of Sam New York City." Connections become even stronger when Pienciak reported, "A law enforcement source [in Minot, N.D.] told me he had evidence that David Berkowitz and John Carr had known each other quite well."

ARLISS PERRY

The Minot link is furthered if we revert back to the brutal ritualistic murder of North Dakota resident Arliss Perry at Stanford Memorial Church in California on Oct. 12, 1974. In a review of Maury Terry's *The Ultimate Evil*, G.M. Kelley offers this illustration: "Arliss Perry's body was found with her legs spread wide apart, nude from the waist down, and the legs of her blue jeans were spread-eagle upside down across her calves, purposely arranged in that manner."

Now, with her death occurring on Oct. 12 (again, Aleister Crowley's birthday), a few more details need to be added. Ms. Perry had been beaten and choked before an icepick was jammed into her skull. Police later found her blouse torn open, arms folded across her chest, with an altar candle placed between her breasts. But the final element of this desecration involved a 30-inch altar candle that had been forced into her vagina.

It seems that Perry had tried "witnessing" to a group of Satanists a few weeks earlier, and the resulting death scene clearly held Masonic implications. If one imagines the Square and Compass of Masonry—essentially an upright "V" overlain by a downward-turned "V," what we have is an incomplete hexagram. In terms of Ms. Perry's death scene, her spread-eagle legs formed one "V," while the folded jeans comprised the downward "V." Then, the candle protruding from Perry equals the "G" (or God) at the center of a Masonic Square/Compass. Finally, if two horizontal lines are placed through this incomplete hexagram (Masonic symbol), it conveniently forms a Star of David.

How, the reader may wonder, does this ritual annihilation relate to Son of Sam David Berkowitz (who was Jewish)? Berkowitz claimed in prison letters that he'd heard about this killing from a man named William Mentzer [aka Manson II]. Jeff Wells in the *Four Pi Movement* explains the significance: "Berkowitz alleged that Perry was killed by Four Pi members as 'a favor' to cultists in her hometown of Bismarck, N.D. Her slayer was named by Berkowitz as Manson II, a professional killer involved with the original Manson and his cult in L.A."

MANSON II

Adam Gorightly's *Death Cults* allows us to become more familiar with this individual. "[Maury] Terry learned that one Son of Sam murder was videotaped, and that the cameraman, Ronald Sisman, was subsequently murdered by cult members when they went to recover the Son of Sam film. Terry pinned this murder on a mysterious figure dubbed Manson II, an 'occult superstar' and hit man who moved through the same late 1960s milieu of sex, drugs and porn as Manson, and who had been intimate with Tate-LaBianca victim Abigail Folger."

Others describe Mentzer as a bisexual who ran Magick Island, a private occult nightclub. He also associated with cocaine trafficker Elaine Greenberger, served as *Hustler* porn legend Larry Flynt's bodyguard, had connections to the Genovese organized crime family, and also knew Spahn Ranch caretaker Shorty Shea (reportedly killed and buried by Charles Manson and his associates). But Manson II's main notoriety derived from the 1983 execution of movie mogul Roy Radin in Los Angeles.

COTTON CLUB MURDER

A variety of researchers have hinted that the Son of Sam cult was actually controlled by a Los Angeles film producer, Roy Radin, who ran sex and drug parties out of his Long Island (Westchester County) mansion called "the Castle." According to Berkowitz, fellow members of his entourage attended these cocaine-laded bashes.

Radin, an ultra-sleazy Hollywood denizen, resorted to using laundered narcotics profits to finance his cinematic productions, including an upcoming filmed based on Harlem's Cotton Club. However, the project tanked after a dispute between Radin and his drug-dealing associates, who placed a contract on his head.

Even more abominable, Radin supposedly obtained a videotape from the underground L.A. film circuit of the Son of Sam/Stacy Moskowitz murder. Radin also employed as an assistant a man named Mickey DeVinko, who had been married to *Wizard of Oz* starlet Judy Garland. As an aside, *Oz* creator—L. Frank Baum—belonged to Madame Blavatsky's Theosophical Society and had a penchant for the occult. If we're to believe victims of CIA trauma-based mind control programming, *The Wizard of Oz* became a primary tool or "magic key" to indoctrinate new members.

At any rate, Radin had links to Satanism, the Process Church and the Illuminati. Due to burning his drug-dealer associates, enter William Mentzer (Manson II), whom the LAPD acknowledged belonged to organized crime hit squads. On Friday, May 13, 1983, Mentzer and an aide shot Radin anywhere from 12 to 20 times. Afterward, to complete the deal, Mentzer shoved a stick of dynamite in Radin's mouth and blew his head off. Later, after being imprisoned for years, David Berkowitz claimed that Mentzer also killed Arliss Perry, and that as the Son of Sam patsy he took the fall for Process Church leader Radin and his friends in high places.

Dave McGowan's *Programmed to Kill: The Politics of Serial Murder* adds credence to this claim: "Police found numerous telephone numbers scrawled on the walls of [Berkowitz's] apartment, including the unlisted private home numbers of prominent doctors living on Long Island, the number for a large Scientology training center in Florida, and the Montauk Gold and Racquet Club (a purportedly closed military base)."

Michael Hoffman concurs in *Secret Societies and Psychological Warfare*: "When Berkowitz left behind a long list of phone numbers in his Yonkers apartment of people in 'high places' linked to the Son of Sam murders, these telephone numbers were never officially investigated by any police agency, at least not for the record."

Is it possible that the Son of Sam hidden cultists consisted of NYPD officers, prominent Jewish homosexuals, and occultists who ordered the ritualistic murders? In Alex Constantine's *The OTO and the CIA*, he describes Berkowitz: "Key decisions in his life were made by leaders of a religious group based in Westchester, a hybrid of OTO members and acolytes from the Process Church of the Final Judgment."

THE PROCESS CHURCH AND WICKED KING WICKER

To understand this phenomenon, we need to trace America's occult underground all the way back to Aleister Crowley devotee Jack Parsons and future Scientology founder L. Ron Hubbard, who began this movement in Pasadena circa the 1940s. In swinging London during the 1960s, Robert Moore (aka Robert DeGrimston)—who had been heavily influenced by Hubbard's Scientology—founded the Process Church of the Final Judgment.

After migrating to America, the Process eventually co-mingled with OTO (Ordo Templi Orientis) elements in New York City. Constantine elaborates on the latter's history: "The OTO was founded between 1895 and 1900 by a pair of powerful Freemasons, Karl Kellner and Theodor

Reuss. Politically, the order was right-wing in the extreme, proposing the creation of a pan-German world based on pagan spiritual beliefs." Reuss then befriended Crowley in 1912, with the Great Beast sporting ties to British spy networks (MI-6) and U.S. intelligence.

Jim Keith's *Mind Control, World Control* takes it one step further by quoting an ex-Process Church member: "A lot of people say the Process is a fascist organization. It's actually half-true. It was founded by the German Democratic Party, a neo-Nazi group in Germany as a front to raise money here in the states."

R.N. Taylor (*The Process: A Personal Reminiscence*) is on a similar wavelength: "[Ed] Sanders [author of *The Family*] claimed that the Process was pro-Hitler and fascist in nature. It was true that they used a variation of the swastika for their symbol. Their social Darwinism was not so far afield from Nazi philosophy. They wore black uniforms and groomed themselves as an elite order."

Maury Terry's *The Ultimate Evil* continues this line of reasoning in regard to Son of Sam's cult: "This group contained a mixture of satanic practices which included the teachings of Aleister Crowley. It was totally blood oriented. The coven's doctrines are a blend of ancient Druidism, the teachings of the Golden Dawn [Crowley's organization] and black magic."

In an October 1979 prison letter, Berkowitz wrote of his association with the Son of Sam cult: "This group contained a mixture of satanic practices which included the teachings of Aleister Crowley and Eliphas Levi. The coven's doctrines are a blend of Druidism, the teachings of the Secret Order of the Golden Dawn, black magick, and a host of other unlawful and obnoxious practices."

Gorightly continues in *Death Cults*: "In a recent segment of A&E's *Investigative Reports: Son of Sam Speaks—The Untold Story*, Berkowitz identified the Process Church as the unifying force behind these various satanic cults, one being 'the Children.'" He further describes how the Children date back to a Nazi-sympathizing doctor who was smuggled into the U.S. via Project Paperclip by the U.S. intelligence community. In this vein, he concludes, "according to Terry, Berkowitz—though admittedly involved in some of the Son of Sam murders—was set up as a fall guy by 'the Children' for the entire series of murders."

In 1997, Berkowitz delved even deeper. "This was not just something they were doing for any type of, necessarily, pleasure, but it was part of an agenda. A very deep, covert and hidden agenda. They were about making war, and they were about bringing some chaos into the world." [i.e. Son of Sam's reign of terror, all linked to hidden elitists].

Paul David Collins's *The Deep Politics of God Revisited* plunges further into this underworld. "The Process provided children for sex and parties held by wealthy people in Westchester, Manhattan, Connecticut, and Long Island. Berkowitz informed Terry that one of these parties was held at [Roy] Cohn's house in Connecticut, and Berkowitz even got to meet the infamous McCarthy aide during the party."

During an August 2002 interview with John Vincent Sanders, Terry agrees that the Yonkers Son of Sam cult was founded by a pedophile demonologist Nazi sympathizer who became associated with the Process Church.

Over the years, Processians have been linked to Satanism, weapons trafficking, pornography, prostitution, drug manufacturing, and Charles Manson. As a part of Adam Parfrey's *Apocalypse Culture* anthology, R.N. Taylor told how Manson appeared in the *Death* issue of a Process magazine, how members visited him in prison, and how "Manson coyly remarked to [Prosecutor Vincent] Bugliosi that he and Robert DeGrimston were one and the same." Charlie also used a Scientology e-meter at the infamous Spahn Ranch, and introduced his Family to the same sort of lifestyle mentioned throughout this article.

Constantine's *The OTO and the CIA* carries this passage. "Charles Manson passed through the Lodge. In the L.A. underworld, the OTO spin-off was known for indulgence in sadomasochism, drug dealing, blood drinking, child molestation and murder. The Riverside OTO, like the Manson family, used drugs, sex, psycho-drama and fear to tear down the mind of an initiate and rebuild it according to the desire of the cult's inner-circle."

In a January 1982 interview, Berkowitz admitted to harboring an interest in Scientology (as did Michael Carr), while in his autobiography—*Son of Hope: My Story*—he recounted the influence of *Rosemary's*

Baby, Anton Lavey's *Satanic Bible*, books about Jack the Ripper, and engaging in various occult rituals. These notions were exhibited in his letter to columnist Jimmy Breslin. Beneath his signature "Son of Sam" appeared an occult sign created by the 19th-century black magician Eliphas Levi. Interestingly, Aleister Crowley claimed to have been the reincarnation of Levi.

Berkowitz's Jewish heritage also plays a role in his maladjusted mindset. In *Blood on the Altar: The Secret History of the World's Most Dangerous Secret Society*, Craig Heimbichner notes, "Judaism's foundational role as the basis for the OTO's Cult of the Beast is little known." In a 1973 movie, *The Wicker Man*, a hexagram—symbolic of the Kabbalah's god—appears on two different occasions. Also, in drawings of this legendary figure, the Wicker Man holds the hexagram of kabbalistic Solomonic sorcery.

Other researchers have postulated that "Sam" is actually a shortened version of "Samael," whose first wife happened to be Eve's predecessor—the evil Lilith. Lilith so happened to be the mother of all demons, and her marriage to Samael was arranged by the Blind Dragon. On the other hand, Samael is frequently referred to as the Angel of Death—and along with the monstrous Moloch—is in charge of dirty deeds. Could all this occult lore account for why Berkowitz referred to himself as a demon?

Hoffman dissects *The Wicker Man* film where an "occult group is involved in pagan ritual sacrifice to an effigy of the demon entity, King Wicker." If the Wicker Man represents an ancient symbol for ritual murder and human sacrifice, then it makes Alex Constantine's observations in *Crowley and the CIA* even more valid. "The Wicked King Wicker alludes to the Druid Wicker Man set aflame during the celebration of Samhain, the Celtic Lord of the Dead. The Wicker Man was a hollow effigy filled with sacrificial victims, and then set aflame. 'The Son of Sam' alludes to Samhain."

Samael (Son of Sam), the demon, along with Moloch, devours the young as sacrificial victims. Samhain (Son of Sam): Lord of the Dead. David Berkowitz—hollow effigy (mind control victim) murdering sacrificed young women like a Lord of the Dead on New York

City's darkened streets.

But the big question remains: did Berkowitz act alone? In *Dead Names: The Dark History of the Necronomicon*, an author (simply going by the name Simon) confesses, "When the Son of Sam murders began to take place, those of us in the occult milieu in New York knew very well that more than one person was responsible for them." Clearly, such a revelation explains why so many vastly different composite sketches of the "killer" surfaced—most of which looked nothing like Berkowitz. In addition, eyewitnesses described different cars at the murder scenes, not belonging to Berkowitz.

On Aug. 12, 2002 Sarah Wallace became curious of these discrepancies in *Are the 'Son of Sam' Killers Still Out There, or Is It Just a Conspiracy Theory?* After uncovering new evidence, New York City detectives "say that top police brass ordered their investigation shut down and wouldn't let [them] pull the original case files."

Queens District Attorney John J. Santucci agreed: "I believe David Berkowitz did not act alone—that others did cooperate, aid and abet him in the commission of these crimes." R.N. Taylor adds further credibility to this thought: "[Maury] Terry suggests that the Process is part of a vast cryptocracy of serial murderers who have links with the police and judicial establishment." He continues, "Terry attempted to link murderers, drug dealers, Satanists, child pornographers and members of the entertainment industry as part of a widespread satanic underground."

Roy Radin, Roy Cohn, Roman Polanski, Larry Flynt, and those in Los Angeles-New York City high places come to mind.

Dave McGowan refers to Maury Terry in *Programmed to Kill*. "Rather than the random work of serial/mass murderers, many were contract hits carried out for specific purposes by an interlocking network of satanic cults." Newton strikes a similar chord. "Newsman Maury Terry believes there were at least five different gunmen in the Son of Sam attacks, including Berkowitz, John Carr, and several other suspects. Terry also notes that six of the seven shootings fell in close proximity to recognized occult holidays."

UNTERMYER PARK

Similar to *The Wicker Man* film where secretive covens convened, Hoffman illustrates how "the Son of Sam cult held their first rituals in Untermyer Park . . . planning for the murders occurred in a fire-charred abandoned mansion which had once belonged to the estate of the Warburg-Rothschild family."

Located in Yonkers, New York near where the Carr brothers and David Berkowitz resided, Process founder Robert DeGrimston also lived near Untermyer Park in the mid-1970s. Founded in 1903 by Zionist Samuel Untermyer—also a reputed Satanist—the park was connected to an array of underground aqueducts where witnesses described seeing torches, fires, dead dogs, and chanting robed and hooded cultists. Not surprisingly, this site had a long history of ritualistic activity, satanic lore, occult graffiti and bloodletting, while sporting a "temple" and "Devil's Cave."

Even more intriguing is an allegation from Fritz Springmeier that Samuel Untermyer belonged to Aleister Crowley's Golden Dawn, which he also characterized as the Rothschilds' personal coven. As an ardent Zionist, Untermyer played a key role in forcing America into World War I. After obtaining proof of Woodrow Wilson's adulterous affair with a neighbor, Untermyer blackmailed the president into appointing fellow Zionist Louis Brandeis to the Supreme Court. The Justice (along with Colonel House and Bernard Baruch) then played a pivotal role in urging Wilson to send forces to Europe.

As insider Benjamin Freedman so expertly disclosed, one of the primary motives behind luring America into WW I was to ultimately create a Jewish homeland in Palestine. This movement gained steam in 1882 when Baron Edmond de Rothschild funded Jewish colonizers in the Middle East.

As Israel's patron saint, Rothschild collaborated with Zionist founder, Theodore Herzl, to create world wars which would eventually cause such chaos and bloodshed that their people—the Jews—would, via subterfuge, obtain a new homeland. It should also be noted that a version of the Rothschild's family crest—a red hexagram—symbolic of Moloch the monster who biblical Israelites sacrificed their children to, became the symbol for Israel's flag—the Star of David hexagram.

The Rothschild agenda becomes clear. In *The Creation of Israel*, David Icke spells it out. "The 'Jewish homeland' in the former Palestine was from the start a Rothschild fiefdom engineered through the global secret society network controlled by interbreeding families known as the Illuminati. They called their plan 'Zionism.'"

Following WW I, the Rothschild-crafted Treaty of Versailles guaranteed WW II. Again, occultist and Rothschild agent Samuel Untermyer used his manipulative leverage to cause global terror and bloodshed. As President at the July 1933 Jewish World Congress, Untermyer bellowed, "Jews of the world now declare a holy war against Germany. We are going to use a worldwide boycott against them that will destroy them." Fully intent on starving the German people, headlines blared, "Judea Declares War on Germany."

MIND CONTROL

Possibly the biggest secret of World War II is that Hitler's Nazi Party worked hand-in-hand with Rothschild's Zionist network to force Jews out of Germany (and Europe), eventually to settle in a yet-to-be-formed country called Israel. As the war wound down in 1945, U.S. intelligence agents—via Project Paperclip—smuggled Nazi scientists out of Germany to become integral in the formation of America's CIA. In addition, Israel's Mossad also folded into the CIA.

Now, with Europe "reshaped" via WW I and II (*solve et coagula*— "break down and re-form"), the Central Intelligence Agency and other furtive secret societies became the prime movers of mind control in hospitals, the military, prisons, mental institutions, and cults. The result: a string of "lone-nut" assassins and societal chaos that the mass media used to keep the citizenry in a perpetual state of fear.

A tiny example of how this network operates can be found in the common thread of mind-benders who continue to treat each patsy. Psychiatrist Daniel Schwartz examined both David Berkowitz and Mark David Chapman, who was also treated by hypnotist Bernard Diamond, who diagnosed Sirhan Sirhan, who fell under the sway of the Process Church, as did Charles Manson.

Of course, Manson used drugs to program his followers, which leads to Adam Gorightly's analysis in *The Shadow Over Santa Susana*. "According to [John] Judge, [psilocybin derivative EA1729] is the same 'acid' that a buddy of David Berkowitz's named Terry Patterson—who served with him in Korea—claimed Berkowitz was given by the 'brass' while in the Army when he was placed in a special program reportedly for 'profiled' candidates. Mae Brussell was convinced that Berkowitz was another in a long list of MK-ULTRA patsies, and more correctly, referred to him as 'son of Uncle Sam.'"

Fueled by MK-ULTRA LSD, cult activity, mind control, and the nefarious agenda of their hidden persuaders, the Summers of Sam subjected us to their media-controlled fear-conditioning and programming. Columbia Jones, in an editorial for *MK Zine* in the Spring/Summer of 2003 wrote, "Twilight language includes the intentional use of language and images so as to lock on to a twin correspondence in the subliminal mind . . . mass media is a branch of ritual magic whose aim is public mind control."

Jim Keith brings this subject to closure in *Mind Control, World Control*. "By the creation of controlled chaos, the populace can be brought to the point where it willingly submits to greater control. [Professor Kurt] Lewin maintained that society must be driven into a state equivalent to an 'early childhood situation.' He termed this societal chaos 'fluidity.'"

During Son of Sam's reign of terror, young women refused to leave their homes, people didn't park along darkened streets, paranoia and tension filled the city, while newscasters and columnists continued to fuel the hysteria. With Berkowitz as the disposable fall guy, his masters reigned supreme in the shadows—successful yet again in debilitating the public.

CHAPTER 12

JOHN LENNON

JOHN LENNON: ENEMY OF THE STATE

I remember the moment with a clarity that's crystallized inside my mind. My buddy Duke and I sat in a darkened parking lot near Mercyhurst College outside of Erie, Pa. We'd driven in his blue Camaro to meet some buddies, but since they weren't home, we waited and listened to the radio. Then a newscaster's words cut through the uncharacteristically warm nighttime air. "John Lennon has been shot." The date: Dec. 8, 1980, one month after Ronald Reagan and George Bush Sr. had been elected president and vice president.

Later reports stated that a lone-nut assassin, Mark David Chapman, pulled the trigger and killed the former Beatles front man outside his home at the Dakota Apartments in New York City. But did he? Although he eventually changed his plea to guilty, there was no trial, courtroom testimony or eyewitnesses. Lennon's wife Yoko didn't see the shooting, and similar to Sirhan Sirhan, Chapman avowed no actual memory of riddling the star's body with bullets.

Details get even murkier. Supposedly, Chapman called out Lennon's name to get his attention, yet no one heard him utter a word.

At his sentencing hearing, Justice Dennis Edwards asked Chapman if he made any comments to Lennon before the shooting. "No, your honor," served as his response. This point is essential, for there was no reason for Lennon to turn in Chapman's direction. Chapman also purportedly crouched into a combat stance prior to firing five rounds from his .38 caliber revolver, but no one saw him do that, either.

All of Lennon's fans had left by the time of his return to the Dakota, so what did Chapman do after allegedly killing the most famous musical legend in America? He dropped his gun, sat down, and began reading reclusive author J.D. Salinger's *The Catcher in the Rye*.

Lt. Arthur O'Connor, commanding officer of the NYPD's 2nd Precinct, commented on his odd behavior. "If the assassin wanted to get away with it, he could have got away with it. There was a subway right on the corner and no one around to stop him."

Patrolman Peter Cullen, an officer in the first car reporting to the scene, felt Chapman being the shooter was implausible. He, in fact, determined that it may have been someone *inside* the Dakota, until doorman Jose Perdomo fingered Chapman. In 1988, during an interview with filmmaker Kevin Sim for the documentary, *The Man Who Shot John Lennon*, Chapman described his mental state at the time. "He walked past me and then I heard in my head, 'do it, do it, do it.' I don't remember aiming. I must have, but I don't remember drawing a bead or whatever you call it. And I just pulled the trigger steady five times. There was no emotion; there was no anger; there was nothing. Dead silence in the brain—dead cold quiet."

Detective O'Connor added this insight. "It's definitely illogical to say that Mark Chapman committed the murder to make himself famous. He did not want to talk to the press from the start. It's possible Mark could have been used by somebody. I studied him intensely. It looked as if he could have been programmed."

Programmed to kill, or programmed to *think* he killed? In *Rethinking John Lennon's Assassination*, researcher Salvador Astucia creates an intriguing scenario whereupon Chapman may have simply acted as another mind-controlled patsy, almost identical to Sirhan Sirhan. Consider that by all accounts, Chapman stood *behind* Lennon and *to the*

Police lead Mark David Chapman from the 20th Precinct stationhouse after arrest for killing John Lennon.

right. Yet all four bullet wounds were located on the *left side* of Lennon's body. Astucia writes, "Lennon's wounds are on the wrong side of the body. The autopsy indicated he sustained four wounds on the left side of his upper body, but Chapman was standing behind him and to his right when the shots were fired."

After being fatally struck with four bullets, Lennon is said to have then dragged himself twenty-five feet, crawled up six steps through some glass doors, and then straggled another ten-fifteen feet into the lobby. But what if another scenario is more realistic? Located directly across from the stairs inside the Dakota is a doorway leading to a service elevator. Astucia postulates that the actual gunman hid inside this doorway, and then when Lennon walked past, fired twice into his left shoulder. As Lennon ran toward the steps, he was hit twice more in the left side of his back. After being critically wounded, Lennon merely dragged his body up a few steps into the lobby, a far more probable scenario than the official story.

If the gunman emerged from this door leading to the service elevator directly across from the stairway, it explains Lennon's wounds in the left side of his body, in addition to the three bullet holes found in the glass lobby doors. It would have been *impossible* for Chapman to strike these doors from where he stood in the Dakota entranceway.

Astucia summarizes, "If the elevator operator shot Lennon from the service elevator doorway as Lennon approached the main lobby, then the left side of Lennon's body would have faced the assailant."

He then concludes, "The emergence of a phantom elevator operator introduces a more believable scenario that the elevator operator was the real assassin and Chapman was merely a mind-altered patsy."

JOSE PERDOMO

By the time John and Yoko returned home from the recording studio on Dec. 8, his fans had already cleared out. The only ones present were Mark David Chapman, front doorman Jose Perdomo, and a photographer. On March 2, 1987 *People* magazine ran the following passage. "When photographer Paul Goresh left, Chapman had only the Dakota's night doorman, Jose Perdomo, to keep him company. Jose was an anti-Castro Cuban, and they talked that night of the Bay of Pigs and the assassination of John F. Kennedy."

Wait a second. Here are two complete strangers who'd supposedly never met before, and one of them is allegedly planning to kill the guitarist and singer for the world's most popular band ever. Now, considering how many anti-Castro Cubans were peripherally involved in the murder of President Kennedy, not to mention later recruited by George Bush, Sr.'s cronies into the Iran-Contra operation, doesn't it seem even remotely peculiar that these men would discuss the disastrous Bay of Pigs failure, which forever incensed the CIA and contributed to their involvement in the Dallas massacre of John Kennedy?

But that's only one element of the picture. Jose Perdomo was also an anti-Castro Cuban exile with long-standing connections to U.S. intelligence agencies. On Dec. 7, 2005 Jerry Mazza provided further clues in *Of John Lennon's Assassination, Imagine.* He notes that Perdomo (aka

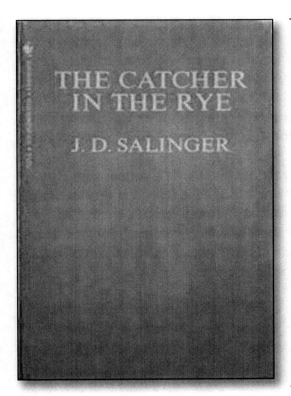

Catcher in the Rye became a seminal book for alienated 1950s adolescents. As a precursor to James Dean and *Rebel Without a Cause*, J.D. Salinger's novel is quite possibly the first moment when "teen culture" emerged. Decades later, it became a staple for high school students. As the book sold millions, its author increasingly became a recluse and refused to give interviews or make public appearances. Similar to *The Wizard of Oz*, many view *Catcher* as a mind-control tool used by MK-ULTRA psychiatrists to alter the thought processes of patients.

Joaquin Sanjemis, aka Sam Jenis) belonged to Brigade 2506 in the failed Bay of Pigs operation. He also lurked in the shadows with Bay of Pigs operative (and later Watergate burglar for Richard Nixon) Frank Sturgis. On the CIA payroll, Perdomo also came in contact with hit men-for-hire and assorted Mafiosi.

Does any of this information seem suspicious, especially when moments later John Lennon would be shot dead? Then, directly after this tragedy, Perdomo imbeds a trigger thought in Chapman's mind by asking, "Do you know what you've just done?" Astucia attributes this act to a further continuance of Chapman's manipulation. "The first thing that needed to be done after Lennon was shot was to plant the idea in Chapman's mind that he committed the murder, even if he did not." Finally (and inexplicably), Perdomo issued a command to Chapman. "Leave! Get out of here!" Why would anyone conceivably issue such a directive?

CATCHER IN THE RYE

Prior to visiting New York City, the unemployed Chapman with a sporadic work record had traveled extensively to many parts of the world, yet his income could not have covered these costs. While in the Big Apple, he roomed at the Sheraton Centre Hotel in Manhattan and had $2,201.76 in his pocket after shooting John Lennon. Similar patsies before him also spent lavishly (i.e. Lee Harvey Oswald, Arthur Bremer) without any visible means to pay for it.

Conspiracy researcher Mae Brussell found a pattern with all these individuals. Once a decoy is established, a legend is created around them via letters, diaries, and various travels. As such, a cover story and "motive" can be created to show how they became "lone nut killers." The patsy ultimately "serves a purpose to direct all attention away from those people who have armed him and located him at the scene of the crime."

Mark David Chapman spent time in Fort Chaffee, Arkansas at a CIA-affiliated military base, then in Beirut, where Brussell alleges that George Abash and the CIA fostered assassination teams. Also, Jerry Mazza discovered that "Chapman began working at a Laotian refugee camp. The camp was run by World Vision, an evangelical charity . . . that was assisted in numerous CIA operations . . . World Vision appears to be an elaborate cover for the recruitment, training, and placement of assassins worldwide."

Even more interestingly, John Hinckley Sr. was World Vision's President of the Board, and also a close acquaintance of George Bush, the elder. Hinckley's son, of course, was framed as a fall guy who tried to kill Ronald Reagan, a move that would have elevated Bush to the presidency eight years earlier. In his book, *The Covert War on Rock*, Alex Constantine writes, "In Cuba, World Vision camps concealed the agitations of Alpha 66, the anti-Castro brigands of Bay of Pigs fame." Lastly, Mae Brussell contends that in Hawaii, Chapman underwent a federally sponsored mind control operation conducted by the U.S. military.

Such travels and experiences certainly aren't typical, but could Chapman really have been another mind-controlled patsy and not the actual triggerman? To answer this question, Chapman originally claimed innocence, then inexplicably switched his plea to guilty because he heard a "small male voice" in his prison cell tell him to do so.

Where did these voices originate? Alex Constantine describes how Chapman's attorney, Jonathan Marks, appointed three separate Jewish psychiatrists to his client: (1) Hypnosis authority Dr. Milton Kline said that he could create a mind-controlled assassin within six months. (2) Dr. Bernard Diamond acted as the defense psychiatrist for another famous patsy, Sirhan Sirhan. (3) Dr. Daniel Schwartz—who counseled David Berkowitz, the Son of Sam killer—who similarly attributed his actions to hearing foreign thoughts in his head.

The reason why these patsies aren't placed on the scene as the real killers is due primarily to an uncontrollable risk factor. Astucia contends that these Manchurian fall guys are merely decoys. "Most do not believe this is a viable technique for political assassination because it is too unreliable."

He continues, "I believe Chapman was the victim of government sponsored mind control where an obsession was placed in his mind to kill Lennon."

In other words, Chapman didn't actually shoot the pop star; he simply was led to believe that he did. How did his handlers accomplish such a feat? Dr. Dorothy Lewis theorizes that Chapman may have been subjected to some sort of "command hallucination." What could have served as the trigger device for his programming? How about J.D. Salinger's *Catcher in the Rye*, the same exact book that John Hinckley clutched at his assassination scene?

CHARLES MANSON AND ROSEMARY'S BABY

One of the most deceptive fables surrounding John Lennon concerns Charles Manson, and how messages sent from the Beatles propelled him on a path of psychotic destruction. Lawyer Vincent Bugliosi floated this outlandish "motive," but Manson always dismissed it as nonsense. In November 1970 he clearly explained during his murder trial:

> Helter Skelter is ridiculous. Helter Skelter means confusion. Literally. It doesn't mean war with anyone. It doesn't mean people are going to kill other people. Helter Skelter is confusion. Confusion is coming down fast. If you don't see the confusion coming down fast, you can call it what you wish. It's not my conspiracy. It's not my music. I hear what it relates. It says "Rise!" It says "Kill!" Why blame it on me? I didn't write the music. I'm not the person who projected it into your social consciousness.

The links between Manson, Lennon, Chapman and the occult branched off in other directions, too. The Family called one of their houses *The Yellow Submarine*, while Charlie nicknamed Susan Atkins *Sexy Sadie* (akin to Lennon's derogatory song about the Maharishi). Then, of course, Atkins murdered Sharon Tate, wife of Roman Polanski, who directed the film *Rosemary's Baby*. Mia Farrow starred as Rosemary, and she traveled with the Beatles to India to meet Maharishi Mahesh Yogi. Reportedly, the last person Mark Chapman saw before killing Lennon was Mia Farrow. In addition, Farrow's husband during the filming of *Rosemary's Baby* was Frank Sinatra, a pivotal factor in the Marilyn Monroe murder.

The newlywed couple in *Rosemary's Baby* lived at the famous Dakota apartments in New York City, the same place where John and Yoko resided. In this movie, an angry mob killed a character named Adrian Mercato for being a devil worshipper (the same locale where Lennon was slain as a "sacrificial lamb"). The Beatles' famous *Sergeant Pepper* album cover contained a picture of occultist Aleister Crowley. Alex Constantine writes in *The Covert War on Rock*, "Months before the murder, Chapman visited Satanist filmmaker Kenneth Anger at a screening in Hawaii, shook hands and handed over two .38 caliber bullets: 'These are for John Lennon.'" Kenneth Anger was a devotee of Aleister Crowley, and featured Crowleyesque themes in many of this works.

Crowley's mother called him "The Great Beast 666" as a child, and Jewish author Ira Levin's book, *Rosemary's Baby*, had a release date that closely coincided with a famous *Time* magazine cover asking, *Is God Dead* in April 1966. When the Jewish Polanski researched *Rosemary's*

Baby, he met with Church of Satan founder Anton Lavey to discuss the specifics of satanic rituals, then cast Lavey as Satan in the famous rape scene where the devil impregnates Rosemary. The Manson Family killed Polanski's pregnant wife, while authorities later arrested Polanski for the statutory rape of a thirteen-year-old girl.

ANTI-SEMITISM

In an earlier article about Charles Manson, it's contended that Roman Polanski may have been targeted for his unflattering depiction of Jewish characters in *Rosemary's Baby*. Did the same fate befall John Lennon? In Albert Goldman's critical *The Lives of John Lennon*, he proposes that the rock star harbored a great deal of anti-Semitism. A 1967 Lennon movie entitled *How I Won the War* displayed an obvious tinge of sympathy toward Germany and the Nazis. Lennon also spent a great deal of time during the early Beatles years in Germany, and had a number of German friends.

In a 1970 interview with *Rolling Stone* magazine, Lennon chastised Paul McCartney's in-law, John Eastman (a potential Beatle manager). "They're f***ing bastards. Eastman's a WASP Jew, man! And that's the worst kind of Jew on Earth. That's the worst kind of WASP, too—he's a WASP Jew. Can you imagine it!" Could this derisive attitude be due to the fact that both Beatles managers (Brian Epstein and Allen Klein), as well as those who run the music industry, were all Jewish and stole their money?

Even Lennon's attitude toward the "unquestionable" Holocaust seemed flippant and irreverent. In a song called *God* on the 1971 album, *Plastic Ono Band*, Lennon sings, "I don't believe in Hitler." Like every other concept and person mentioned in this song, the Holocaust doesn't hold a "sacred" meaning that the Jews insist it should have.

YOKO ONO

Depicted as a conniving "dragon lady" by fans and rock critics, Yoko Ono is blamed for breaking up Lennon's first marriage, poisoning him against the Beatles and causing them to disintegrate, destroying his public image, addicting him to drugs, ruining his political activism, forcing him underground, and ultimately leading Lennon to quit the music scene.

During the mid-1970s until his triumphant return in late 1980, Lennon did become a near-total recluse. Jokingly referring to himself as Greta Hughes (Greta Garbo + Howard Hughes), Albert Goldman partly attributes this hermit-like state to Yoko encouraging and supporting Lennon's huge heroin addiction. A major devotee of the occult [she later named one of her albums, *I Am a Witch*], Yoko lured her husband into a bizarre realm where many of the decisions she made for them were based upon Tarot cards (business deals, investments, etc). This manipulation also led to séances, consulting witches, an interest in paranormal activity, and New Age mysticism.

Of course, John familiarized himself with many of these topics on his own, for he had great interest in Eastern religions, UFOs, conspiracy theories, primal scream therapy, Hare Krishna, Madame Blavatsky, numerology, astrology, and psychics.

But Yoko took matters to an entirely new level. In 1965, she crafted a piece of conceptual art prophetically referred to as a "Danger Box"—"a machine from which you will never come back the same." Was this device indicative of her presence in Lennon's life, where once he entered her web, he could ultimately never escape?

Fittingly, Ono's second husband, Anthony Cox, practiced hypnotism, which leads to an interesting story told by former Lennon girlfriend, May Pang. Living with John during his breakup with Ono, she spoke of their plans to purchase a home together, and how Lennon wanted to start recording once again with Paul McCartney. Then, Yoko intervened by getting John to participate in a stop-smoking session. The technique used—hypnosis.

Pang also felt that John was either drugged or placed in a trance because from that day forward he never returned to her. She did see him once later, describing him as being in a zombie-like state. The next half-decade found Lennon in his Dakota seclusion, cut-off from friends, music, politics, and the outside world ("staring at shadows on the wall").

ENEMIES LIST

Eventually, in December 1980, Lennon emerged with his final album, *Double Fantasy*. Only one month earlier, Ronald Reagan had been elected president (with ultimate insider George Bush, Sr. as his vice president). No doubt, William Casey, Reagan's campaign director and later CIA Director, felt that trouble could be brewing. He and Bush had already engineered the delay of U.S. hostages being released by promising to sell Iran weapons. Iran-Contra would also be initiated within the next year.

Casey, Bush, and others in their cabal knew that if a politically charged radical extremist with a big mouth emerged from his hiatus and started popping off, their nefarious plans might be foiled. Plus, Lennon became well versed in conspiracy research during his years of seclusion, and certainly knew about the government's role in illegal drug trafficking. Specifically, Lennon remarked to *Rolling Stone* magazine (later found in the book, *Lennon Remembers*): "The same bastards are in control. The same bastards are runnin' everything. They're doing exactly the same things, selling arms to South Africa, killing blacks in the street, people are living in f***ing poverty with rats crawling all over them. It's the same. It just makes you puke."

For making such statements during the early 1970s, those who considered Lennon an "enemy of the state" were Richard Nixon, Attorney General John Mitchell, FBI Director J. Edgar Hoover, and Senator Strom Thurmond.

U.S. VERSUS JOHN LENNON

The best documentary in existence that illustrates the Mop Top's radicalized transformation is *The U.S. Versus John Lennon*. As the Vietnam War raged on with millions killed in the Southeast Asian jungles, college students burned their draft cards, marched, and protested. Groups such as the Black Panthers, yippies, Weather Underground, pranksters, and hippies became household names, none of which passed Lennon's notice. Declaring, "The world is run by insane people for insane objectives," he and Yoko entered the realm of politics by first promoting "bagism"—a concept based on "total communication" where people are judged on their qualities and ideas rather than appearance.

His decidedly overt political song *Revolution* on *The White Album* carried the lines, "When you talk about destruction, don't you know you can count me out (in)." They were further fueled by protests and riots in the summer of 1968 at the Democratic National Convention in Chicago where marchers chanted, "The whole world is watching" as policemen bloodied America's youth.

In March 1969 John and Yoko staged a "bed-in" at the Amsterdam Hotel, followed by another one in Montreal two months later. When asked what he'd like to tell President Nixon, Lennon responded, "Declare peace." This concept became their focal point, with Lennon saying that they'd like to sell peace like soap powder. Even the song they created on the spot—with the help of Timothy Leary and Tommy Smothers—revolved around this notion. "All we are saying is, give peace a chance."

Becoming a national anthem for the anti-war movement, Lennon next erected posters and billboards all over the world with the words, "War is Over." On the other hand, in April 1970 Nixon's war machine forces invaded Cambodia, then indiscriminately riddled students with bullets at Kent State on May 4. In all, more than 40,000 U.S. soldiers died in Vietnam on Nixon's watch.

To keep a lid on dissenters, J. Edgar Hoover used the FBI as his secret police force. Their tactics included tapping phones, widespread surveillance, harassment, frame-ups, and even Gestapo-like assassinations. An April 10, 1972 FBI memo from J. Edgar Hoover instructed, "Initiate discreet efforts to locate subject [John Lennon] and remain aware of his activities and movements." Further, more than a decade later, in March 1983, Yoko Ono's head of security, Dan Mahoney, located listening devices planted inside the Lennon's Dakota apartment.

In September 1971 the Lennons moved to New York City, and according to John, "The first people who got in touch with me were Jerry Rubin and Abbie Hoffman." Potentially acting as Jewish *agents provocateurs*, TV newsman Geraldo Rivera described these two as "highly evolved political activists." The still naïve Lennon and Ono became "instruments and tools of these political masters" by introducing America to Rubin and Black Panther Bobby Seale on the Mike Douglas and Dick Cavett TV talk shows.

Pushing the envelope by becoming even more radicalized, Lennon joined and spoke at actual street protests. The highlight arrived when he and Yoko performed at a "Free John Sinclair Freedom Rally" at the University of Michigan campus on Dec. 10, 1971. The twelve-hour concert—broadcast live—found Lennon singing about "The CIA selling dope." That following Monday, the Michigan Supreme Court freed White Panther leader John Sinclair (who had been imprisoned for selling two joints to an undercover narc).

Seeing Lennon's influence and power increase exponentially, the FBI freaked-out, labeling him an enemy of the state. Worse, now that eighteen-year-olds could vote via passage of the 26th Amendment, Lennon could seriously imperil Nixon's reelection, especially if he joined a proposed "radical tour" across America, culminating with a free three-day concert at the Republican National Convention in Miami. This "political Woodstock" conceived by Jerry Rubin never came to fruition, but it still sent shockwaves through Tricky Dick's paranoid mind.

Panicked, the Nixon administration found relief in GOP Senator Strom Thurmond, who wrote to the White House and proposed stopping Lennon by canceling his visa and deporting him via the INS (Immigration and Naturalization Service). Calling him an "undesirable alien," members of the Nixon team (including G. Gordon Liddy and John Dean) admitted to FBI surveillance and wiretapping. In response, Lennon warned, "They were coming for me. If anything happens to Yoko and me, it wasn't an accident."

Even with the feds hounding him, Lennon continued to poke them in the eye. On April 22, 1972 he spoke at a huge outdoor peace rally in New York City, then photographed himself standing beside a poster depicting "USA surpasses all genocide records." To fight back, INS dragged out Lennon's legal battle from March 1972 until July 1976— a harrowing ordeal which documents later proved extended through the FBI, CIA, all the way up to the president's office. Years later (found deep inside INS files), letters sent from J. Edgar Hoover to H. R. Haldeman proved that a concerted effort existed to get Lennon out of the country.

Watergate journalist Carl Bernstein said of Richard Nixon, "His was a rogue, criminal presidency based on wholesale criminality." Like a battering ram against these forces, novelist Gore Vidal described John Lennon as "a born enemy of those who govern the United States."

MOTIVE

So, why was John Lennon murdered by shadowy elements of the American political organized crime syndicate? Sean Lennon described his father as a "counterrevolutionary" killed by a "government conspiracy."

As for Mark David Chapman, researcher Fenton Bresler provides this overview. "The killer was merely a tool. A human gun used and controlled by others to destroy a uniquely powerful radical figure who was likely to prove a rallying point for mass opposition to the policies soon to be implemented."

Implemented by whom? Because they feared Lennon would emerge from his Dakota darkness and begin speaking out against their criminal foreign policy (Iran-Contra, Mena drug running, etc), Jerry Mazza provides the final word. "Former CIA head and operative George H.W. Bush and company put together a preemptive strike against Lennon. As usual, they needed a certified nut" to serve as the prerequisite patsy.

JOHN LENNON—*Give Me Some Truth*

I'm sick and tired of hearing things
From uptight, short-sighted, narrow-minded hypocrites
All I want is the truth
Just gimme some truth

I've had enough of reading things
By neurotic, psychotic, pig-headed politicians

All I want is the truth
Just gimme some truth

No short-haired, yellow-bellied, son of Tricky Dicky
Is gonna mother hubbard soft soap me
With just a pocketful of hope
Money for dope
Money for rope

I'm sick to death of seeing things
From tight-lipped, condescending, mama's little chauvinists
All I want is the truth
Just gimme some truth now

I've had enough of watching scenes
Of schizophrenic, egocentric, paranoiac, prima donnas
All I want is the truth now
Just gimme some truth

CHAPTER 13

JOHN HINCKLEY

JOHN HINCKLEY & THE 'BUSHY' KNOLL

"Expedience is the first law of nature. The wolf knows nothing about morality. It tears out the throats of sheep and then eats them. That does not make it evil. Animals can always be trusted to do what's expedient. With man, you have to assume the worst."

—Craig DiLouie

On March 30, 1981 at approximately 2:00 in the afternoon, President Ronald Reagan completed a speech before the AFL-CIO at the Washington Hilton. Outside this hotel, John Hinckley stood with a .22-caliber Rohm R6-14 revolver. After yelling, "Mr. President, look over here," he fired six shots, not one of them directly striking the commander-in-chief.

In fact, according to official sources, the sequence of shots purportedly produced the following results:

Bullet One: Blasted into the skull of Press Secretary James Brady, crippling him.

Bullet Two: Struck Officer Thomas Delahanty in the back.

Bullet Three: Zipped over Reagan's head and harmlessly hit a building.

Bullet Four: Lodged in the chest of Secret Service Agent Thomas McCarthy.

Bullet Five: Careened off the bulletproof glass of the president's limousine.

That leaves one remaining bullet—number 6—which we're told struck Reagan. Newscasters reported that this shot ricocheted off the president's vehicle and then followed a circuitous route similar to Arlen Specter's "magic bullet theory" in the JFK assassination. To make the logistics work, the bullet supposedly flattened itself into the size of a penny, took a sharp ninety-degree turn, snuck in the narrow gap of the limo's open back door, and finally entered the president's body beneath his left armpit. But that's not all. The bullet next propelled itself off his ribcage, turned over yet again, skirted around his heart, before ultimately lodging in his left lung. Of course, all this activity occurred while a Secret Service agent tackled Reagan and pinned his arms down as they frantically dove for cover inside the car.

Naturally, critics don't buy this story. Rather, as Charles Overbeck wrote in an article for *Parascope* entitled *Reagan, Hinckley, and the 'Bushy Knoll' Conspiracy*, "If a sniper were positioned on the 'Bushy Knoll,' he would have had a clear shot at Reagan along the exact angle at which the bullet entered his body.

A second shooter? In *Of John Lennon's Assassination, Imagine*, independent journalist Jerry Mazza made this observation. "Imagine the correspondent Judy Woodruff appearing on *NBC Special Reports* that ran right after the shooting. She said she saw at least one shot fired from the hotel overhang above Reagan's limousine. She later added that a Secret Service agent had fired that shot."

A bona fide second gunman? David Southwell and Sean Twist write in *Conspiracy Files*, "More than one witness reported that at least one shot came from a Secret Service agent who was stationed on the overhang behind Reagan's limousine." They continue, "If you inspect video footage of the shooting it is clear from the position Hinckley was standing in when he opened fire, he would have needed to shoot through a car door to hit Reagan where he did. This impossibility is explained by the 'ricochet theory' which is as implausible as the infamous 'magic bullet theory' in the JFK shooting."

If one inspected photos from that day, it's perfectly clear that a man is positioned on the hotel's overhang with his hand on a rail near the top of a wall. This locale has come to be dubbed "the Bushy Knoll." Plus, since media cameramen captured this hit from several angles, it also becomes evident that Hinckley probably didn't shoot some of the other victims either. Ballistics tests further proved that the "lone nut gunman" had not used devastator ammunition as was initially announced.

Closer examination reveals that Hinckley stood in the middle of a crowd that prevented him from taking a direct shot at Reagan as she exited the Hilton. Then, when Hinckley drew his revolver, carpenter and union president Alfred Antenucci lunged out at the assailant from behind—therefore lessening his ability to take an accurate shot. His daughter later described the situation. "[My father] decided: nobody is going to kill the president in front of me. And he started hitting Hinckley on the back of the neck and grabbed him and pulled him to the ground, and Hinckley kept firing."

Picture all the obstructions to Hinckley's line of fire—a crowd of people, Secret Service agents, an open limousine door, and being thrust to the ground in mid-shot. Lee Proctor, Roger Shoffner, and Robert C. McCartor provided invaluable analysis in *John Hinckley Jr. and the Attempted Assassination of Ronald Reagan.*

• From the video, one can see how close Hinckley was to [policeman] Delahanty. Hinckley would have had to point almost straight up to shoot him.

• [Secret service agent] McCarthy was hit on his right side, the side away from Hinckley. The angle and force of the shot indicate that it was unlikely to have come from Hinckley's weapon.

• By the fifth shot, Reagan is inside the limo with [Secret Service agent Jerry] Parr on top. Reagan cannot be wounded without a bullet hitting Parr.

Parr was indeed *not struck* by any bullets. So, who shot Reagan? Proctor, Shoffner, and McCartor reach a crescendo in their investigation. "Another shooter with a rifle inflicted the wounds. For a bullet fired at this time to hit Reagan following the path the government described, it would have had to climb to hit the limo, slide down the car body, jump between the body and the window, make a U-turn, drop two feet, pass through Parr and Reagan's left arm without making a mark, then hit Reagan under the left arm, glance off his seventh rib, and travel through his lung stopping one inch behind his heart and one inch from his aorta."

They make three final conclusions:

• Hinckley did not shoot Reagan.

• Reagan was hit with the first shot [from the Bushy Knoll], not the last [from Hinckley's gun].

• Hinckley perfectly fits the mold of a "lone nut" assassin, making him the perfect patsy for a larger conspiracy.

A LARGER CONSPIRACY

Colonel Fletcher Prouty once remarked that the only way a president can be assassinated is if his Secret Service detail is commanded to *intentionally stand down*—in other words, to allow a direct hit on the target. In this context, one must wonder why the Secret Service selected a doorway from the Hilton Hotel that led directly to a site that blindly allowed the president to be ambushed by an attacker. In *Conspiracy Files*, Southwell and Twist ask, "It is possible the agency wished to put one of their own men into the White House early to help them strengthen their position in the drug trade and secret wars they were conducting in Central America."

Who could they be referring to in regard to the agency? All one needs is a copy of my book, *Hillary (And Bill): The Drugs Volume* to arrive at an answer. Former CIA Director, Skull and Bones member, and penultimate insider George Bush, Sr. was the man lurking in Reagan's shadow, and as vice president, he needed only one bullet to realize this dream. In Dallas, a "magic bullet" eliminated JFK, and in the nation's capital, a "ricochet bullet" almost placed Poppy Bush in the Oval Office.

Since we're on the subject, Lee Harvey Oswald of course assumed the role of fall guy on Nov. 22, 1963. His handler in Texas was a Russian émigré named Baron George DeMohrenschildt, a government asset connected to the oil industry. If we fast-forward to 1978, Gaeton Fonzi of the House Select Committee on Assassinations summoned the Baron to describe his peculiar relationship with Oswald. Conveniently enough for the CIA, DeMohrenschildt placed a .20-gauge shotgun to his head and "suicided" himself. What makes this arrangement even odder is, according to Jim Marrs in *Rule by Secrecy*, "George Bush Sr.'s name, address, and phone number were found in [his] personal notebook."

It's been exhaustively documented that Bush Sr. became peripherally involved in the Bay of Pigs fiasco, JFK's murder, Watergate, and served as CIA director from 1976-77. Plus, as Charles Overbeck notes, "On Nov. 23, 1963 J. Edgar Hoover wrote a memo regarding the briefing of a 'Mr. George Bush' on the reaction of anti-Castro Cubans to the Kennedy assassination."

So, Bush obviously dwelled in the world of skullduggery, subterfuge, and political assassinations. He also proudly proclaimed during a speech on Sept. 11, 1990, "Out of these troubled times, a New World Order can emerge." Now is it clearer why Reagan's handlers led him to a blind exit where patsy John Hinckley, Jr. awaited?

To more fully understand the dynamics, we need to revert back in time yet again. After Richard Nixon's Watergate fall, Bilderberg attendee and Warren Commission member Gerald Ford held the reins of power. But what few realize is that Bush and Nelson Rockefeller both vied for the vice president slot. After Rocky won the spot, Bush purportedly fumed over being snubbed. This point becomes more important for one specific reason: within a span of seventeen days, two assassination attempts were made on Ford's life by Squeaky Fromme and Sarah Jane Moore. Had Bush been selected as vice president, and had either of these female mind-control victims been successful, Bush the Elder would have been president in 1975—an entire thirteen years before he succeeded Reagan in 1988.

To his credit, Reagan didn't trust Bush in the least. Again, Jim Marrs explains. "Reagan lambasted Bush's membership in both the Trilateral Commission and the Council on Foreign Relations, and pledged not to allow Bush a position in a Reagan government." In the expose *Hinckley: Hit Man for the Secret Government* from the *Northstarzone* website, the author writes, "The shadow government did not care for Reagan when he first ran for president. He would sometimes speak out against the Trilateral Commission and other secret organizations." In addition, "At the very moment the assassination was to take place Bush was on his way to speak before the globalist Trilateral Commission." Unreceptive to Reagan's free market principles, Bush made headlines during the 1980 campaign by calling his views "voodoo economics."

From the CIA's perspective, they desperately needed to get one of their own (i.e. Bush) back in control because of Jimmy Carter's decimation of their counter-intelligence operations. Trowbridge H. Ford even goes so far as to say in *Why John Hinckley Jr. Almost Assassinated Ronald Reagan*, "Hinckley was programmed to assassinate President Carter just in case he was able to secure the release of the hostages [held in Iran]." Naturally, such an event did not transpire because George Bush, Sr. and his cronies orchestrated the "October Surprise" and delayed their release until the day of Reagan's inauguration. This one pivotal move secured Jimmy Carter's political demise.

Trowbridge Ford elaborates by drawing a comparison to Bobby Kennedy. After winning the California primary and essentially becoming the Democratic Party's nominee, this trigger event caused the shadow elite to order his assassination, with patsy Sirhan Sirhan being their mind-numbed robot. Had Carter made a similar "surprise announcement" regarding a hostage release, it would have brought adulation and a sense of heroism to his tepid presidency. Reagan would have been defeated, and the CIA's future plans for Iran-Contra foiled.

If this scenario sounds far-fetched, consider *The Trial of John Hinckley Jr.* where Doug Linders reveals, "In a three-day period, Hinckley visited three cities where Carter rallies were held: Washington, D.C., Columbus, and Dayton." Hinckley also appeared simultaneously in other cities where Carter spoke: Lincoln, Denver, Dallas and Nashville. Hinckley's handlers even tried to hook him up with a member of the

American Nazi Party in Nebraska to strengthen his resolve.

But Hinckley proved to be inept. In Charlotte Grieg's *Cold-Blooded Killings*, she recounts how officials arrested Hinckley in 1980 at an airport in Nashville. President Carter was scheduled to speak there that day, yet Hinckley—with three concealed weapons and ammunition concealed in his luggage—simply received a small fine and was released shortly thereafter. Here was a potential assassin transporting weapons across state lines, and he's freed with merely a slap on the wrist. Shades of Arthur Bremer cannot be denied.

In the end, however, Reagan came around, as I described in *The New World Order Exposed*. "In 1980, two months before the November election, a party was thrown for Reagan in Middleburg, Virginia. Reagan sat in the seat of honor, and beside him to his right sat a very important man . . . David Rockefeller, head of the CFR and Trilateral Commission. Somewhere along the line, Reagan was told that his bid for the presidency on the Republican ticket would be thwarted unless he chose George Bush as his vice president."

HINCKLEY FAMILY

The day after John Hinckley's arrest for attempting to kill Ronald Reagan, the *Houston Post* ran a headline story by Arthur Wiese and Margaret Downing: *"Bush's Son Was to Dine With Suspect's Brother."*

"Scott Hinckley, the brother of John Hinckley, Jr., who is charged with shooting President Reagan and three others, was to have been a dinner guest Tuesday night at the home of Neil Bush, son of Vice President George Bush."

This disclosure indeed raised eyebrows, but there's more. The Bush and Hinckley families had been associates since the 1960s, when all of them became wealthy in the oil business. The Hinckleys also contributed substantial amounts of money to George Bush's presidential campaign against Ronald Reagan in 1980. Interestingly enough, Neil Bush also served as George W. Bush's campaign manager in 1978 during his unsuccessful congressional bid. While doing so, he resided in Lubbock, Texas—the exact same place where John Hinckley Jr. lived at the time.

Other skeletons exist. In 1980, Scott Hinckley was employed as Vice President of Operations at the CIA-connected Vanderbilt Energy Corporation—just as his father had been. On the morning of Reagan's near-fatal hit, three U.S. Department of Energy representatives strolled into his office with some damning information. Again, according to the *Northstarzone* article, "Auditors had uncovered evidence of pricing violations on crude oil sold by the company from 1977 through 1980. The auditors announced that the federal government was considering a penalty of $2 million. Scott Hinckley reportedly requested several hours to come up with an explanation of the serious overcharges. The meeting ended little more than an hour before John Hinckley Jr. shot President Reagan."

More strange ties have surfaced. Not only were the Hinckleys connected with nefarious Texas oilman H.L. Hunt (tied to both the JFK and Martin Luther King assassinations), but Webster Tarpley and Anton Chaitkin also question the relationship of John Hinckley, Sr. to the U.S. intelligence community in *George Bush: The Unauthorized Biography*. Similarly, these two authors also connect Hinckley, Sr. to World Vision, Inc., which "is one of the notorious non-government organizations that function as a de facto arm of U.S. intelligence." For decades, World Vision has been rumored to be involved in clandestine mind-control operations for the CIA.

Did one hand wash the other between the Hinckleys and Bushes in regard to Ronald Reagan's attempted assassination? John Hinckley, Jr. clearly exhibited signs of being a mentally unstable, deranged drifter. Plus, son Scott faced impending fines and possible imprisonment due to his illegal activities at Vanderbilt. Did the Hinckleys sacrifice their son at the altar as a patsy so that an Agency shooter could take out Reagan? Consider that after Hinckley's trial, Judge Barrington D. Parker declared him, "not guilty by reason of insanity." The Judge then relegated Hinckley to a country club mental institution, where he eventually received privileges to leave the premises for visits. As a reward, President George W. Bush nominated Parker to be one of eleven appointees on the prestigious federal appeals court.

TAXI DRIVER

To support Hinckley's status as an unstable lunatic stalker, media sources focused their attention on the young man's obsession with film star Jodie Foster. Specifically, Hinckley lusted over the actress in her breakthrough role as Iris, a thirteen-year-old prostitute in Martin Scorsese's *Taxi Driver*. According to Stephen J. Spignese's *In the Crosshairs: Famous Assassinations and Attempts*, Hinckley viewed the film at least fifteen times.

Some other peculiarities arose from this movie, which screenwriters based loosely on the life and diaries of Arthur Bremer. First, Hinckley's mother—Jo Ann—went by the nickname Jodie. Secondly, Foster had originally landed the role of Alice Sutton in Mel Gibson's *Conspiracy Theory* before relinquishing it to Julia Roberts. Her reason: Mel Gibson's character played a taxi driver, and the ramifications were too eerily similar to real life.

Likening himself to the Zodiac killer, Bremer, and Son of Sam, Hinckley mailed a slew of letters to Foster while she attended Yale University (home of Skull and Bones). Also mirroring Travis Bickle's preoccupations in *Taxi Driver*, Hinckley spoke with Foster via telephone on two occasions, and actually moved to New Haven, Connecticut for a three-week period.

CATCHER IN THE RYE

Purported Lennon assassin Mark David Chapman, Rebecca Schaeffer assailant Robert John Bardo, and Hinckley all possessed a copy of J.D. Salinger's groundbreaking teen novel *The Catcher in the Rye*.

This literary work is important on a number of different levels. For beginners, those working in the furtive world of intelligence services are called "catchers in the rye" (i.e., members of a secretive clique). In terms of mind control and mental illness, especially regarding "lone nut" killers, the reference is very telling: when someone nears the state of insanity, they're "ready to go over the deep end" or "off the edge."

In Salinger's book, the teen protagonist—Holden Caulfield—fantasizes about being a "catcher in the rye"—someone who catches little children as they're about to fall off a cliff. The reference is incorrectly lifted from a Robert Burns poem: "Gin [If] a body meet [changed to catch] a body, comin' thro' the rye, . . ."

Caulfield explains: "I keep picturing all these little kids playing games in this big field of rye . . . thousands of little kids, and nobody's around . . . and I'm standing on the edge of some crazy cliff . . . I have to catch everybody if they start to go over the cliff."

If the Agency is used as a backdrop, let's examine this passage in the context of 1950s mind control experiments.

Little kids—Victims, innocent, experiments conducted unbeknownst to them.

Playing games—LSD doctors performing psychedelic tricks.

Big field of rye—Their minds, which will be harvested in the laboratory.

Nobody's around—No government oversight, a law unto themselves.

Edge of some crazy cliff—Insanity . . . similar to the time when unwitting military scientist Frank Olson purportedly committed suicide by plunging from a tenth-story hotel window after MK-ULTRA mindbenders dosed him with LSD. In reality, investigators discovered that Olson had been struck on the head and shoved from the window to conceal the ties between his nervous breakdown and their LSD tests.

Catch everybody—The patsy lured with a honey pot into falsely thinking they're some sort of savior or accomplice, when in reality they're being set-up as a duped fall guy.

This analysis makes even more sense when we realize that author J.D. Salinger—a complete recluse since the 1960s—suffered a nervous breakdown after WW II and spent several months recovering in a Nuremberg, Germany hospital. Furthermore, Holden Caulfield tells his *Catcher in the Rye* story from a mental institution after suffering a nervous breakdown. His collapse is caused by a sickly realization that society—at least from his perspective—is depressingly corrupt and evil, and he can't do a thing to change it. Thus, when the little children in his fantasy leap over a cliff, he can't rescue them.

It gets even stranger. Ian Hamilton's *In Search of J.D. Salinger* revealed that the hermetic author had connections to Defense Intelligence during the war, and within the Counter Intelligence Corps, he interrogated captured Nazis. Some have even used the term "denazification" of these specific German doctors and scientists.

Adam Gorightly explains the significance of his role in *Is the Catcher in the Rye a Mechanism of Control?* "Denazification could be construed as a code word alluding to the importation of high-level Nazi spies into the highest ranks of the American intelligence community under the auspices of Project Paperclip, the top secret operation—which at the war's end—smuggled hundreds of Nazis out of Germany. These 'reformed' Nazis were then given new identities, in time forming the core of the new U.S. intelligence, defense, and aerospace establishments."

Thus, the book itself takes on special importance. Gorightly delves deeply into the rabbit hole with some brilliant analysis. "When I refer to *The Catcher in the Rye* as a 'mechanism of control' I mean in the sense of a triggering device, which sets off a post-hypnotic suggestion, much like the queen of hearts in Richard Condon's *Manchurian Candidate*, unleashing within its mind-controlled subjects the command to kill."

MIND CONTROL

The big question, of course, is: did Hinckley fall victim to any such mental manipulation prior to playing the fall guy for Reagan's attempted killers? The answer is a resounding yes. For beginners, Hinckley read an array of books on another hypnotized patsy, Sirhan Sirhan, and obsessed over the Arthur Bremer-inspired film *Taxi Driver*. Plus, in true zombie fashion, Hinckley continued to repeatedly pull the trigger of his revolver, even after wrestled to the ground—exactly like Sirhan did at the Ambassador Hotel in Los Angeles. Even stranger, Gorightly writes in *Death Cults*, "John Hinckley, Jr. stated that he met David Berkowitz [Son of Sam] in Colorado during the 1970s."

Then, Trowbridge Ford claims that during a trip to Hollywood in 1976, Hinckley met a Dr. Janiger, upon which time he resumed taking LSD again. L.A. psychiatrist Dr. Oscar Janiger—known to associates as "Oz"—conducted LSD experiments in conjunction with "Operation Kachina Doll." These tests were conducted under the auspices of the CIA's MK-ULTRA "Operation Midnight Climax" where subjects were unknowingly dosed with LSD. Janiger also synthesized the monster-like super-hallucinogenic drug DMT, which Charles Manson provided to his followers.

Janiger became so infatuated with psychedelics that he once boasted, "My initial contact with the drug LSD-25 was so remarkable that it moved me to spend the next 45 years of my life studying it." He received his supply of the drug from CIA asset Captain Al Hubbard, affectionately known as the Johnny Appleseed of LSD.

One other element peculiar to Janiger is his moniker, Oz. In Cathy O'Brien's *The Trance-Formation of America*, she describes how words are used as a form of mental mind play. "CIA cryptic language is manipulation of the English language such that words have a double meaning (aka 'double binds' in mental health terminology)."

She provides examples such as:

Transform = Trance-Form: to change or alter a person via hypnosis.

Communion: a sexual reference placed in religious terms to signify the takeover of mind-controlled sex slaves.

Service Entrance = Serve-Us En-Trance: a patsy or female "presidential model" is indoctrinated into slavish, docile obedience via the compartmentalization of her mind, ultimately creating a multiple personality disorder (MPD) automaton.

After traveling extensively around the country (with no visible means of support—just like Arthur Bremer), Curt Rowlett fits the final pieces to this puzzle in *Project MK-ULTRA: Did the U.S. Government Actually Create Programmed Assassins?* He begins, "It is known through court records that Hinckley underwent psychiatric treatment just prior to his attempt on Reagan, and that at the time of his shooting he was under the influence of psychiatric drugs." Similar to Sirhan and Bremer, he too scribbled in a diary (surely to "prove" his intentions by creating a "legend").

However, realizing that Hinckley may not be emotionally stable enough to fill the role of fall guy, his handlers introduced a new twist on an old theme. Similar to doubles and alternative patsies for Lee Harvey Oswald (such as the enigmatic Kerry Thornley), his handlers conjured up an alternative lone nut gunman named Edward Richardson.

On March 30, 1981, President Reagan was shot and seriously injured outside a Washington, D.C., hotel allegedly by John W. Hinckley Jr., the son of a wealthy oil executive. Hinckley was tried and found not guilty by reason of insanity.

Charles Overbeck provides the narrative. "Richardson traced Hinckley's path from Connecticut to Colorado, writing demented love letters to actress Jodie Foster, just like Hinckley. A week after Hinckley's infamous attack, Richardson was arrested in New York's Port Authority bus terminal with a .32 caliber revolver after threatening the lives of both Reagan and Foster. So both men are obsessed with the same actress from the same film. Both of them were intent on re-creating Travis Bickle's crazed assassination scheme from the movie *Taxi Driver*. They even looked a lot alike. What are the chances of two separate mentally unstable individuals, with so many exotic similarities, reaching critical mass at the same time?"

And, to top it off, Edward Richardson also had links to Hinckley's father's World Vision, Inc. If Hinckley so happened to melt down at the last minute, his handlers had a second man at the ready to take an unceremonious fall.

CHAPTER 14

PORT ARTHUR MAYHEM

THE PORT ARTHUR MASSACRE

April 28, 1996—a date forever cemented into the minds of Australians. The place—Port Arthur, Tasmania—as remote a locale as you could ever find in Australia. One of the greatest Aussie writers ever—Ms. Hero Cee—described this event on Feb. 28, 2001 for *Babel* magazine.

"I remember being stunned when I heard the news report that a gunman had gone berserk in the tourist town of Port Arthur. In a tragedy that shook Australia, 35 innocent people died and 22 were injured. Like most other Australians, I cried for the mother who begged the gunman to spare her two little girls before all three were gunned down. I cried for the old man whose wife died in his arms."

Naturally, authorities placed blame for the carnage on a lone-nut killer—28-year-old Martin Bryant—who was eventually convicted (without a trial) and sentenced to 1,035 years in a maximum-security prison. But did Bryant actually pull the trigger that day or, as Hero Cee asks, could it have been "a highly organized terrorist strike undertaken with the apparent complicity of the Australian government?"

This question is undeniably valid for a number of reasons. First,

Bryant scored an abysmally low 66 on standard IQ tests. That places him in the mental retardation category. Writing for *Nexus* magazine in 2006, Arthur Cristian quoted psychiatrist Ian Joblin's assessment of Bryant's limited intelligence as being "roughly equal to that of an 11-year-old." Secondly, he'd had absolutely no knowledge or training in the use of high-powered semi-automatic rifles. Lastly, Bryant persisted in declaring his innocence; and, as Cristian states, in interviews with Inspectors Ross Paine and John Warren, he not only denied carrying out the massacre, but also related an entirely different narrative of the events on April 28, 1996.

This same author then stresses, "Martin Bryant is adamant that he never visited the PAHS [Port Arthur Historic Site] on the day of the massacre." Further, "neither Bryant's fingerprints nor his DNA has ever been found at PAHS. This much has effectively been conceded by Sergeant Gerard Dutton, officer in charge of the Ballistics Section of Tasmania Police [December 1988, *Australian Police Journal*]."

Evidence of a frame-up continues. Hero Cee highlights five other areas:

> 1. There is a 30-year embargo on all evidence relating to the incident.
> 2. No one has formally identified Martin Bryant."
> 3. He was "so intellectually impaired that he received a full disability pension from the government since leaving school.
> 4. Although survivors described the shooter as being right-handed and shooting expertly from the hip, Bryant is left-handed, and has been assessed by police as having little or no ability to operate an assault weapon.
> 5. There are no fingerprints or DNA evidence to link Bryant with the Broad Arrow Café [where one of the shootings occurred], or any of the weapons said to have been used.

EXPERT MARKSMAN

To fully understand the Port Arthur phenomenon, we must revisit the actual shooting on that tragic day. As Cee summarized, "A young man with long blond hair opened fire on a crowd of diners inside the

Broad Arrow Café. Using a Colt AR15 and shooting from the right hip without using sights, he killed 20 people with clean shots to the head, and injured another 12. Official reports stated that the shooting lasted no longer than 90 seconds, and that the gunman killed the first 12 victims in the first 15 seconds. This speed and accuracy is astonishing to the verge of being impossible. It is well beyond the level of any sporting shooter, or any regular Army personnel." In addition, the noise within this confined area would have been deafening and prohibitive to the shooter. Cee notes, "Only very sophisticated hearing protection would have enabled him to continue, yet he wasn't wearing a headset."

In all, there was actually an array of other crime scenes at PAHS that day where the rampage ensued. Interestingly, inside the Broad Arrow Café (where most of the carnage occurred), investigators discovered incorrect ammunition at the crime scene. In *Deceit and Terrorism: The Port Arthur Massacre*, Andrew S. MacGregor writes, "There were live .308 rounds found on the floor inside the café. The only weapon used . . . was the AR15, which uses .223 ammunition."

Similar to Lee Harvey Oswald's inexplicable feat using his Italian Manlicher rifle, experts in the field were astounded by Bryant's supposed precision. Acclaimed researcher Joe Vials put the matter into context in *Australia's Port Arthur Massacre: Government and Media Lies Exposed*: "Whoever was on the trigger in Tasmania managed a kill rate well above that required of a fully trained soldier, an impossible task for a man with Martin Bryant's mid-60s IQ and his total lack of military training." He continued, "Though Australia has tens of thousands of skilled sporting shooters, it has very few combat veterans, and even fewer special-forces personnel trained to kill large numbers of people quickly in an enclosed space." Vials concluded, "Whoever was on the trigger that fateful day demonstrated professional skills equal to some of the best special-forces shooters in the world. His critical error lay in killing too many people too quickly while injuring far too few, thereby exposing himself for what he was: a highly trained combat shooter probably ranked among the top 20 such specialists [trained counterterrorist marksmen] in the Western world."

Others concurred with this assessment. Eyewitness victim Neville

Quinn observed, "He [the gunman] appeared to be the best-trained army guy I've ever seen; his stance was unbelievable." Arthur Cristian asserted that the "gunman managed to shoot the first 19 out of 20 people dead with single-shot accuracy to the head." Finally, Cristian references Brigadier Ted Serong, ex-commander of the Australian military in Vietnam. "There was an almost satanic accuracy to that shooting performance. Whoever did it is better than I am, and there are not too many people around here better than I am."

All this, as Joe Vials reminds us, from "an intellectually impaired registered invalid with no training in the use of high-powered assault weapons."

MORE BEDLAM

After leaving Port Arthur's Broad Arrow Café, the gunman executed 15 more innocent victims, wounded 10 others, then stole a BMW and drove to Seascape Cottage. Oddly enough, Martin Bryant purportedly arrived at PAHS in his own Volvo, which contained some much-needed items if he wanted to continue his rampage. When arriving at the Broad Arrow, the killer carried two gym bags—one with his gun and ammunition, the other containing a cumbersome video camera. Then, after the shooting, MacGregor documents that "several witnesses saw the gunman carry the Prince Sports bag out of the café and put it in the boot [trunk] of the Volvo. This was even captured on James Balasko's video."

As Hero Cee asks, "If Bryant's car [Volvo] was at Port Arthur, why did he steal the BMW to get to Seascape Cottage, abandoning the much needed shotgun and ammunition? And why the passport?"

Some interesting points must be discussed. First, similar to 9-11 where a pristine passport was found at Ground Zero near the WTC rubble, police conveniently discovered Bryant's "passport" in his Volvo. But some observers aren't even sure now that the Volvo in question was Bryant's, but possibly an identical model to give the appearance that Bryant drove to PAHS.

After holing up in Seascape Cottage for the night, a man calling himself "Jamie" (supposedly Martin Bryant) kept police at bay by firing at them from his hideout. But now, something quite enthralling took place. It seems Bryant's precision failed him; or, as Hero Cee wrote, "The gunman's accuracy suffered a remarkable change. He fired an estimated 250 rounds that night at police. He hit nothing." Could it be that the *real* Martin Bryant had never been at PAHS, but instead an imposter? To close this section, MacGregor tells us, "The following morning, Martin Bryant was arrested naked after he fled from a fiery Seascape Cottage, unarmed, dressed in black, and with his clothes alight." It appears a blaze broke out at his bunker, so Bryant fled, easily arrested by awaiting officials.

Still, was it actually Bryant inside the Broad Arrow Café? Every eyewitness on the scene described the shooter as being in his late teens to early 20s in age (18-22); anywhere from 6-10 years younger than Bryant. Only one individual at the café personally knew Bryant, and that was former owner Jim Laycock. Was he able to identify him as the killer? No. "I did not recognize the shooter as Martin Bryant."

Another man, Vietnam Vet John Godfrey, stood outside the café when the gunman emerged. Not only did he see him then, but also after stashing his goods in the Volvo. Was this man Martin Bryant, as the police and media alleged? "In my opinion," responded Godfrey, "the picture I saw in the newspapers was not the same person." Another survivor—Wendy Scurr—also refused to acknowledge Martin Bryant as the shooter.

What are we left with? The only man who was a friendly acquaintance of Bryant before the rampage couldn't identify him as the shooter, nor did others. So, as Arthur Cristian concludes, "It is only when one realizes that Bryant has never been positively identified as the PAHS shooter that one begins to understand why a court trial was never held."

FALSE EVIDENCE

There are so many pieces to this puzzle that don't fit (or fit too conveniently) that the entire case is flimsier than a three-legged table. For starters, why did the local police purchase a specially refrigerated morgue transport vehicle (capable of holding 22 dead bodies) a year prior to the Port Arthur shootings? This question is especially valid since, on average, only six murders a year occur in Tasmania. No other police department owned a similar truck, and two years later, when no longer needed, they sold it. As one writer pondered, "Isn't it a strange coincidence the number of dead in the Broad Arrow Café closely matches the capacity of this morgue truck?"

Let's examine a few other anomalies. Officials told the Australian people that the shooter [purportedly Martin Bryant] sat eating at the Broad Arrow Café before beginning his onslaught. Waitresses remember serving him, and police recovered the tray, plate, cup and utensils he used. Yet Arthur Cristian observes, "Although the tray would have contained fingerprints, thumb prints, palm prints, saliva, sweat, skin and possibly hair from the shooter, there is no evidence that it yielded anything that came from Martin Bryant."

This seemingly monumental absence of fingerprints and DNA at the crime scene was quickly suppressed and ignored by the government. But what do we make of there being no fingerprints or DNA samples removed from the Volvo at PAHS—the car supposedly owned by Martin Bryant? Didn't he drive this vehicle for years? Cristian states the obvious: "Fingerprints and DNA from the Volvo therefore represented the most reliable means of determining whether the greatest homicidal maniac in Australian history had really been Bryant." How did police explain this discrepancy? "Overnight moisture eliminated all traces of fingerprints and DNA," was the official response from the police.

Moisture! Let's cut to the chase. Martin Bryant wasn't even at PAHS or the Broad Arrow Café. An impostor with a look-alike Volvo filled that role. Tasmanian officials botched the crime scene because, again, as Cristian relates, they "did not want evidence to survive that would have proven that Bryant had not been the person using the car that afternoon."

Other facts have also been disclosed. When diners were soon to be massacred at the café, Bryant filled his Volvo at a gas station 10 miles north of PAHS (between 11:40 and 11:45 a.m.). Nearly an hour and a half later, he visited a friend when more dead bodies piled up at PAHS.

BRAINWASHING

Following his arrest the next day (whereupon authorities sequestered this "despised monstrous murderer" Martin Bryant away from virtually everyone), an intensive brainwashing program developed. To begin, Arthur Cristian establishes a vital point: "Bryant vehemently resisted the idea that he had perpetrated the murders at Port Arthur. He maintained that he had not even visited PAHS on the day in question, and he had difficulty understanding how police obtained a picture of the vehicle that seemed to be his own yellow Volvo parked at the PAHS tollgate when he only recalled driving past it."

Virtually all quotes (unless otherwise noted) will be derived from Cristian's excellent analysis from this point forward. To "re-educate" their subject, mind-benders specializing in brainwashing like the Tavistock Institute's Dr. Fred Emery entered the scene. They then began to break down Bryant's resistance, artificially induced memories, and made him more susceptible via various psychological ploys to the notion that he'd been the triggerman. One tactic involved using videotaped footage from the Broad Arrow Café (remember that the shooter retrieved a bulky videotape camera from his duffel bag, then left it for police to conveniently find). "The entire sequence of events would have been filmed for the purpose of brainwashing Bryant into believing that he had been the actual perpetrator; that he was the man shown in the film."

To intensify these thoughts, expert mind-controllers "were in total control of Bryant's environment—and after his arrest, [he] was subjected to weeks on end of virtual solitary confinement. Government agents specializing in mind control convinced Bryant that, due to the traumatic nature of the events in which they alleged he had been involved, he was suffering from psychogenic amnesia [memory blockage]." After repeatedly watching the bloody footage, the nearly retarded Bryant eventually thought the movies were his own memories. In a recorded interview, Bryant fully realized, "they are trying to brainwash me to not have a trial." As such, "A concerted effort was made to implant false memories in Bryant's mind that would represent a first step toward having him accept responsibility for the Port Arthur murders."

THE CONSPIRACY EXPLAINED

Again, all credit must be given to Arthur Cristian of *Nexus* magazine for his ingenious efforts to explain what *really* happened in Australia on April 28, 1996.

To reconstruct the conspiracy, we must first look at what on-duty police officials were doing while a gunman shot up the Broad Arrow Café and other venues. It just so happens that, conveniently enough, the only two policemen on the Tasman Peninsula were dispatched miles away to a call that turned out to be a hoax.

Meanwhile, Martin Bryant was beginning some errands until he suddenly disappeared. Without delving too deeply into his lengthy article, Cristian proposes that Bryant was "intercepted, abducted, and drugged into unconsciousness" during one of his stops. Could it be that the Tasmanian police—instead of racing to a bogus call—actually pulled Bryant over and apprehended him for a minor infraction (i.e. failure to use his turn signal)? Then, after drugging him, he's taken to Seascape much later while Bryant's yellow Volvo is driven to PAHS and parked—"proving" he was there.

As this part of the plan unfolds, the actual gunman (disguised to look like Bryant) is seated within the café until he notices that Bryant's yellow Volvo appears. As Cristian affirms, this sign means the massacre is to proceed. In other words, Bryant is in police jurisdiction as the designated patsy. "According to [researchers] Michael Beckman and Rebecca McKenna, the Port Arthur gunman was watching the car-park anxiously in the period between 1:10 and 1:15 p.m." While chit-chatting about inconsequential subjects, he suddenly leaped into action and began his killing spree—his move coinciding with the Volvo's arrival.

Even stranger is the fact that "there was a sizeable contingent of members of the Australian police, military, and intelligence establishments on hand, including the secretive ASIS (Australian Secret Intelligence Service) and ASIO (Australian Security Intelligence Organization) [their version of the CIA]." Why were there so many spooks and other official establishment members present? For three reasons: (a) to keep control of the crime scene once all hell broke loose; (b) to speak with the press and begin the official "spin"; and (c) positively identify "Martin Bryant" as the killer. The same *modus operandi* has been utilized countless times before, so why not continue it at Port Arthur?

GUN BUY-BACK

When all is said and done, why would the Australian government conspire to kill and wound nearly 60 innocent victims? Quite simply, after public outrage erupted over the senseless violence, a concerted media and government campaign was ratcheted into high gear to disarm the Australian citizenry. Due to this "psy op," the people were psychologically manipulated to surrender their weapons as draconian gun laws were immediately shoved down their throats. As writer Joe Vials shows, "the gun control proposals accepted by police ministers in May 1996 were prepared before the massacre by an ideological senior bureaucrat with United Nations connections." The exact same tactics were used in the U.S. via the OKC bombing and with Patriot Act legislation prior to Sept. 11, 2001.

In all, Australians forfeited a total of 640,000 guns due to this disaster called the "Gun Buy Back Scheme." Prime Minister John Howard did his part by demanding that some of the structures at PAHS be destroyed, thereby eliminating all evidence. Astute observers know that this same technique was utilized at Waco, in OKC, and with the WTC towers in New York City after 9-11.

CHAPTER 15

THE CULT OF DIANA

THE CULT OF DIANA: DNA PRINCESS

"The more I look into it, the more I have to say that I, personally, cannot dismiss the possibility of premeditated murder."
—Patricia Cornwell, crime writer

"The so-called 'road traffic accident' in which Diana died was no accident. It was a pre-planned, calculated and well-practiced assassination operation perpetrated by MI6, together with the CIA, and executed by a highly trained, mercenary-style special-forces unit hired specifically for the task."
—JON KING and John BEVERIDGE
Princess Di: Hidden Evidence

I remember the news flash with vivid clarity. After getting up at 3:20 am to prepare for an early work shift, I turned on the TV to see an urgent bulletin: "Princess Diana dies in Paris car crash." Fully aware of all the vitriol going on between her and the royal family, I immediately sensed that the world's most beautiful woman had been deliberately killed.

Later that day, I explained to my buddy that since Di was dating (and might soon marry) an Arab, the British throne murdered her because they couldn't tolerate the two princes (William and Harry) possibly having a "dark-skinned" stepfather. My friend said I was crazy; but now, all these years later, my original suspicions have been proven correct by a variety of different sources.

OFFICIAL STORY

In simplest terms, after Di's crash, authorities quickly arrived at the following version of events. Limousine driver Henri Paul—excessively drunk at the time—sped at over 90 miles per hour to avoid pursuing paparazzi, and in the process caused a horrific accident that killed two other passengers, and himself, while severely injuring a fourth.

Test results showed Henri Paul's blood alcohol level to be three-times the legal limit. But was he actually inebriated? Videotape footage from the Ritz Hotel shows him acting completely sober, while colleagues said they never detected any erratic behavior or smelled alcohol on his breath. Authors Peter Hounam and Derek McAdam write in *Who Killed Diana*, "Bodyguard Trevor Rees-Jones, trained to spot unusual behavior, stated quite unequivocally that he appeared absolutely normal that night." Jones himself testified, "I had no reason to suspect [Paul] was drunk. He did not look or sound like he had been drinking."

A cause of further suspicion centered on the level of carbon monoxide in Paul's blood, which registered at a whopping 21%. Since the tests were conducted two hours after the accident took place, Paul's carbon monoxide level during the crash would have been 30%, which is lethal.

CO levels at or above 20% (where the brain is deprived of oxygen) could cause intense headaches, vomiting, an inability to walk, and general incapacitation. Driving an automobile in any way, shape, or form would be unimaginable. In *The Murder of Princess Diana*, Noel Botham quotes a group of professors and doctors who studied Paul's carbon monoxide levels. "The pathologists' findings and conclusions on the issue are: physically impossible."

Realizing they had a major problem on their hands, officials blamed Paul's CO levels on the limousine's burst air bags. But Mercedes Benz flatly denied that the excessive amounts of CO originated from

The car in which Princess Diana was a passenger.

any source on the car they manufactured.

The only other possible explanation is that a 20%-plus carbon monoxide result arose from someone who committed suicide via car-exhaust fumes. This point is vital because if Paul wasn't drunk, and there weren't any visible sources of CO poisoning, could his results have been deliberately switched with someone else's? Different researchers have speculated that the driver may have been injected with a concentrate of drugs and alcohol after the fact, but this option doesn't explain the CO. In haste, did a corrupt coroner exchange test results with another man who killed himself that very same evening (via carbon monoxide poisoning inside his car) without considering the toxic levels of CO? It just so happens that a man *did* commit suicide by this very method in Paris on the night of Princess Diana's murder.

Another aspect of the official story that doesn't hold up under scrutiny is Paul's purported speed. To reinforce this claim, the public was told that the limo's speedometer locked at 121 miles per hour after the crash. But again, Mercedes Benz engineers entered the picture and refuted this allegation, later proving that the speedometer reverted back to zero.

In actuality, Paul traveled at exactly 64 miles per hour. This fact surfaced when CCTV cameras speed-stamped the limo only seconds prior to entering the tunnel. Supposedly, the dozen or more cameras lining the route were mysteriously disabled that evening, but drivers later complained that they'd received speeding tickets only minutes before Diana's crash. Therefore, were the cameras actually turned off, or did officials not want anyone to see the actual footage of Diana's limousine because it would utterly crush their deceptive explanations?

THE BIG SURPRISE

In the ensuing years following her separation from Prince Charles, Diana and the royals engaged in an ongoing tit-for-tat public spat that scintillated the British press and its readers. With each side vying for one-upmanship, Diana frequently prevailed due to her charm, looks, and wit. Of course, she took her fair share of blows, too, but the princess teased shortly before her death, "You are going to get a big surprise, you'll see. You are going to get a big surprise with the next thing I do."

Some have speculated, rightly so, that had Princess Diana and Dodi Fayed not died in Paris, they were set to announce their engagement the following day. Further, Diana had not followed established protocol imposed by the royals by seeking the Queen Mother's permission to get married.

Irritating them to an even greater degree was Diana's excursion on Dodi's yacht where paparazzi snapped pictures of her in a bikini kissing her lover. Underworld denizen Peter Scott, author of *Gentleman Thief*, commented, "She was getting photographed in skin-tight bathing suits with Arabs on the yacht. I thought she was off her rocker, or hell bent on self-destruction."

The royals weren't fond of Dodi or his family. For one, they felt the Fayeds obtained their wealth via questionable means, while Dodi's uncle—Adnan Khashoggi—reigned as one of the world's most vilified arms dealers. Plus, they were *foreigners* of Arab descent. Now one of them wanted to marry the future King of England's mother.

Dodi had already ordered a $200,000 engagement ring, then told his step-uncle, Hussein Yassin, "Diana and I are getting married. We are very serious. You'll know about it officially very soon." One of the reasons for the trip to Paris involved picking up this engagement ring. Once Diana informed her sons, they intended to break the news publicly.

PREGNANCY?

Could there be more? Rumors swirled about the UK that Diana already carried Dodi's child. In the swimming suit photos, did they see a tiny tummy bulge that confirmed her pregnancy? Worse, the Royals were supposedly fuming about being disgraced via their link to a mixed-race baby.

The evidence is quite substantial in support of Diana's condition:

• Noel Botham, *The Murder of Princess Diana*—"In 2003 it was revealed that the Princess went into a London hospital only days before her last trip with Dodi to undergo a pregnancy test."

• Frederic Maillez, SOS Medecins emergency responder—as the first paramedic to reach the tunnel, he was told by colleagues that Diana rubbed her stomach and said she was six weeks pregnant.

• Hounam and McAdam, *Who Killed Diana*—"It is said that a British television company acquired evidence never broadcast that when in London before her second trip to the Mediterranean, Diana visited a Harley Street clinic for a scan which showed she was pregnant."

• Dr. Coriat, in a Dec. 29, 1997 letter—blood tests indicated that Diana was in a "state of pregnancy of 9-10 weeks."

• *Agence France-Presse*, December 1997—Diana was at least six weeks pregnant when her crash occurred.

• Noel Botham—"The medical assistant from University College Hospital who helped prepare her body for embalming believed Diana was pregnant at the time of her death. The baby would have been an illegitimate half-brother, or half-sister, for William and Harry, and his father would have been neither British-born nor Christian."

• Dr. Pierre Coriat, Pitie-Salpetriere Hospital, head of anesthesiology—treated Diana on the night of her death and confirmed she was 9-10 weeks pregnant.

• Hounan and McAdam—medical records showed that blood tests

revealed Diana was pregnant. All of these test results mysteriously vanished from her file.

PREMONITIONS

Princess Diana fully realized that her primary purpose all along had been to produce pure-blooded sons for Prince Charles. In *The Murder of Princess Diana*, Noel Botham plays on this revelation: "After the birth of Prince Harry, Princess Diana lived with the constant fear of being murdered." In October 1996 Diana wrote a letter which reflected her grave concerns: "This particular phase of my life is the most dangerous. My husband is planning 'an accident' in my car . . . brake failure and serious head injury in order to make the path clear for him to marry."

In the documentary *Lady Die*, director Chris Everard seconds this notion: "The film explores the hand-written note which Diana gave to her brother—and another given for safe keeping to her lawyer—which explicitly said that a fake car crash, one which would result in death, was being planned by people working for Prince Charles."

In *Royal Conspiracy: Princess Diana Names Her Killer*, reporter Uri Dowbenko relates how Diana told friend Paul Burrell, "I'm going to date this [letter] and I want you to keep it. Just in case."

Diana made no secret of her concerns. Businessman and friend Roberto Deverik recalls, "She was convinced she was going to be killed. She said, 'When it's not convenient anymore, I will—they will blow me [up] in a car or in a helicopter.'" Similarly, the *Sunday Mirror* carried this passage on Jan. 4, 1998: "One day I'm going to go up in a helicopter and it'll just blow up. MI5 will do away with me."

The princess was terrified of British intelligence, the palace "watchdogs" who protected the royal family, and especially her husband. Noel Botham summarized the situation: "Diana lived constantly with the fear of being assassinated, and put her thoughts in writing one year before her death. She believes she was the subject of comprehensive surveillance by an unseen enemy."

To combat these attackers, Diana assembled what came to be known as the "crown jewels"—a cache of secret tapes and videos. This highly damning information held the potential to decimate the monarchy if ever made public. This supposed insurance policy against her assailants clearly denoted a point of no return. Lines had been drawn, and resentments ran deep. Dowbenko conveys Princess Diana's inner turmoil. "I have been battered, bruised and abused mentally by the System for years now." In light of their unrelenting attacks and incriminations, Diana snarled, "After all I've done for this fucking family."

To protect herself against the press and potential assassination attempts, she became fixated on leaving England. Diana told Richard Kay of the *Daily Mirror* about her plans to withdraw as a public figure. "I have decided to radically change my life," she said. But even these measures weren't enough to protect her, or the crash's only survivor, bodyguard Trevor Rees-Jones. Speaking of his memory loss, it likely appears that this rendered state is a form of self-protection. "If I remember, they'll kill me," he said. "Every single day I fear for my life."

INTELLIGENCE AGENCIES

"Diana's Death: Intelligence Agents Were in the Hotel"
—Headline, Germany's *Bild*
Sept. 9, 1997

In Jon King and John Beveridge's *Hidden Evidence*, they provide an overview of the Hotel Ritz where Diana and Dodi were staying. "There were several people picked up on the hotel's security videos who appear to have been there most of the day and were still watching events quietly from the edge of the crowd. They did not appear to be either press photographers or casual onlookers. Their identity has never been satisfactorily explained."

It has been established that at least six MI6 agents were in Paris on Aug. 31, 1999. Furthermore, security cameras at the Ritz captured seven unidentified persons posing as paparazzi. Then, when Diana and Dodi snuck out a back door to avoid detection, these intel-paparazzi were already lying in wait, primed to trail their back-up Mercedes.

Of course, paparazzi members were blamed for Diana's crash, but

King and Beveridge quoted a British intelligence source in 1997: "The paparazzi in London and Paris are crawling with British intelligence. Some are freelancers on the MI6 payroll; others are our own deep-cover agents."

Clandestine operatives weren't limited to the press. Noel Botham writes, "Former MI6 Officer Richard Tomlinson revealed that during his time with the British intelligence service he learned that there was unofficial but direct contact between certain senior and influential MI6 officers and senior members of the royal household, including those who practiced their dark arts in St. James Palace."

The subject of occult practices and secret societies among the royals and British intelligence agencies is a great concern, even to the Queen Mother, who commented, "There are powers at work in this country about which we have no knowledge."

Considering these subversive forces, it's incomprehensible to imagine that a hit on Princess Diana would have taken place without intel involvement. Former MI5 Officer David Shayler admitted, "There is compelling evidence to indicate that an intelligence service was involved in the crash."

King and Beveridge explain how these groups also performed surveillance on Diana's beau. "There had been a full MI6 work-up order on Dodi, and there was to be a meeting at Balmoral Castle of 'The Way Ahead Group' (the inner circle that advises Queen Elizabeth and Prince Philip) to receive a briefing from MI6 on the Dodi investigation." Senior MI5 and MI6 officials were also present inside the tunnel following Diana's crash. [Note: Britain's MI5 is the equivalent of America's FBI, whereas MI6 equals the U.S. CIA.]

Similarly, cooperation from French intelligence, specifically the General Directorate of External Security, would obviously be necessary for an operation such as this to occur in Paris. One significant area of proof is the fact that a few moments before Diana's accident, every police channel in Paris conveniently shut down and became inoperative.

They weren't the only ones involved. On Dec. 12, 1998 the *Washington Post's* Vernon Loeb wrote, "The National Security Agency has disclosed that U.S. intelligence is holding 1,056 pages of classified information about the late Princess Diana." By using the Echelon electronic surveillance system (among other bugging devices), the NSA admitted to trailing Diana for years, up until the day of her death.

In addition, the State Department possesses extensive files on Diana that have been sealed indefinitely. The reason: their release would seriously jeopardize American national security.

This unabated surveillance led to a paranoid, Big Brother atmosphere in England and the U.S. On May 16, 1993 James Whitaker of the *Mirror* addressed this situation: "They [MI5] do it regularly. They have literally hundreds of hours of transcripts. They are bugging all the royals from the queen downwards." Such a presence obviously had its darker ramifications. Mike Grey, a personal security officer for the royals, provided this observation: "Clandestine surveillance by the security services on the most intimate of situations was to culminate later in the assassination of Diana, princess of Wales, of this I have no doubt."

HENRI PAUL

As previously noted, chauffeur Henri Paul gave every appearance of being sober prior to driving Diana and Dodi. Security guard Kez Wingfield confirmed his state, as did CCTV footage. Further, had his carbon monoxide blood-level actually been 20.7%, he would have been incapacitated by crippling headaches and nausea.

Paul became a limited hangout and scapegoat for one essential reason—his ties to numerous intelligence agencies. Investigative reporter Gerald Posner told *Talk* magazine, "Paul was on the payroll of several security services: the French, the British, and perhaps, the Israelis." MI6 officer Richard Tomlinson confirmed this information, claiming Paul was funneled $200,000 by MI6.

King and Beveridge further magnify this point with data exposing the fact that Paul juggled a dozen bank accounts with a net worth of over $100,000. Yet, his annual salary totaled only $20,000 per year, while he made sizeable deposits during the months preceding Princess Diana's crash.

Paul's best friend, Claude Garrel, admitted that he worked for French and British intelligence for ten-plus years; a claim seconded by

Tomlinson during testimony before the French magistrate. "I firmly believe [his MI6] files will contain evidence of crucial importance to the circumstances and causes of the incident that killed M. Paul together with the princess of Wales and Dodi al-Fayed," said Tomlinson.

Paul's actions become even more suspect after learning that he cancelled a weekend vacation upon discovering that the famous couple would be arriving in Paris. Meeting them at LeBourget Airport, Paul later disappeared on the evening of Aug. 30 from 7-10 p.m.—hours before returning to chauffeur Diana and Dodi from the Ritz. Gerald Posner quotes an American law enforcement official that said Paul met with the DGSE (France's version of the CIA). There, he received 2,500 francs—money which officials discovered in his pocket following the tunnel crash.

In light of these developments, it's easy to determine Paul's involvement in the events that night. For starters, the alternate limousine he selected—a Mercedes S280—weighed much less than the one used to pick them up at the airport. Obviously, its size made them much more vulnerable during a collision.

More importantly, rather than taking the most direct route from their Imperial Suite to the apartment, Paul selected a longer, more circuitous route. So, instead of following the Champs Elysees—the broadest, safest street in Paris—he went out of his way to direct them into the fateful Pont l'Alma tunnel.

On top of that, Paul made the decision to have *no backup security vehicles* in their entourage, plus only one bodyguard—Trevor Rees-Jones (who he initially tried to prevent from coming along). In all, Paul took every step possible to directly disregard standard security procedures that had been put in place for years by Mohamed al-Fayed. It was he who shunned extra personnel, selected the death route, and drove the princess to her demise.

DEATH SCENE

As Henri Paul steered their Mercedes S280 through the Paris streets, a motorcycle with a pillion rider followed them the entire way from the Ritz Hotel. Contradicting the official story, eyewitness Eric Petel stated that there were *no* photographers following the limo at this point. As their car approached Pont l'Alma tunnel, the cyclist pulled slightly ahead of them, then the pillion rider aimed an anti-personnel light into their front windshield. Within moments, he unleashed a blinding burst of light at the driver, completely incapacitating Paul.

This dramatic move is fundamental to understanding what caused the crash. Noel Botham describes this *weapon* that was developed for the U.S. and UK Special Forces: "Lights such as these are used as weapons by the SAS in surprise raids. They blind and mentally disorient the enemy for up to a full minute. The effect on a driver, at night particularly, is catastrophic. He is totally blinded and mentally stunned. He would be incapable of steering a car."

Eyewitness Francois Levistre was actually inside the tunnel when he noticed a motorcycle speed past Diana's limo, then blast them with a brilliant flash of light before the crash. Levistre described it as more intense than any camera flash.

Simultaneously, a white Fiat Uno lay in wait at a virtual standstill near the tunnel entrance. After the pillion rider zapped Paul with his blinding light, the Fiat pulled alongside, then bumped into the limo, causing it to spin out of control into the 13th pillar.

Another eyewitness, Gary Hunter, viewed the white Fiat getaway car. He said: "These people were in a hurry not to be there. I am confident that the car was getting off the scene. It was obvious they were getting away from something and that they were in a hurry. It looked quite sinister."

Upon impact inside the tunnel, Henri Paul and Dodi Fayed died immediately, while Trevor Rees-Jones had his face literally ripped-off as he lay unconscious. The only passenger inside the vehicle to survive intact was Princess Diana.

Dr. Frederic Mailliez, who happened to be driving home, examined her first. He described her condition as "not catastrophic" and said, "I thought this woman had a chance." He added, "The woman in the back seemed to be in the best shape. She looked pretty fine." Eric Petel crawled into the backseat and found Diana bleeding, but semi-conscious and talking. Likewise, Dr. Jean-Marc Martino—a resuscitation specialist for SAMU (Service d'Aide Medicale Urgente) described

Diana's condition as "severe but not critical."

Diana had clearly survived the crash, but what happened next is sickening beyond comprehension. As she lie bleeding in the limo's backseat, a group of vulture paparazzi shoved their telephoto lenses only inches from her face and snapped countless rapid-fire shots at her with blinding flashbulbs. Imagine Diana's horror at this gruesome scene. She'd experienced a high-speed crash, her fiancée lay dead beside her, she's in a state of shock, bleeding, while a bodyguard has his face shredded and the driver is slumped dead over the steering wheel.

Obviously wracked with pain, these monsters stick their lenses practically in her face and fire off a strobe effect of blinding light. How grotesquely sick.

NO SENSE OF URGENCY

With the most photographed woman in the world lying partially conscious in the backseat of a crashed limousine, it took an ambulance fifteen minutes to reach the scene. Being well past midnight, Parisian streets were not by any means congested or stifled by traffic jams.

In *Introgenocide: An Ambulance Ride to Hell*, John Lee quotes a French trauma doctor. "As soon as a lady witness called police at 12:26, every ambulance in Paris heard the call. And believe me, it didn't take that long before everyone knew who was in the crash. For the SAMU ambulance to take between twelve and fourteen minutes to arrive is unbelievable. In that area, and at that time, it should not have taken more than five minutes."

Then, when paramedics did arrive, nearly *an hour* passed before Di was loaded into the ambulance. Since she wasn't trapped inside the vehicle, why did doctors attend to her on a stretcher inside the tunnel for such a long time?

Even more incredibly, once the ambulance finally departed with Diana, they went to La Pitie Salpetriere, a hospital further away than any other from the crash scene. A total of five different medical centers were closer in proximity. Again quoting the French trauma doctor, John Lee writes, "I would have taken her within a quarter of an hour to Val de Grace, which is much closer than La Pitie. That is a military hospital.

Every political figure who is in a car crash or is injured is taken there."

The brazen disregard for Diana's life continued. La Pitie was approximately five miles from the tunnel, yet 43 minutes elapsed between the ambulance's departure from the crash site and its arrival at the hospital. This time span averages out to a driving speed of approximately seven miles per hour! It gets worse. When the ambulance reached Paris's Natural History Museum—located directly across the street from La Pitie—it stopped for another unexplained ten minutes. They were literally a stone's throw away from the emergency room.

In all, the entire process from crash time to her entrance into the trauma care unit took one hour and 46 minutes. "She died moments before she was brought into surgery," writes Jeffrey Steinberg in *Al Fayed Charges Murder in Anniversary Lawsuit*.

In this same vein, Dr. Wolf Ulrich, head of the European Commission on Crime, lamented, "Diana could still be alive had it not been for the doctors' incompetence. They simply let her bleed to death." The glaring mistake in his assessment is the word "incompetence." The extended delay in transporting Princess Diana five miles didn't arise from simple negligence, but was instead deliberate. The controlled setting didn't allow physicians who weren't bought and paid for to save Diana's life. She had to be murdered prior to ever reaching the hospital.

WHITE FIAT UNO

After Diana's death, investigators traced the mysterious white automobile seen racing from the scene to Mr. James Adanson. Jeffrey Steinberg describes him as such: "Adanson was not only one of the leading paparazzi who had stalked Princess Diana and Dodi Fayed during the final weeks of their lives, Adanson was also at the time of the crash the owner of a white Fiat Uno."

Steinberg continues, "French authorities did, in fact, seize the white Fiat Uno owned by Adanson, which he had painted and sold shortly after the crash. Forensic tests on the car confirmed that the paint and bumper scratches matched those on the Mercedes, strongly suggesting that Adanson's car had been involved in the crash."

Even more incriminating is how Adanson boasted to friends that he not only witnessed Diana's death inside the tunnel, but also photographed and taped her. He was, without doubt, part of the hit squad dispatched to murder Princess Diana. More telling is the fact that he's now been tied to MI6 as a contract worker, as well as being a member of the UKN British intelligence network.

Richard Tomlinson states knowingly, "MI6 has a whole cadre of people like Adanson who simultaneously do their own job—their own profession. They happen to have skills that can be used occasionally by MI6 on a contractual basis."

To eliminate this smoking gun, eight months later—in May 2000—authorities found Adanson's body in the charred wreckage of his car in southern France. The auto had been locked from the outside, and Adanson's body could only be identified via DNA due to its grotesquely burned condition. Police ruled his death "suspicious."

COVER-UP

With lightning speed, those behind Diana's death began making efforts to conceal their foul play. For starters, a mere six hours after the crash, the French Department of Transportation completely reopened the tunnel to traffic without any sort of investigation. They also claimed that the CCTV system outside Alma tunnel had malfunctioned, yet other motorists passing through this gateway later received speeding tickets stamped only minutes prior to when Diana crashed. To state otherwise is a deliberate act of distraction to prevent the public from viewing Diana's crash footage.

Moreover, French judges refused to order DNA tests on driver Henri Paul's urine and blood samples to determine whether they were actually taken from his body. In addition, Paris police commander Jean-Claude Mules, who signed Diana's death certificate, acknowledged that the rush to embalm Diana came from an authority higher than him.

MOTIVE

Following her separation from Prince Charles, the royal family distrusted Diana and considered her a loose cannon. With the queen's fortune conservatively estimated at $3 billion, they had plenty to lose, especially when pitted in a test of wills with the popular princess.

They were also troubled by rumors that Diana threatened to leave Britain and take her children along. She told well-known journalist Richard Kay, "My destiny is to go abroad." Paul Majendie of *Reuters* confirmed this notion, saying, "She planned to quit Britain." If so, the royals and Prince Charles would have had even less influence on their two teenage princes, William and Harry.

Another hot-button issue that infuriated the Establishment as a whole revolved around Diana's campaign against land mines. Noel Botham provides an excellent overview of the repercussions: "In the Pentagon in Washington, and among some of America's wealthiest arms dealers, it began to dawn on people that the princess of Wales had not only become the most visible and intractable opponent of their policies, but she now represented the most serious current threat to their agendas."

What would she next speak out about that highlighted the war machine's atrocities—Gulf War Syndrome? How about the organizations and corporations that shared the same bed with the royal family? Moreover, who could ignore her comment during an interview with *Panorama* magazine in 1995 where she said Prince Charles was not fit to be king? She even got—at least perfunctorily—President Bill Clinton on her side to abolish U.S. involvement in the sale of land mines.

Still, none of these pressing matters rivaled her involvement with Dodi al Fayed. If she were indeed pregnant, the bulge would begin showing within weeks. The House of Windsor's racism bubbled to the boiling point. How could they allow the future King William to be linked to a brown Arab half-brother?

If anyone isn't convinced, the *Sunday Mirror* was to run a story on the morning of the crash—Aug. 31, 1997—with the following news item: "Prince Philip [has] been banging on about his contempt for Dodi and how he is undesirable as a future stepfather to William and Harry. Diana has been told in no uncertain terms about the consequences should she continue the relationship with the Fayed boy . . . Now the royal family may have decided it is time to settle up." Other sources had Philip calling him an "oily little bed-hopper."

The Fayeds belonged to an enemy camp, and those who lurked within the royal secret cabal realized that photographs of Diana in a bikini embracing Dodi was an affront to their self-created Illuminati superiority. Worse, instead of backing down under the weight of their objections, Diana basked in making them squirm.

Rayelan Allan (of *Rumor Mill News* and wife of former CIA agent Gunther Russbacher) characterized the battle in these terms: "Diana was dictating the pace of events, as she loved, and the Royals hated every minute of being overshadowed again. Diana was rubbing it in and she knew it, and so did the Royals. The British establishment had reached zero tolerance with Diana and her risqué relationship with the son of their arch-enemy al Fayed."

When Prince Charles voiced his displeasure with Diana's affair, she publicly laughed at him. When Charles's mistress, Camilla, celebrated her birthday, Diana trumped her by appearing in a bikini on Dodi's yacht. They were arm-in-arm, a completely in-your-face gesture to the royals.

Hounam and McAdam consider the impact of an Anglo/Arab half-brother for the future king: "The scenario opening in front of their horrified eyes was of a possible marriage to an Egyptian playboy followed almost inevitably by a conversion to Islam. It was unthinkable that the heir to the throne and his younger brother should have a Muslim stepfather."

On Oct. 12, 1997, the *Independent's* Robert Fisk carried the following item: "Had I heard what the Lebanese were saying about Diana's death? They had convinced themselves that it was a plot. The British establishment could not stomach the idea that Diana—in love with an Egyptian Muslim—might herself convert to Islam. So they got rid of her."

Because they feared these people may exert *any* type of influence on heirs to the throne, King and Beveridge were told by an MI6 source in 1998, "Her removal would have become almost a necessity the minute her divorce from Prince Charles was made final, never mind her subsequent relationship with a Muslim. That would most certainly have been the final nail in her coffin."

ISRAEL AND THE MOSSAD

"Mossad's business is spying and killing. Mossad does that in the USA just as freely as in Great Britain, France or Germany."
—Frankfurter Allgemeine Zeitung

The unaware may wonder: what concerns did the state of Israel have with a seemingly British affair? If Diana had extended her land mines campaign to target Israeli war crimes against Palestinians, she could turn public sentiment against this terrorist nation. Journalist Nicholas Davies, in a German documentary, spoke of Diana's larger plans as an icon for the less fortunate: "She intended to start a campaign in a Palestinian refugee camp in Gaza or the West Bank. 'This misery must come to an end, and these children must no longer live under such conditions,' was to be her message."

With Dodi being a Muslim, what if Diana rightfully compared Israeli atrocities in the Middle East to what purportedly occurred to them during WWII. If she meddled too boisterously, all of Israel's genocidal practices would be exposed for the world to see. Botham writes, "In Israel, it was widely believed the union of Diana and Dodi signaled a change in world opinion in favor of Arabs and consequently against Israeli interests."

Picture Princess Diana strolling along the West Bank with Dodi and the two princes while holding a brown Muslim baby as hundreds of thousands cheered her on worldwide television. The Mossad could, under no circumstances, tolerate such a visual image, especially if proof of their destructive militarism against innocent civilians and children was inter-spliced.

It's already been established that MI6 played an integral part in Diana's murder, and since they've been intimately connected to both the CIA and Mossad for decades, an interesting picture begins to emerge. Jewish financiers dating back to Amschel Rothschild have been funneling money to the monarchy, thus exerting a vast amount of control.

Well-known Israeli National Security Advisor Ari Ben-Menashe disclosed the contents of what he saw in the Mossad files: "They explain many things about the intelligence presence around Diana. They reinforce her own claims she was the subject of intense scrutiny by Britain's security services, the CIA and French intelligence. The American National Security Agency was also involved with satellite surveillance of her."

In the end, the Mossad, royals, and American arms dealers all had a vested interest in silencing Diana. In *Who Killed Diana*, underworld hit man Peter Scott said unequivocally, "It wasn't an accident. The Israelis were involved."

JON KING'S "SOURCE"

"Give me control over a nation's currency, and I care not who makes its laws."

—MAYER AMSCHEL ROTHSCHILD

In *Princess Diana: Hidden Evidence*, Jon King extensively quotes a deep intelligence source who claimed that the murder in question was ordered "beyond normal channels" and was carried out by private mercenary firms hired by various spy agencies.

Among these, of course, was the CIA, which the source said "became the corporate world's own intelligence agency. It was funded by corporate money, and so it was obliged to serve corporate agendas. It was never run by the White House."

This concept of corporatism leads to the root of real power on our planet. "For the past fifty years administrations in the West have become infected with a cancer called corporate government. It all began immediately after the Second World War, when the corporate monopoly that funded the war effort really began to impose itself on peacetime administrations. The banks and loan companies that had loaned money to the U.S., to Britain, *and* to Hitler for the manufacture and supply of arms suddenly began to call in their debts."

Although the timeline stretches back further into the past than WWII, what we're viewing is a global government organized crime syndicate. This operation "is run by some of the world's most powerful financial and industrial godfathers. . . . Remember, the CIA was formed by MI6."

King's source continues: "I always refer to these people as 'godfathers' because that is what they are. They are the owners, directors, and manipulators of the world's largest financial institutions and multinational arms, drugs, fuel and technology companies. These people are rarely seen on a public stage."

Finally, referring to the role of MI6 and the CIA, he reveals, "The assassination had been planned for a good many months . . . the target had to go because they had been carcinogenic to the system." Diana's suspicions had been correct all along that her life was in danger.

"Behind the plot sat an extremely powerful cabal of financial, industrial, and political godfathers who wanted this 'loose cannon' out of the way, once and for all." The truth has now been disclosed.

BLOODLINES

To truly understand Diana's murder, we must delve even deeper into the psyche of those who committed this horrendous deed. In simplest terms (in the context of an extremely complex subject), for centuries a ferocious battle has been waged by the Windsor Dynasty to keep control of the royal throne. The primary matter of contention that they've desperately tried to keep concealed is that the German Hanover-Windsors—aka the Establishment or "the Firm"—is actually the product of an imposter bloodline.

More importantly, the House of Windsor resulted from a bastardized, genetically modified Judaic strain of blood. On the other hand, Princess Diana's family—the Spencers—is said to be traceable back to a "pure" bloodline. Without getting any more specific, the Stuarts (from which Diana's own heritage arose) would be considered Britain's true royal family, while the Windsor's Judaic bloodline was usurped by Rome for political ends (i.e. control).

In *Princess Diana: Hidden Evidence*, King and Beveridge provide three invaluable quotes which illuminate this intriguing subject.

One: "The Windsor bloodline is the result of an ancient alliance of Germanic and Judaic royal bloodlines that is, and always has been, predominantly Judaic."

Two: "This same Judaic royal bloodline is the very authority upon which the most powerful right-wing U.S./European faction of Masonic government was—and remains—founded. And moreover, the House of Windsor remains this faction's titular head."

Three: "High-level intrigues and machinations have conspired across centuries to keep this Judaic strain precisely that: Judaic. The inference being that had the future Queen Mother of the House of Windsor ever married an Arab Muslim, then the House of Windsor's decades-long struggle to survive the unification of Europe as this bloodline's titular head would have been severely compromised."

With their usurped, fake royal bloodlines dating back to the Jewish dynasties of ancient Israel, the Windsors, in effect, could not tolerate Diana's romance with a Muslim. The jealous god Jehovah became pitted in a genetic-political war with Allah.

In the middle—unknowingly (at least originally)—sat Princess Diana, who the royals carefully selected to be their baby maker. It's not her they wanted—just her womb and pure DNA. Once she produced two fitting male sons, Diana's usefulness had been exhausted. Of course, if she'd simply remained quiet and didn't open her mouth, they'd have allowed her to stick around. But, as HRH Prince Michael James Alexander Stewart suggested, this rebellion is precisely why Diana had to be assassinated. "It is all to do with the question of blood. Diana was a Stuart by descent, and the Windsors felt threatened by this."

OCCULT DESIGNS

In *Lady Die*, filmmaker Chris Everard describes "occult cocktail parties at the Cliveden Estates in the 1960s," and how Diana's "crash in Paris was the beginning of a gruesome occult ritual—with the time and place of the crash being chosen carefully to coincide with ancient satanic rites."

To close the circle and complete the silencing of Diana, Rayelan Allan describes the significance of her death locale. The tunnel—Pont de l'Alma, "was a pagan sacrificial site." The reason her killers selected

Dodi and Diana had been enjoying a holiday before they went on their fatal trip to Paris, where they both were killed in the Pont D'Alma underpass.

---

this specific spot was because "it had been a temple to the goddess Diana, the goddess who was known as the queen of heaven. They knew the temple had been used for human sacrifice. The religion they were going to create was based on human sacrifice, not just the ritual murder that was performed in the temple, but the sacrifice of the person's entire life to the New World Order's new religion."

She concludes, "Pont de l'Alma was a sacred portal which led directly to the throne of heaven . . . 'Pont' means 'bridge,' and 'alma' means 'soul.' Pont de l'Alma, the site of the accident which killed Princess Diana, means 'Bridge of the Soul.'"

CHAPTER 16

COLUMBINE

OCCULT RITUAL AT COLUMBINE

Why Columbine? According to official reports, two semi-lone-nut teenage killers—Eric Harris and Dylan Klebold—stormed into their high school and fatally shot 13 students and teachers, while wounding 23 others before turning the guns on themselves. Again, the question is: why? A number of possible motives have been provided, such as:

• They were under the hypnotic influence of prescription drugs, such as Luvox.

• Marilyn Manson and other satanic heavy metal groups corrupted them.

• The two were homosexuals and were tired of being ostracized.

• Gun control advocates used this killing spree as an excuse to abolish the Second Amendment.

• Violent video games and movies spurred them on, desensitizing them to the effects of murder.

• Since the date of this shooting fell on April 20, their act was a tribute to Adolf Hitler.

• Membership in the now-notorious "Trenchcoat Mafia" propelled their sense of revenge against society.

- Satanism drew them away from the proper path in life.
- Jocks and bullies continually picked on the duo.
- The teenagers were unknowingly part of a bizarre government MK-ULTRA mind-control experiment.

Arguably, each of these explanations could have been a contributing factor to the Columbine massacre. But as you'll discover, a much wider conspiracy and cover-up were at play, leading to one of the most shocking displays of occult-based ritual that America has been subjected to.

LONE-NUT MAD BOMBERS?

Legitimate suspicions about the official version of events arise immediately when examining the number of explosive devices that were discovered inside the high school. A total of approximately 90-100 bombs were identified, including 27 pipe bombs, 48 dry ice bombs, a dozen propane canisters, 40-gallon jugs of incendiary liquids, plus 20-pound liquid petroleum gasoline tanks.

Although some of their explosives were quite crude and simplistic (what one would expect from amateurs), others obviously required a degree of expertise. Captain Phil Spence, an investigator for the Arapahoe County Sheriff's Department, stated, "Some of the bombs were more sophisticated, equipped with timing devices . . . one blew a hole clear through a wall in the library."

Two other factors must also be considered. First, Denver's *9News* filed an exclusive report where a Columbine night janitor saw "someone in a black trench coat inside the school the night prior to the shooting." This largely overlooked information is crucial because not only does it lead to pre-knowledge of the rampage, but is also reminiscent of the Oklahoma City bombing where witnesses noticed a group of men in the Murrah building's underground parking garage appearing to "plant bombs" near the huge cement girders.

Secondly, about 45 minutes before the shooting began inside Columbine, a construction worker named Roger Anderson told authorities that "he saw an older-model black BMW carrying four teenagers about a block from the school. The driver made a U-turn and drove off, followed closely by a tan sedan carrying two more teenagers."

Anderson later said he saw the same BMW—which carried Dylan Klebold—sitting in the Columbine parking lot after the melee began.

These were the very same cars that were later found to have pipe bombs, extremely large gasoline cans, and 20-pound propane tanks inside them, along with other flammable liquids. Then, at 11:20 a.m., when other students began their lunch break, Klebold and Harris exited the school and went straight to these cars before commencing with their shooting rampage.

Let's pause a moment and ask, as one researcher did, "Could two high school kids trudge this much firepower and pyrotechnics into a school unnoticed, not to mention their additional firearms? Plus, over 50 different eyewitnesses claimed to have seen additional participants in this massacre other than just Klebold and Harris."

Investigator and author Dave McGowan puts the matter into perspective in an article entitled *Anatomy of a School Shooting*. "Picture, if you will, two teenagers strolling unnoticed into a high school, each carrying two firearms, a propane tank bomb, and some fifty other explosive devices, as well as an abundant supply of ammunition. Picture them then proceeding to carefully place each of these 95 bombs throughout the school, still unnoticed and undisturbed by faculty or other students."

It's incomprehensible to believe that two high school kids planted nearly 100 bombs that day, especially when they participated in a school-related bowling class at 6:30 that morning. Fellow classmates said neither Klebold nor Harris wore trench coats, and that they were laughing and joking with no visible signs of aggression. These are the lone-nut mad bombers?

Sheriff John Stone doesn't believe so: "I've never thought it was just two suspects because of the amount of stuff that was brought in." Jefferson County D.A. Dave Thomas agreed. He told the *Denver Post* on May 5, 1999, "It is obvious to me that they couldn't have carried them all [the bombs] in at the same time, plus the four weapons." A spokesman for the local sheriff's department, Steve Davis, concurred, telling the *Associated Press* on May 14, 1999, "From day one we've always felt like there was a very good possibility that more people were involved."

MULTIPLE SHOOTERS

Sheriff John Stone spoke for many when he continued to challenge the official version of events at Columbine: "I've said all along there were more people involved, and nothing has changed my thinking." His perspective matches the initial live broadcasts that emerged from the high school on April 20, 1999 where students inside the war zone reported seeing men (not teenagers) in black trench coats during the shooting. As most seasoned investigators know, these "on the fly" telecasts are often the most accurate before government spin doctors begin altering the story to fit their ends.

STUDENTS

Cutting edge publisher Russ Kick encapsulated the existence of wider involvement in a March 27, 2001 article for *The Village Voice*. "If Eric Harris and Dylan Klebold acted alone in slaughtering thirteen people and wounding many others at their high school, why did the police and press originally report that many students were saying up to eight gunmen were involved? Why do investigators say Harris and Klebold killed themselves at 12:05 p.m., but live coverage indicated shots were being fired in the school until approximately 3:45? Who was the still unidentified student in a black jacket who was arrested at gunpoint during the siege?"

Reporter John Quinn spoke with one of these students—Chris Wisher—who told him that the third young man led away from the school in handcuffs four hours after the attack was "one of the ones who shot at us." Wisher added that he was "personally acquainted with another witness who saw a group of 7-8 assailants upstairs at Columbine in black trench coats with weapons when Harris and Klebold were downstairs."

Tales of multiple shooters proliferated among the students, such as those who simultaneously heard gunfire both inside and outside the school. The mother of student Kim Sander described to KUSA-TV what her daughter had seen: "She looked up and saw a gunman in a black trench coat with a very huge gun in front of him. He had dark brown hair, thick bushy eyebrows, and was very ugly. She didn't recognize him as a student."

Another student, Cathy Parks, told MSNBC that while two shooters were upstairs in the library, bombs were being detonated on the floor below. CNN ran a similar account: "Another male student who said he was about 100 yards away from the shooters said there were three of them, including one fellow student he recognized and another boy dressed in white throwing bombs on top of the school—some kind of grenade." *USA Today* added, "Beyond the two dead gunmen, students described seeing another youth dressed in a white shirt throwing bombs that looked like soda cans. A youth matching that description later was seen being led away by police."

All of the above accounts originate from *mainstream* sources, including the *Denver Rocky Mountain News* on July 29, 1999. "Dozens of witnesses interviewed by police after the crime claimed that from five to eight individuals participated in the shooting that left 15 people dead, including the killers, and more than 20 injured." One student positively identified as being among the school shooters was Chris Morris (a friend of Eric Harris), while Sunnee Hoppe was "100% sure" that a graduate named Robert Perry participated in the attacks because she "had known him for six years."

MASKS AND AMMUNITION

Parent Michael Shoels, who has a vested interest in the truth because his son Isaiah was killed on April 20, 1999, told the Columbine Research Task Force (CRTF) that from the numerous eyewitnesses he had spoken with, "Everyone was talking about shooters in black masks. According to authorities, Harris and Klebold weren't wearing masks at any point."

Chris Wisher confirms that when he saw Harris and Klebold inside the school, neither wore masks. A teacher at Columbine, Patti Nielson, who was also shot during the assault, described seeing masked gunmen in the school's lower level while other shooters were upstairs. Another glaring inconsistency concerns the amount of ammunition found afterward inside the school. The Jefferson County Sheriff's claim that "853 pieces of ballistic evidence was recovered during the investigation," whereas "other officials currently say Harris and Klebold fired about 200 rounds."

SWAT AND NATO FORCES

The most obvious questions at this point are: who was wearing the black masks that day; and who were the additional shooters that fired the more than 600 remaining shots? Some parents, such as Brian Rohrbough, whose son Daniel was killed at Columbine, are convinced that law enforcement agents were the culprits. According to investigator John Quinn, Jefferson County District Judge Brooke Jackson felt there was enough evidence to have Rohrbough's autopsy reports released. After this ruling, Mr. Rohrbough stressed, "I think it is important for people to understand Daniel was running from the gunmen who were on the hill behind him, and he was shot and killed *from the front*. The fatal bullet could not have come from Klebold and Harris. It had to come from law enforcement at the bottom of the hill."

It is now known from verifiable sources that SWAT teams were inside Columbine shortly after the shooting began. When asked why there was such a slow response by law enforcement, sheriff's spokesman Steve Davis refuted these claims. "It was *not* two hours before a SWAT team went in. Several officers responded within three minutes, and the first SWAT team was in the building in about 20 minutes."

In June 1999, John Quinn penned an article claiming that live television viewers of FOX-WFLD in Chicago saw a NATO bomb truck parked outside Columbine as the rampage ensued. One chilling account was as follows:

> Numerous people from around the country have reported to John Quinn and the CRTF that they saw a large blue NATO truck located on the Columbine High School grounds at about 11:30 am. It was shown from a helicopter. The cameraman zoomed in and immediately the video feed was cut.

If these reports are accurate, it is eerily reminiscent of confirmed reports from Oklahoma City where a bomb squad truck was seen by many witnesses parked around the corner from the Alfred P. Murrah Building only hours before the structure was rocked by explosives.

Another equally bizarre anecdote comes from the Columbine Research Task Force:

> *KUSA's* Kyle Dyer emphatically states, "It seems we've heard so many eyewitness accounts that so many students saw these men . . . they must have been all over the school." A cameraman focuses on a number of officials in the staging area, from a SWAT guy dredging around a body shield that says "NATO-3" in white letters on its front, to a man wearing sunglasses and a black suit—possibly the FBI's Dwayne Fuselier. [Correspondent] Greg Moss then reports, "At one point, police officers thought they [the gunmen] were on the roof."

SWAT teams, FBI agents, and NATO. Were any of these entities actually participants at Columbine? In *Hillary and Bill: The Murder Volume*, it was proven beyond any doubt that BATF, Delta Forces, FBI, and the elite Combat Applications Group partook in the massacre of 86 individuals at Waco—many of them innocent children. Is there a chance—as some have speculated—that an organization such as the SOG (Strategic Operations Group) was present, along with other rogue units?

Before dismissing this possibility, consider the words of Jefferson County SWAT Team commander Terry Manwaring in the March 2000 issue of *Playboy*: "I just knew the killers were armed and were better equipped than we were." Jefferson County Sheriff John Stone sarcastically echoed this sentiment. "We have initial people there right away, but we couldn't get in. We were way out-gunned by two kids who couldn't aim?"

Author Dave McGowan analyzed this scenario, then made the following assessment: "Stranger still is the notion that two teenagers with limited firearm training and armed only with shotguns and 9mm handguns would be able to outgun a veritable army of law enforcement officers, many with advanced paramilitary training and weapons." On top of that, McGowan adds, "Articles from the *Associated Press* reveal that ballistics evidence shows that six of the thirteen victims in the massacre were possibly killed by the SWAT Team."

Is this why most law enforcement personnel waited four hours before entering the school? As John Quinn pointed out, "They and other authorities were well aware that there were far more than two gunmen inside." Further, on the *Unite 4 Justice* website, "The *Associated Press* reported that a SWAT member was on the roof of a home facing the school library after the owner found spent bullet casings in the roof's gutter. Some windows in the library were shot from the *outside* and the glass was all over the carpet. Did a SWAT sniper shoot the killers before they killed anyone else?"

This case gets even more twisted. Dr. William Deagle, a Denver physician employed by the Englewood Fire Department, was dispatched to Columbine on April 20, 1999. Exactly ten months later, on Feb. 20, 2000, he testified:

> The Jefferson County sheriffs threatened my firefighters with deadly violence if they tried to rescue [teacher] Dave Sanders. They were told if they tried to enter the building, they would be shot.
>
> Did you know there were twenty-six federal and state agencies at Columbine? There were BATF in the building. I have three children's accounts that were shot, that I personally interviewed, that said the BATF were shooting children. There were Denver SWAT teams inside the building at the time of the shooting that didn't engage them.
>
> I had firefighters crying in my office telling me how they arrived in eight minutes and were willing to go in without a Kevlar flak jacket and helmet and were told, "If you go in, we'll shoot you."

SELF INFLICTED SUICIDES?

The public was told that after running rampant within the school for 45 minutes, the two teenage killers committed suicide at 12:05 p.m. But yet again, the facts don't quite fit reality. Dave McGowan clarifies the situation. "Another question that could be cleared up by the release of the autopsy reports is the alleged suicides of the two shooters, seeing as how Klebold was shot once in the left side of the head, apparently by one of two 9mm weapons . . . The wound's location puzzles some investigators. They believe that if the right-handed Klebold had shot himself, the wound should have been on the other side." (*Denver Rocky Mountain News,* June 13, 1999)

This point is extremely crucial because, as filmmaker Evan Long points out, "Klebold's injury indicates that a bullet went through his skull from the left to the right. The gun he was holding is difficult to hold to one's own head, and was found next to his right arm."

Long continues, "Bits of Klebold's brain and skull were ejected on Harris's left pant leg. Likewise, Harris's wound appears to have resulted in a trajectory of blood onto the lowest shelf of the bookcase immediately behind his head." The following words are vital: "This would appear to indicate that Harris and Klebold were lying in this exact position at the time of the shots being fired." In other words, the boys were already down on the ground—prone—when the shots were fired that killed them.

THE ASSAULT CONTINUES

Inexplicably, even though Harris and Klebold were killed at 12:05 p.m., on April 20 the *Denver Post* reported, "By 3:45 p.m. shots still rang out inside the school as more than 200 law enforcement officers and four SWAT teams tried to stop the gunmen and evacuate wounded high school students."

It's obvious that something is awry with this timeline, as Dave McGowan indicates. "The official report contends that the lunchtime rampage ended after 45 minutes and that 'sometime after noon the killers stood near the library windows and turned their guns on themselves' (*Los Angeles Times,* May 16, 2000). Strange, then, that there would be shots ringing out some three-and-a-half hours later."

Others inside the school also conveyed this seeming inconsistency. Columbine art teacher Patti Nielson, who was wounded in the library, crawled into a cupboard to escape being killed. More than an hour later, she exited her hiding place, then looked at her watch. It read 1:00 p.m. At this point, she heard more gunfire, an entire hour after Klebold and Harris were killed.

In *The Columbine Cause*, Evan Long describes another teacher, Lois Kean, who also hid during the assault: "Sometime between 1:00 and 1:30 p.m. she and [teacher] Carol Weld went back into the RNN (audio/visual department) sound booth. She stated that five minutes after getting back into the booth, they heard more shooting. She stated it was a round of shots, definitely more than two, and had an automatic sound to it."

FURTHER ARRESTS

While this continued shooting occurred, a significant event occurred in a field behind the Columbine High School. According to the Columbine Research Task Force, "At 1:42 p.m., three young men were arrested at gunpoint in the west corner of Clement Park Field. They were wearing hats, black jackets, and camo pants. During the course of the next few hours, it became more and more clear that these young men had prior knowledge that the shooting was going to take place."

On April 20, 1999, Robert Weller of the *Associated Press* confirmed this information. "Three youths wearing black—but not trench coats— were stopped by police in a field near the school. The Colorado Bureau of Investigation said the three were friends of the gunmen who were being taken in for questioning."

CNN videotapes substantiate these arrests, showing three teenagers with hands clasped behind their heads as police cars and officers surround them. Named Matthew Christianson, Matt Akard, and Jim Branetti, did they have any connection to the shooting rampage, especially when student Chris Wisher "repeatedly told investigator John Quinn in phone interviews that he personally saw a third shooter on the scene, and that friends of his saw a half-dozen trench-coated assailants with weapons."

DWAYNE FUSELIER—COVER-UP COMMANDER

Considering that Columbine was the deadliest high school shooting in U.S. history, what if you knew somebody that had a son that attended this very same school, belonged to the Trenchcoat Mafia, and made a graphically-violent movie about teenage killers going on a rampage? What if this same individual had a second son who held membership in the exact same Trenchcoat Mafia to which Dylan Klebold and Eric Harris belonged? Would you make this person the FBI's lead investigator at Columbine? Do you feel there would be any potential conflict of interest?

Unbelievably, as if straight out of *The Twilight Zone*, this scenario is precisely what occurred. FBI agent Dwayne Fuselier's eldest son, Scott, graduated from Columbine high school in 1997. He also helped produce a student movie that was described by Kevin Vaughan and Hector Gutierrez of the *Associated Press* as follows: "The film depicts gun-toting, trench coat-wearing students moving through Columbine's halls and ends with a special-effects explosion of the school." The *Denver Rocky Mountain News* provided a similar description. "Trenchcoat-wearing students armed with weapons moving through the school's halls. The film ends with four students walking away from the school as it explodes in flames."

On May 13, 1999, the *Denver Post* carried a story that stated that Fuselier's "youngest son, Brian, was in the school cafeteria at the time [of the massacre] and managed to escape after seeing one of the bombs explode." More amazingly, Brian Fuselier belonged to the Trenchcoat Mafia, alongside Klebold and Harris. Is this the reason he was *allowed* to escape instead of being slaughtered like the other students? Further, one of the Trenchcoat Mafia's closest allies—a student named Brooks Brown—was with Harris and Klebold only moments before the boys entered Columbine and began shooting. Then, when news organizations like CNN arrived on the scene, Brooks Brown provided on-the-spot interviews to each and every one of them, providing a specific spin. Brown also told Vaughn and Gutierrez of the *AP* that Scott Fuselier's gory Columbine movie "was a parody, done in humor." Could his assessment be due to the fact that, according to the *AP* on May 13, 1999,

Brooks Brown "helped in the production of the film"?

To put this matter into perspective, Dave McGowan writes, "First, we have the son of the lead investigator, who was obviously a member of the so-called Trenchcoat Mafia, involved in the filming of a pre-en-actment of the crime. Then we have the second son of the lead investigator being at ground zero of the rampage. And finally, we have a close associate of both the Fuselier brothers and of Harris and Klebold (and a co-filmmaker) being in the company of the shooters immediately before they entered the school, by his own admission." McGowan continues, tongue-in-cheek, "There's certainly nothing unusual about that. It's actually standard FBI procedure to have your son shoot a training film for a high school slaughter a couple of years beforehand."

So, who was this lead investigator? Dwayne Fuselier was an FBI special agent, a member of the Special Operations and Research Unit, and belonged to an elite squad called the Crisis Management Unit. As such, Fuselier's own resume lists him as a:

> Senior member of the FBI's Critical Incident Negotiation Team where he responded to most of the major hostage/barricade incidents handled by the FBI, including the Atlanta Prison Siege (1987), the Branch Davidian Siege in Waco, Texas (1993), the Montana Freeman Siege (1996), and the arrest of the Texas Seven (2001).

Similar to FBI gunman Lon Horiuchi, who killed Randy Weaver's wife during the Ruby Ridge siege (1992), then moved on and became involved in the Waco masacre, Fuselier too seems to have been a key operative during shadowy government black ops.

POLICE COVER-UP

The deeper one delves into the Columbine case, the more you realize how the bizarre turns into the truly twisted. In addition to FBI agent Dwayne Fuselier's direct ties to the Trenchcoat Mafia (via his sons), the Jefferson County Sheriff's office also had previous connections with Klebold and Harris. According to a *CBS/AP* story, "Authorities had at least 15 contacts with the Columbine high school killers dating back two years before their murderous attack, the state attorney general [Ken Salazar] said in a report that angered families of the victims."

For starters, the sheriff's office first came in contact with Eric Harris in 1997 for a criminal complaint. The paperwork for this incident has since vanished. Then, in 1998, Deputy Tim Walsh arrested Harris and Klebold for breaking into a van. For reasons that will become clear shortly, after the Columbine shooting in 1999, Walsh never mentioned to investigators that he'd had contact with the teenage gunmen. Why?

One of the reasons is that in 1998, the sheriff produced a warrant to search Eric Harris's home for *bomb-making* materials. More importantly, the Columbine Research Task Force uncovered a police file (#JC-001-010589) entitled "Walsh Butt-Rape." After being arrested on one occasion, authorities compiled a report that, after showing a diagram of the Columbine High School shootings, includes a hand-scribbled stick-figure drawing composed by Eric Harris wherein he is being sodomized by a police officer (hence the file name).

Did Jefferson County officials sexually molest either of the Columbine shooters? At this time, nobody can answer that question with any degree of certainty. But, there is now evidence that a cover-up was orchestrated following the Columbine incident. In an article by Alan Prendergast of the *Denver Westword News* on Sept. 30, 2004, he described the results of a grand jury investigation:

> Although the probe of missing police documents resulted in no indictments, it did raise questions about "suspicious" actions by the Jefferson County Sheriff's brass, including the shredding of a large pile of Columbine files. Most stunning of all, the report charged that a few days after the massacre, several high-ranking officials met secretly and resolved to suppress key documents stemming from the JCSO's earlier investigation of Harris, to treat them as if they didn't exist—in short, to lie about them.

Was he referring to the Walsh "Butt-Rape" files, or Dwayne Fuselier's association with the Trenchcoat Mafia? It's clear from the Columbine *Basement Tapes* that the teens harbored a strong dislike for Deputy Walsh, as Klebold snarls a disdainful "fuck you" into the camera at him, indicating that they'd obviously had previous contact with the officer.

Further proof of this past association between the teens and local police can be found on 911 dispatch calls made on April 20 when the Columbine rampage took place. In an exclusive from Denver's *7News*, the following conversation occurred:

> Officer Dave Baldwin: Just so you know, Rich, while you're driving down there, our suspect—he's supposed to still be in the school shooting people. He's wearing . . . he's an 18 year-old wearing all black. Uh, that's all we have at this time.
> Sergeant Rich Millsaps: Is this the sheriff's guy?
> Officer Dave Baldwin: Yes.

Now, how would *anyone* definitively know the shooters' identity only minutes after the melee began? *7 News* continues.

> Walter Gerash, an attorney representing two families suing the sheriff's department, says that a phrase like "the sheriff's guy" is how officers typically refer to their informants. "It's important to note that when that dispatch conversation was taking place, the sheriff's department had already figured out that Harris was one of the shooters," [*7News* reporter] Julie Hayden said. Gerash speculated that Harris might have been an informant for someone in the department.

An informant, or was his relationship with the sheriff's department more nefarious? Also, was Millsaps referring to Tim Walsh, or someone else? When asked about this matter by *7News*, Jefferson County Sheriff John Stone refused to answer any questions, precisely the same tactic Dwayne Fuselier used when refusing to speak about his son's membership in the Trenchcoat Mafia.

MIND CONTROL

Rumors have swirled for over a decade involving some type of extreme mind control experimentation involving the Columbine teenagers. While much has focused on subliminal programming in violent video games, satanic heavy metal, and gory Hollywood movies, another aspect also reared its ugly head. Could Eric Harris have been a Manchurian killer who became an unwitting pawn in this twisted ritual?

The theory has credence for a number of different reasons. First, it's been established that Harris had a lengthy relationship with the Jefferson County Sheriff's Department—either as an informant, or as a victim of sexual abuse. Secondly, as a member of the Trenchcoat Mafia, he was in direct contact with the Fuselier brothers, whose father—Dwayne—not only served in an elite FBI squadron, but also filled a role as a top-level government psychologist. Were the Fuselier brothers actually Trenchcoat Mafia "handlers" that set the course for what happened on April 20? This notion could be dismissed if it weren't for Scott Fuselier's Trenchcoat Mafia student movie where Columbine was ultimately destroyed in a blaze of glory.

Another parent in addition to Dwayne Fuselier also enters the picture, namely Wayne Harris, father of Eric. A plethora of conjecture, accusations, and subterfuge has been directed at this man; and in all fairness, it would be beneficial to separate fact from fiction. Unfortunately, similar to so many others associated with the Columbine massacre, he too refuses to answer any questions. Why is this trend so prevalent, and why are so many reticent to speak about what happened before and during that fateful day?

At any rate, it is known that for most of his career, Wayne Harris was a pilot stationed at Plattsburgh Air Force Base in northeast New York. From here, everything becomes murkier. Some researchers have speculated that Plattsburgh was a multi-level underground MK-ULTRA base used for mind control experiments. Others link it to Dr. Ewen Cameron, one of the most infamous mind-benders of all-time. From this information, conspiratologists posit that Eric Harris was subjected to bizarre psy-op experiments until his family moved from New York to Colorado in 1996—three years before the massacre.

Are these fantastic claims accurate? Did Wayne Harris have connections to the FBI's Delta Force or other intelligence agencies? Could he have used his son as a guinea pig for chemical and/or drug manipulation? How much input did Mr. Harris have on his son's Internet website, and did he assist Eric in learning to detonate explosives?

Regrettably, no substantiated evidence is available in regard to these claims that could stand up in a court of law. However, it must be admitted that a freakish scene existed at Columbine, especially in regard to the Trenchcoat Mafia. With direct ties to the FBI (Fuselier), local police (Tim Walsh), the Air Force (Wayne Harris), and possibly some of the CIA's most demented mind-controllers (Cameron), there's enough circumstantial evidence to make one wonder why such a wall of silence surrounds each of the parties listed above.

RAGE

Considering the number of factors outlined in this article, one conclusion is certain: the teenage killers at Columbine were bursting with rage, especially Eric Harris. Whether abused at Plattsburgh AFB, sodomized by a police officer, or indoctrinated by twisted Trenchcoat Mafia rhetoric, Harris seethed with contempt, as can be witnessed by journal excerpts that the 17 year old wrote shortly before the Columbine massacre.

But beware, as Dave Cullen writes in *The Depressive and the Psychopath*, "These are not the rantings of an angry young man picked on by jocks until he's not going to take it anymore. These are the rantings of someone with a messianic-grade *superiority* complex, out to punish the entire human race for its appalling inferiority. It may look like hate," but as Dr. Robert Hare, author of *Without Conscience* concludes, "It's more about demeaning other people."

MOTIVE

Despite hundreds of mainstream media articles written about, analyzing, and dissecting the Columbine shooting, not once did the controlled press pinpoint the hidden motive behind this massacre. On the contrary, these cover-up artists did everything imaginable to conceal the fact that both Dylan Klebold and Eric Harris were Jewish, and that April 20th was actually part of an ongoing occult Talmudic ritual that strangely infected a majority of the Clinton-era presidency.

Understandably, the preceding paragraph packs a huge wallop. So, let's continue step-by-step. For starters, Dylan Klebold's mother—Susan Yassenoff—worshipped at the local synagogue on a regular basis. This woman also received her education in a Jewish *schul*, pursued her secondary education at Temple Israel, while her father, Leo, was a leading force in Jewish affairs and an integral part of Temple Israel. The teenage killer came from a "devout" Jewish household. On April 26, 1999, the *New York Times* wrote, "Dylan Klebold was a practicing Jew, following his Jewish mother's religion. They had a Passover Seder in their home shortly before the shootings, and Dylan actively participated."

Similarly, Eric Harris reveals that his mother is Jewish, while *Salon* magazine quotes him as telling a teacher, "My mother is Jewish!" He also dated a Jewish girl in high school—Sarah Davis—and in stark opposition to the mainstream media smokescreen, his website was very pro-Jewish. At one point he even declared his desire to "rip the arms off racists and neo-Nazis."

In addition to their strong Jewish affiliations, Harris and Klebold also exhibited an undeniable bias against Christians. In their infamous basement videotapes, the boys spoke of killing "Christian, God-loving whores." Klebold then interjects, "I'm glad we killed Christ," and, "I'll shoot Christian girls in the head." Later, when speaking about two classmates, he rants, "I don't like you. You're stuck-up little bitches. You're fucking little Christian, godly little whores. What would Jesus do? What the fuck would *I* do?" Fueled by his accomplice, Eric Harris interjects, 'I would shoot you in the motherf***ing head!" Go, Romans! Thank God they crucified that asshole." To this, Klebold cheers, "Go, Romans!"

The corporate media painted these teens as devil worshipping, Marilyn Manson neo-Nazis. In actuality, they hated nazis and instead were closer in their views to the violently supremacist JDL (Jewish Defense League). Furthermore, the Trenchcoat Mafia consisted of many members who were also Jewish, and strongly anti-Christian. It's also rumored that FBI lead investigator Dwayne Fuselier is Jewish, thus making his two sons—also associated with the Trenchcoat Mafia—Jewish. To support this point, Scott Fuselier—who co-produced the explosive Columbine student film in 1997—went on to become a director for *Jewish Impact Films* and won a second place prize from the Bronfman Center and Avoda Arts at the third annual New York Jewish student film festival on March 2, 2006. The Bronfmans, of course, are recognized as one of the world's most powerful Jewish families.

This violent, Talmudic, anti-Christian perspective was reflected in an account given by a girl who survived the Columbine onslaught. According to an article written by journalist Ken Walker on May 10, 1999, after a temporary halt in the shooting, "One of the gunmen asked, 'Does anybody in here believe in Christ?' The girl then described that, to her surprise, her friend who was hiding beside her, stood up and said, 'I do. I believe in Jesus.' 'He shot her right then, and she fell down beside me.'"

To crystallize this morbid event, we need to recall the specific date of these shootings—April 20, 1999. Previously, when did the Waco massacre occur? April 19, 1993. Two years later, the OKC Bombing took place on April 19, 1995. April 19 is the Jewish Passover, also known as the Pasach.

Men, women, and innocent children at Waco were burned to death as government tanks with CS-gas flamethrowers incinerated their compound in rural Texas on the Jewish Passover.

Exactly two years later, as innocent children were dropped off at a daycare center in the Alfred P. Murrah Building, they were crushed to death on the Jewish Passover. Then, four years and one day later, a multitude of masked, trench coat-wearing killers slaughtered innocent teenagers at Columbine High School, only one day after the Jewish Passover commenced.

Each of these acts was blamed on lone-nut killers (David Koresh, Timothy McVeigh, and Harris/Klebold). But the larger picture is now clear. Three times in just six years during the Clinton presidency, extremely traumatic mass-murders were committed on the Jewish Passover. What are the odds that such high-profile atrocities would just "coincidentally" happen on this precise date on the calendar? The timing is no accident. Columbine was simply another occult, Talmudic ritual played out in all its ghastly detail before the American public.

BIBLIOGRAPHY

Allen, Gary, *The Rockefeller File*. Seal Beach, CA: '76 Press, 1976

Astucia, Salvador, *Rethinking John Lennon's Assassination: The FBI's War on Rock Stars*. Gaithersburg, Maryland: Ravening Wolf Publishing Company, 2004

Berkowitz, David, *Son of Hope: My Story*. Overland Park, KS: Morningstar Communications, 2006

Bernays, Edward, *Propaganda*. New York: H. Liveright, 1928

Botham, Noel, *The Murder of Princess Diana*. New York: Pinnacle Books, 2004

Breitman, George, Porter, Herman, and Smith, Baxter, *The Assassination of Malcolm X*. New York: Pathfinder Press, 1976

Brussell, Mae, *The Mae Brussell Reader*. Santa Barbara: Prevailing Winds Research, 1991

Bugliosi, Vincent, *Helter Skelter: The True Story of the Manson Murders*. New York: W.W. Norton and Company, 1974

Burleigh, Nina, *A Very Private Woman: The Life and Unsolved Murder of Presidential Mistress Mary Meyer*. New York: Bantam Books, 1998

Canevani, Leonore &Van Wyhe, Jeanette and Dimas, Christian and Dimas, Rachel, *The Murder of Marilyn Monroe*. New York: Carroll and Graf Publishers, 1992

Carter, Dan, *The Politics of Rage: The Origins of the New Conservatism, and the Transformation of American Politics*. New York: Simon and Schuster, 1995

Colodny, Len and Gettlin, Robert, *Silent Coup: The Removal of a President*. New York: St. Martins, 1991

Condon, Richard, *The Manchurian Candidate*. New York: Four Walls Eight Windows, 1959

Constantine, Alex, *The Covert War on Rock*. Los Angeles: Feral House Publishers, 2000

Davis, Deborah, *Katharine the Great: Katharine Graham and Her Washington Post Empire*. New York: Sheridan Square Press, 1979

Dieugenio, James and Pease, Lisa, *The Assassinations: Probe Magazine on JFK, RFK, MLK, and Malcolm X*. Los Angeles: Feral House Publications, 2003

DiLouie, Craig, *Paranoia*. Bend, OR: Salvo Press, 2002

Evanzz, Karl, *The Judas Factor: The Plot to Kill Malcolm X*. New York: Thunder's Mouth Press, 1992

Foreman, Laura, *True Crime: Serial Killers*. Alexandria, Virginia: Time Life Books, 1992

Freedman, Benjamin, *Facts are Facts*. Carson City, NV: Bridger House Publishers, 1954

Gates, Daryl, *Chief: My Life in the LAPD*. New York: Bantam Books, 1992

Goldman, Albert, *The Lives of John Lennon*. New York: Bantam Books, 1988

Gordon, Robert J. and Wecht, Cyril, *The Search for Lee Harvey Oswald*. New York: Penguin Books, 1995

Gordon, William, *Four Dead in Ohio: Was There a Conspiracy at Kent State?* Laguna Hills, CA: North Ridge Books, 1995

Gorightly, Adam, *Death Cults.* State College, PA: Sisyphus Press, 2004

Gorightly, Adam, *The Shadow Over Santa Susana: Black Magic, Mind Control and The Manson Family Mythos.* New York: Writers Club Press, 2001

Gorightly, Adam, *The Best of Adam Gorightly: Collected Rantings (1992-2004).* College Station, TX: Virtual Bookworm Publishing, 2005

Gorightly, Adam, *The Prankster and the Conspiracy.* New York: Paraview Press, 2003

Greene, Carol, *Test-Tube Murders: The Case of Charles Manson.* Weisbaden, Germany: Dr. B'ttiger Verlags-GmbH, 1992

Grieg, Charlotte, *Cold-Blooded Killings: Hits, Assassinations and Near Misses That Shook the World.* London: Arcturus Publishing, 2006

Haley, Alex, *The Autobiography of Malcolm X.* New York: Penguin Books, 1973

Hall, Manly P., *The Story of Healing, the Divine Art.* Los Angeles: Philosophical Research Society, 1979

Hamilton, Ian, *In Search of J.D. Salinger.* Chicago: Trafalgar Square Books, 1988

Hare, Robert, *Without Conscience: The Disturbing World of Psychopaths Among Us.* New York: The Guilford Press, 1993

Heimbichner, Craig, *Blood on the Altar: The Secret History of the World's Most Dangerous Secret Society.* Coeur d'Alene, ID: Independent History and Research, 2005

Heymann, C. David, *The Georgetown Ladies' Social Club: Power, Passion and Politics in the Nation's Capital.* New York: Atria Books, 2003

Hoffman, Michael A., *Secret Societies and Psychological Warfare.* Dresden, NY: Wiswell Ruffin House, 1989

Hounam, Peter and McAdam, Derek, *Who Killed Diana?* Berkeley: Frog Books, 1998

Jackson, Devon, *Conspiranoia: The Mother of all Conspiracy Theories.* New York: Plume, 1999

Jeffers, H. Paul, *History's Greatest Conspiracies: 100 Plots Real and Suspected.* New York: Barnes and Noble Publishing, 2004

Keith, Jim, *Mind Control, World Control: The Encyclopedia of Mind Control.* Kempton, Illinois: Adventures Unlimited Press, 1997

King, Jon and Beveridge, John, *Princess Di: Hidden Evidence.* New York: S.P.I. Books, 2001

Lavey, Anton, *The Satanic Bible.* New York: Avon Books, 1976

Leary, Timothy, *Flashbacks: An Autobiography.* Los Angeles: J.P. Tarcher, 1983

Lee, Martin and Schlain, Bruce, *Acid Dreams: The Complete Social History of LSD, the CIA, the Sixties, and Beyond.* New York: Grove Weidenfeld, 1985

Leonard, Jerry, *The Perfect Assassin: Lee Harvey Oswald, the CIA and Mind Control.* Bloomington, Indiana: 1st Books, 2002

Levin, Ira, *Rosemary's Baby*. New York: Penguin Books, 1967

Levy, Joe. *The Little Book of Conspiracies: 50 of the World's Greatest Theories*. New York: Metro Books, 2005

Marks, John, *The Search for the "Manchurian Candidate": The CIA and Mind Control*. New York: W.W. Norton and Company, 1979

Marrs, Jim, *Rule by Secrecy: The Hidden History That Connects the Trilateral Commission, the Freemasons, and the Great Pyramids*. New York: Perennial, 2000

McGowan, Dave, *Programmed to Kill: The Politics of Serial Murder*. Lincoln, Nebraska: iUniverse, 2004

McMillan, George, *The Making of an Assassin: The Life of James Earl Ray*. New York: Little, Brown and Company, 1976

Moorhouse, Frank, *Satanic Killings: Inside the Satanic Minds of Some of the Most Unpredictable and Dangerous Killers in History*. London: Allison and Busby Limited, 2006

Newton, Michael, *The Encyclopedia of Serial Killers*. New York: Checkmark Books, 2000

Norris, Joel, *Serial Killers*. New York: Anchor Books, 1989

O'Brien, Cathy and Phillips, Mark, *The Trance-Formation of America: The Life Story of a CIA Mind Control Slave*. Las Vegas: Reality Marketing, 1995

Parfrey, Adam, *Apocalypse Culture*. Los Angeles: Feral House Publishers, 1990

Pepper, William, *An Act of State: The Execution of Martin Luther King*. London: Verso, 2003

Piper, Michael Collins, *Dirty Secrets: Crime, Conspiracy and Cover-up During the Twentieth Century*. State College, Pa: Sisyphus Press, 2005

Piper, Michael Collins, *Final Judgment: The Missing Link in the JFK Assassination Conspiracy*. Washington: The Center for Historical Research, 2000

Ray, James Earl, *Who Killed Martin Luther King: The True Story of the Alleged Assassin*. New York: Marlowe and Company, 1992

Ray, John Larry and Barsten, Lyndon, *Truth at Last: The Untold Story Behind James Earl Ray and the Assassination of Martin Luther King*. Guilford, Connecticut: The Lyons Press, 2008

Ross, Colin A., *Bluebird: Deliberate Creation of Multiple Personality by Psychiatrists*. Richardson, TX: Manitou Communications, 2000

Salinger, J.D., *The Catcher in the Rye*. New York: Little, Brown and Company, 1951

Sanders, Ed, *The Family: The Story of Charles Manson's Dune Buggy Attack Battalion*. New York: E.P. Dutton and Company, 1971

Schechter, Harold and Everitt, David, *The A to Z Encyclopedia of Serial Killers*. New York: Pocket Books, 1996

Scott, Peter, *Gentleman Thief: The Recollections of a Cat Burglar*. New York: Harper Collins, 1995

Simon, *Dead Names: The Dark History of the Necronomicon*. New York: Avon Books, 2006

Smith, Matthew, *Marilyn's Last Words: Her Secret Tapes and Mysterious Death*. New York: Carroll and Graf Publishers, 2004

Southwell, David and Twist, Sean, *Conspiracy Files*. New York: Gramercy Books, 2004

Spence, Richard B., *Secret Agent 666: Aleister, British Intelligence and the Occult*. Port Townsend, WA: Feral House, 2008

Speriglio, Milo, *Marilyn Monroe: Murder Cover-up*. Van Nuys, CA: Seville Publishing, 1982

Spignesi, Stephen J., *In the Crosshairs: Famous Assassinations and Attempts*. New York: Barnes and Noble Books, 2003

Sprague, Richard, *The Taking of America, 1-2-3*. Roslindale, Mass: Rat Haus Reality Press, 1976

Talbot, David, *Brothers: The Hidden History of the Kennedy Years*. London: Simon and Schuster, 2007

Tarpley, Webster and Chaitkin, Anton, *George Bush: The Unauthorized Biography*. Washington: Executive Intelligence Review, 1992

Terry, Maury, *The Ultimate Evil: An Investigation Into a Dangerous Satanic Cult*. New York: Doubleday, 1987

Thomas, Kenn, *Popular Paranoia: A Steamshovel Press Reader*. Lilburn, Georgia: IllumiNet Press, 1995

Turner, William and Christian, John, *The Assassination of Robert F. Kennedy: The Conspiracy and the Cover-up*. New York: Thunder's Mouth Press, 1993

Thorn, Victor, *Hillary (and Bill): The Drugs Volume*. Washington: American Free Press, 2008

Thorn, Victor, *Hillary (and Bill): The Murder Volume*. Washington: American Free Press, 2008

Thorn, Victor, *Hillary (and Bill): The Sex Volume*. Washington: American Free Press, 2008

Thorn, Victor, *The New World Order Exposed*. State College, PA.: Sisyphus Press, 2003

Valentine, Douglas, *The Phoenix Program*. New York: William Morrow and Co., 1990

Vankin, Jonathan and Whalen, John, *The 70 Greatest Conspiracies of All Time: History's Biggest Mysteries, Cover-ups and Cabals*. New York: Citadel Press, 1998

Victorian, Armen, *Mind Controllers*. London: Vision Paperbacks, 1999

Wheeler, Cisco and Springmeier, Fritz, *The Illuminati Formula to Create an Undetectable Total Mind Control Slave*. Fritz Springmeier, 1996

Wolfe, Donald H., *The Last Days of Marilyn Monroe*. New York: William Morrow and Company, 1998

Wyllie, Timothy, *Love Sex Fear Death: The Inside Story of the Process Church of the Final Judgment*. Port Townsend, WA: Feral House, 2009

Zepezauer, Mark, *The CIA's Greatest Hits*. Tucson: Odonian Press, 1994

Newspaper and Magazine Articles

Ali, Tariq, *Power to the People*

Allan, Rayelan, *Diana, Queen of Heaven: The New World Order Religion*

Allan, Rayelan, *Princess Diana's Death and Memorial: The Occult Meaning*

Bartels, Lynn, *Police Step Up Search for Others Involved*

Bashir, Martin, *Princess Diana Interview: Panorama Magazine*

Branson, Allen, *Psychopaths, Psyops, and Cointelpro*

Bresler, Fenton, *Who Killed John Lennon?*

Breslin, Jimmy, *Breslin to.44 Killer: Give Up Now!*

Brussell, Mae, *Charles Manson and the Crushing of the Counter Culture*

Butler, Ed, *Did Hate Kill Tate?*

Canfora, Alan, *U.S. Government Conspiracy at Kent State*

Cee, Hero, *The Next Round in Gun Control*

Cee, Hero, *The Port Arthur Massacre*

Collins, Paul David, *The Deep Politics of God Revisited*

Constantine, Alex, *Crowley and the CIA*

Constantine, Alex, *The OTO and the CIA*

Cothran, George and Hegarty, Peter, *Spies for Zion*

Cristian, Arthur, *Port Arthur Massacre*

Cullen, Dave, *The Depressive and the Psychopath*

Damore, Leo, *The Meyer Conspiracy*

Davis, Deborah, *Steamshovel Press # 6 Interview*

Davis, Tom, *Interview with Mae Brussell on the Assassination of John Lennon*

Denver 7News, *Tape Suggests Police Knew Columbine Shooter Before Attack*

Douglass, James W., *The Murder and Martyrdoms of Malcolm X*

Dowbenko, Uri, *Royal Conspiracy: Princess Diana Names Her Killer*

Elson, John T., *Theology: Toward a Hidden God*

Emory, Dave, *The Assassinations of Dr. Martin Luther King, Jr. and Malcolm X*

Feldman, Bob, *Who Eliminated Malcolm X?*

Fisk, Robert, *Her Majesty the Terminator*

Fitrakas, Bob and Wasserman, Harvey, *The Lethal Media Silence on Kent State's Smoking Guns*

Ford, Trowbridge H., *Why John Hinckley, Jr. Almost Assassinated Ronald Reagan*

Fulsom, Don, *The Unsolved Murder of JFK's Georgetown Mistress*

Gaines, James, *The Man Who Shot John Lennon*

Gorightly, Adam, *Is the Catcher in the Rye a Mechanism of Control?*

Guyatt, David, *Princes of Plunder*

Hayes, Ben, *The Death of Mary Pinchot Meyer*

Hersh, Seymour, *1971 Tape Links Nixon to Plan to Use 'Thugs'*

Horrock, Nicholas, *CIA Documents Tell of 1954 Project to Create Involuntary Assassins*

Hutchison, Earl, *Revisiting the Malcolm X Assassination*

Icke, David, *The Creation of Israel*

Johnson, Dirk and Wilgoren, Jodi, *Terror in Littleton: The Gunmen*

Jones, Columbia, *MK Zine Editorial*

Jura, Jackie, *RFK Assassination Puzzle Pieces*

Kerr, Jane, *My Husband is Planning an Accident*

Ketcham, Christopher, *Bigger than Watergate: The Cover-up That Succeeded*

Kick, Russ, *Witness to a Massacre*

Krock, Arthur, *The Intra-Administration War in Vietnam*

Krupey, G.J., *The High and the Mighty: JFK, Mary Pinchot Meyer, LSD and the CIA*

Leary, Timothy, *High Times Interview*

Lee, John, *Introgenocide: An Ambulance Ride to Hell*

Life Magazine, *The Love and Terror Cult*

Linders, Doug, *The Trial of John Hinckley, Jr.*

Loeb, Vernon, *NSA Admits to Spying on Princess Diana*

Long, Evan, *The Columbine Cause*

MacGregor, Andrew S., *Deceit and Terrorism: The Port Arthur Massacre*

Maier, Timothy W., *New Chapters in the Assassin's Diary*

Majendie, Paul, *Princess Diana Planned Move Abroad, Court Told*

Mazza, Jerry, *Of John Lennon's Assassination, Imagine*

McGowan, Dave, *Anatomy of a School Shooting*

McGowan, Dave, *Celluloid Heroes: The Tangled Web of Charlie Manson*

McMillan, George, *The Making of an Assassin*

Murphy, Jarrett, *Columbine Report Stirs Anger*

Overbeck, Charles, *Reagan, Hinckley, and the 'Bushy Knoll' Conspiracy*

Pease, Lisa, *Bremer and Wallace: It's Déjà vu All Over Again*

Pease, Lisa, *Sirhan Says 'I Am Innocent'*

Pease, Lisa, *The RFK Plot Part II: Rubik's Cube*

Pienciak, Richard, *Son of Sam: New York's Summer of Terror 30 Years Later*

Piper, Michael Collins, *Mossad Linked to Martin Luther King Assassination*

Posner, Gerald, *Al Fayed's Rage*

Prendergast, Alan, *Columbine: Anatomy of a Cover-up*

Proctor, Lee and Shoffner, Roger and McCartor, Robert C., *John Hinckley, Jr. and the Attempted Assassination of Ronald Reagan*

Quinn, John, *The Columbine Massacre Conspiracy and Cover-up in Littleton*

Quinn, John, *The Rocky Mountain Horror Show: The Littleton Massacre's Hidden Mind Control Connections*

Mark Riebling, *Tinker, Tailor, Stoner, Spy*

Rowlett, Curt, *Project MK-ULTRA: Did the U.S. Government Actually Create Programmed Assassins?*

Ruppert, Michael, *Bobby, I Didn't Know!*

Sanders, John Vincent, *I am the Son of Sam!*

Schwartz, Greg A., *Was a Government Conspiracy Responsible for the Kent State Massacre?*

Smith, Brice, *The Buried Truths of Martin and Malcolm*

Steinberg, Jeffrey, *Al Fayed Charges Murder in Anniversary Lawsuit*

Stern, Sol, *A Short Account of International Student Politics and the Cold War*

Thomas, Charles, *The Kent State Massacre: Blood on Whose Hands?*

Thomas, Kenn, *JFK News*

Thompson, Hunter S., *He was a Crook*

Tomek, Aaron, *All the President's Men*

Tompkins, Stephen G., *Army Feared King, Secretly Watched Him*

Vaughn, Kevin and Gutierrez, Hector, *FBI Investigator's Son Linked to Case*

Vials, Joe, *Australia's Port Arthur Massacre: Government and Media Lies Exposed*

Vidal, Gore, *The Art and Arts of E. Howard Hunt*

Wallace, Sarah, *Are the 'Son of Sam' Killers Still Out There, or is it Just a Conspiracy Theory?*

Walker, Ken, *Gunmen's 'Do You Believe in God?' Posed to Several Columbine Students*

Ward, Bernie and Toogood, Granville, *JFK Two-Year White House Romance*

Weller, Robert, *Gunmen Open Fire in Colorado High School*

Wells, Jeff, *Four Pi Movement*

Wenner, Jann, *Rolling Stone Interview with John Lennon*

Wernerhoff, Carl, *The Assassination of Robert F. Kennedy*

Wiese, Arthur and Downing, Margaret, *Bush's Son Was to Dine with Suspect's Brother*

Wolfson, Jill, *Hurting Young Men Put Pen to Rage*

X, Malcolm, *Malcolm X on Zionism*

INDEX

You thought mind-control killings were only experimental? Think again!

NEW WORLD ORDER ASSASSINS

After eight years, the final installment of Victor Thorn's *New World Order* trilogy has finally arrived. This collection (including *New World Order Exposed* and *New World Order Illusion*) examines recent history's most spectacular assassinations in a fashion that dramatically differs from the cover-up versions provided by government sources and their allies in the mainstream media. From Marilyn Monroe's "suicide" in 1962 to 1999's Columbine high school massacre, Thorn exposes a host of lawless intelligence agencies, mind control projects and occult underpinnings that serve as a thread to connect each case. Readers will enter a realm where: sexual set-ups and tell-all diaries are used for blackmail; cults provide a breeding ground for Manchurian Candidates; and "lone nut shooters" act as patsies, while the real killers remain cloaked in shadows. *New World Order Assassins* unfolds within the context of turbulent political events where the Cuban Missile Crisis, Vietnam, Watergate and Reaganomics provide a compelling backdrop. Not only limited to American violence (includes uncensored information on the Manson Family murders, the Son of Sam murders, the killings of Martin Luther King Jr. and Malcolm X, the assassination of John Lennon, the unsolved murder of JFK mistress Mary Pinchot Meyer, the mysterious slaying of Bobby Kennedy and many more), this book also contains the foreign intrigue of Princess Diana's murder and Australia's Port Arthur slayings. To complete the picture, the influence of pop culture "trigger mechanisms" provides a subtext via the music of the Beatles rock group, movies such as *Taxi Driver* and literary classics like J.D. Salinger's *The Catcher in the Rye*. An unparalleled work of investigative reporting, tying together hundreds of otherwise diverse events and relying upon the work of more than 300 respected conspiracy researchers, *New World Order Assassins* is destined to be one of the most highly quoted books of the decade.

Softcover, 280 pages, #NWA, **$30 plus $5 S&H** in the U.S. Available from AMERICAN FREE PRESS, 645 Pennsylvania Avenue SE, #100, Washington, D.C. 20003. Send payment with the form in back or call 1-888-699-NEWS toll free to charge to major credit cards. Also at www.americanfreepress.net. (Outside U.S. email FAB@americanfreepress.net for bulk order S&H; one copy foreign S&H is $11.)

ALSO AVAILABLE: THE FIRST TWO BOOKS IN THE TRILOGY:

The New World Order Exposed: The Secret Cabal That's Undermining America

By Victor Thorn—There's nothing new about the New World Order. It is a conspiracy—not a conspiracy theory—and its very roots can be found in the Garden of Eden. Today, those who are tilling this soil for their own insidious ends are in positions of power in government, the media and academia. In order to understand the history of and the nature of this monster—this enemy of Liberty—you must read Victor Thorn's *The New World Order Exposed*. **Softcover, 563 pages, #NWE, $26.**

The New World Order Illusion

By Victor Thorn and Lisa Guliani—Book 2 of the NWO trilogy. Peer behind the news to see what the controlled media is not telling you, including: The real reason why U.S. troops attacked Iraq and Afghanistan; who really controls the media; the neo-conservatives' role as frontmen for the New World Order Elite; the unsettling truth about the dismantling of our sacred Constitution; the role of the United Nations in the New World Order; and much more. Forego the illusion and determine your own reality. **Softcover, 132 pages, #NWI, $15.**

GET THE ENTIRE SET OF THREE FOR JUST $60 plus $8 S&H.

In the maverick tradition of one of the great historians of the modern era . . .

No topic is "too controversial" for The BARNES REVIEW, the most interesting history magazine published anywhere today. Commemorating the trailblazing path of the towering 20th Century revisionist historian, the late Harry Elmer Barnes, TBR's mission is to separate historical truth from propaganda and to bring history into accord with the facts. Founded in 1994 by veteran American nationalist Willis A. Carto— a personal friend of Barnes—*The Barnes Review* concurs with Rousseau's maxim that "Falsification of history has done more to impede human development than any one thing known to mankind." TBR covers all aspects of history from the dawn of man to recent events and also places a special focus on the philosophy of nationalism. As such, TBR proudly describes itself as a "journal of nationalist thought" and dares to be

politically incorrect in a day when Cultural Marxism prevails in the mass media, in academia and in day-to-day life. TBR's editorial board of advisors encompasses historians, philosophers and academics from all over the face of the planet, intellectuals united in their desire to bring peace to the world by exposing the lies and prevarications of the past that have brought us to where we are today. If you believe everything you see in the "responsible" media or think that absolutely everything that appears in most college-level history texts is true, you might be shocked by what you see in TBR—but if you are shocked by what you see in TBR, then that's all the more reason you need to join the growing ranks of independent-minded free-thinkers from all walks of life and all over the world who are longtime TBR subscribers.

Isn't it time you subscribe?

The Barnes Review $46 for ONE year (six bimonthly issues—64 pages each); Including this special free bonus: A FREE COPY OF Michael Collins Piper's blockbuster book *The New Jerusalem*. That's a $20 gift free for a one-year domestic subscription. Subscribe for two years at $78 and get *The New Jerusalem* PLUS Mark Glenn's *No Beauty in the Beast: Israel Without Her Mascara*. Outside the U.S. email TBRca@aol.com for international rates and for S&H to your nation.

Call 1-877-773-9077 today and charge a subscription to major credit cards.

Send your check, money order or credit card information (including expiration date) to:

The BARNES REVIEW
P.O. Box 15877
Washington, D.C. 20003

Check us out at barnesreview.org or barnesreview.com

Books from Michael Collins Piper

Share the Wealth: Huey Long vs Wall Street. Edited by Michael Collins Piper. Here's the incredible story of the man they had to kill: Huey P. Long. *Share the Wealth* is a panoramic overview of the life and times of Louisiana's legendary larger-than-life populist. During the 1930s, the big loud voice of Louisiana Governor—and later U.S. Senator—Huey Long spoke out against the plutocrats of New York and London and their puppets in Washington and on behalf of America's farmers, laborers, small businessmen and the hardworking middle class. He posed a major threat to the

rampant predators of the Federal Reserve Money Monopoly. Had he not been gunned down in 1935, it's certain Huey would have played a part in expelling FDR from the presidency. For that, Huey Long had to die. Also a comprehensive overview of the speeches and writings of Huey P. Long. Softcover, 101 pages, #HL, *$20.*

The New Babylon: A Panoramic Overview of the Historical, Religious and Economic Origins of the New World Order. Here are the facts on the Rothschild Empire-controlled "City of London" and its global reach—a "secret history" of the last 200 years and of the Talmudic origins of the New World Order in ancient Babylon. After writing *The New Jerusalem*, Michael Collins Piper realized there was more to the story of Zionist power in the world—there were hidden religious and economic reasons that explained why our republic had fallen into the hands of forces working to establish a New World Order. In this titanic volume—280 pages in length and relying on many hard-to-find historical documents and other materials—Piper explores the hidden history of the New World Order and explains how it all evolved: from the teachings of the Talmud to the rise of the International Money Power to the reign of the House of Rothschild and its control over the Federal Reserve System. Softcover, 280 pages, #NB, *$25.*

The High Priests of War. Here is the book that has the neo-conmen running scared! Author Michael Collins Piper's full-length exposé of the history of the ex-Trotskyite, neo-conservative warmongers at the highest levels of power who orchestrated the war against Iraq and are involved in setting up the U.S.A. Police State. They include names like Wolfowitz, Perle, Feith and Kissinger and they are undoubtedly more dangerous to the future of America than Osama bin Laden. More than 50,000 copies of this hardhitting book have been distributed since its first printing several years ago—even more pertinent now! Softcover, 144 pages, #HP, *$20.*

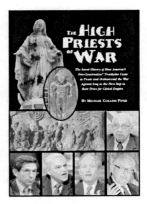

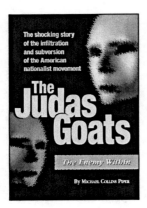

Judas Goats: The Infiltration & Subversion of the American Nationalist Movement. Here is Michael Collins Piper's nationalist blockbuster. This book—perhaps more than any other book ever written—exposes the Mossad, CIA, FBI and Southern Poverty Law Center sabotage of patriotic and nationalist groups in America throughout the last 75 years. Some real shockers in this uncensored exposé including: J. Edgar Hoover ran chapters of the KKK and Communist Party USA; federal agents in Oklahoma City at the time of the bombing; McCarthyism vindicated; FDR's Sedition Trial; the real Roy Bullock—ADL spy; Judas Goats still working in the movement. Much more. Softcover, 375 pages, #JG, *$25.*

The Golem: Israel's Nuclear Hell Bomb and the Road to Global Armageddon. Veteran author Michael Collins Piper pulls no punches in asserting that Israel's nuclear "Hell Bomb" is pushing civilization toward global Armageddon and that the perpetration of this un-controlled weapons program has the world held hostage. Piper explains the danger the planet faces from American collaboration with a nuclear-armed Israel. Israel has worked relentlessly to construct an atomic arsenal—its Golem—as the foundation of its security strategy. Softcover, 198 pages, #G, *$25.*

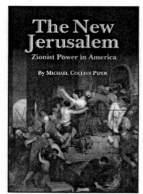

The New Jerusalem: Zionist Power in America—All the data you need to prove beyond a shadow of a doubt that Zionist interests do in fact control Wall Street, the U.S. news industry (print, radio and TV), finance, foreign policy, and more. Names names and organizations. Nothing like it in print today. The irrefutable evidence you need to convince your friends and foes alike that those who claim Zionism is the most powerful force in American politics are not "anti-Semitic," but are stating the dangerous truth. Softcover, 176 pages, #NJ, *$20.*

Target: Traficant: The Inside Story of How the Justice Department Conspired to Take Down Jim Traficant An eye-opening overview of the campaign by high-level forces to destroy the no-nonsense populist congressman. The Traficant case represents one of the most outrageous hit-and-run operations ever orchestrated against an American public official. Piper dissects the intrigues of the Justice Department and the FBI and demonstrates, beyond any doubt, that the congressman was absolutely innocent of all of the charges on which he was convicted. Softcover, 176 pages, #TT, *$25.*

Dirty Secrets: Crime, Conspiracy & Cover-Up in the 20th Century. Based on the writings and interviews of Michael Collins Piper. Compiled and edited by Victor Thorn & Lisa Guliani. This collection includes essays not found on the Internet, previously unpublished writings, interviews (including the long-lost *Final Judgment* tapes), reviews and insights into the JFK assassination, the OKC bombing, the Fed, FDR and Pearl Harbor, Israel's attack on the *USS Liberty*, Israel and Islamic fundamentalism, the murder of MLK, the Holocaust and more. Also includes synopses of three of Piper's major works. Softcover, 250 pages, #DS, *$22.*

More Uncensored Books...

Frontman: Barack Obama's Darkest Secrets Revealed.
In 2008, Barack Obama became the face of hope and change.
Yet lurking behind the scenes is a host of personages who long
ago selected this man to forward their global agenda. *Frontman* reveals the actual powers behind his throne: Bilderberg
plotters, Zionist handlers, global financiers and Marxist activists. To cover their tracks, secrecy has enveloped Obama's
past, including his birth records, college transcripts and employment history. While other books merely scratch the surface, *Frontman* tears away the deceptive smoke and mirrors.
This brutally honest portraits shows how our nation is being
controlled by unseen hands that are leading us perilously close
to disaster. Softcover, 112 pages, #O, *$20.*

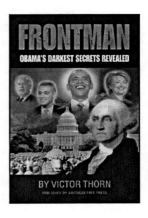

*Ship Without a Country: Eyewitness Accounts of the At-
tack on the USS Liberty.* Thousands of books, articles, essays, documentaries and films have been made concerning
pivotal events in history such as Pearl Harbor and the assassination of JFK. Why has no such attention been given to the attack on the *USS Liberty?* The reason is that the entity
responsible was Israel. In this book, readers will hear from eyewitnesses to the attack and to the high-level cover-up of the attack. All of this testimony has been kept fanatically hidden for
nearly half a century. Had the ship been sunk, it would have
kicked off a military exchange between the U.S. and USSR.
The book paints the ultimate picture of betrayal, and cover-
up. Softcover, 90 pages, #SWC, *$15.*

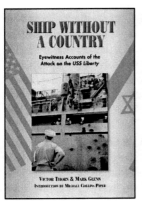

*Jim Tucker's Bilderberg Diary: One Man's Battle to
Shine the Light on the Shadow Government.* In existence
for more than 50 years, acting as a global ruling elite, Bilderberg's very name and activities remain hidden in the shadows,
despite its immense clout in directing the course of world affairs. With the release of *Bilderberg Diary* by veteran journalist
James P. Tucker Jr., those who've never known of Bilderberg
will get a first-hand account of its history from the one journalist who has doggedly tailed the Bilderbergers for the last
quarter of a century. Tucker lays out his entire remarkable history of infiltrating Bilderberg meetings, procuring their private
documents, and working relentlessly to shine the spotlight of
public scrutiny on Bilderberg's shadowy affairs. Many rare
photos. Softcover, 272 pages, #BD, *$25.*

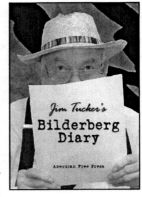

The Bilderberg Files: Rare Research Material on Bilderberg from the 1970s. THE BILDERBERG FILES is a special assembly of rare research material and early reports on Bilderberg that provides readers will find a wealth of confidential Bilderberg documents that prove that this secretive globalist group is operating behind the scenes despite denials to the contrary. These files originally came into the hands of Willis Carto, the founder of the Washington-based populist institution LIBERTY LOBBY, after he traveled to Turkey a quarter-century ago to report on the shadowy organization. At the time, the name Bilderberg was a carefully guarded secret of the global elites. But after three decades of tireless work on

the part of Carto and AFP editor emeritus Jim Tucker, millions of people around the world are now aware of the Bilderberg group and its goal of creating a world government for the benefit of the plutocracy. Softcover, 8.5 x 11 format, 68 pages, #BF, *$20.*

The CIA in Iran: The 1953 Coup and the Origins of the U.S.-Iran Divide. How many Americans know a CIA "dirty-tricks" team overthrew Iran's democratically elected leader in 1953? Here's the inside report from the declassified files that reads like a detective novel. *The CIA in Iran* reveals in shocking detail a once-top-secret CIA report showing how U.S. and British operatives employed bribery, murder and terrorism to topple a government they could not control. It is the true story of how American agents orchestrated the downfall of the democratically elected government of Prime Minister Mohammad Mossadeq and maneuvered the infamous Shah into power. Find out the whole formerly clandestine story. Softcover, 150 pages, #CIA, *$20.*

Phantom Flight 93: And Other Astounding September 11 Mysteries Explored. In *Phantom Flight 93* you will discover how this event in Shanksville is the key to 9-11. Starting with physical evidence, it becomes clear that a passenger jetliner could not have possibly crashed in Shanksville, Pa. where federal officials said it did. Rather, the reality of that fateful morning is far more sinister. Book also examines the cell phone calls purportedly made by individuals on Flight 93, 9-11 passenger list oddities, corrupt officials who were in a position to assist in the plan and more. For far too long, Flight 93 has been overlooked by researchers and commentators in the alternative media. With the arrival of *Phantom Flight 93*, the public will finally get the truth. Softcover, 200 pages, PF93, *$25.*

Debunking 9-11: 100 Unanswered Questions About Sept. 11. All of the best reporting from AMERICAN FREE PRESS newspaper on the Sept. 11 tragedies plus commentaries from survivors and researchers. In AFP's *Debunking 9-11,* you'll get never-before published commentaries from William Rodriguez, the Trade Center's "last man out," and Ellen Mariani, crusading wife of one of the victims killed on 9-11, renowned Pentagon insider Col. Donn de Grand Pré and many more PLUS all of AFP's groundbreaking coverage of the event from the beginning: the spies operating in New York; the many theories put forth by independent researchers who reject the government's explanation of many of the events of Sept.

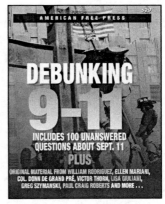

11; alternative theories as to why the twin towers collapsed; detailed information from a dozen sources presenting evidence of foreknowledge by the government and foreign intelligence agencies of the event; scientific debate over what really happened at the Pentagon on Sept. 11 and theories as to the downing of Flight 93. Softcover, 8.5 x 11 format, heavily illustrated, color cover, 108 pages, #DE, *$20.*

AFP Citizens Handbook & Rulebook for Jurors. Back by popular demand in a new, larger format, the AFP Citizens Handbook is loaded with vital information for every American—from elementary school kids to seniors. Besides the full texts of the Declaration of Independence, Constitution and Bill of Rights, the AFP Citizens Handbook also dedicates a key portion to our rights as jurors. This 9-page section has been requested again and again by readers and supporters who find this information invaluable when called for jury duty. This special enlarged edition also includes President George Washington's "Farewell Address," in which he implored future Americans to resist the temptation to become involved in the affairs of foreign nations, and Patrick Henry's reconstructed "Give Me Liberty" speech. Softcover, 57 pages, #CHB, *$6.*

ORDERING and S&H: Order any of the books listed here from AFP/FAB, 645 Pennsylvania Avenue SE, #100, Washington, D.C. 20003. S&H charges apply: Inside the U.S. add $3 S&H on orders up to $25. Add $5 S&H on orders from $25.01 to $50. Add $8 S&H on orders from $50.01 to $75. Add a flat $10 S&H on orders over $75. Outside the U.S. please email FAB@americanfreepress.net for best S&H to your nation. See more books and videos online at AFP and FAB's website: www.americanfreepress.net.

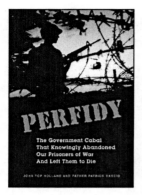

Perfidy: The Cabal That Abandoned Our POWS and Left Them to Die. Most people are unaware that there are many villainous high ranking government officials who have long been involved in the POW/MIA cover-up. Many of their names are mentioned and their nefarious actions are discussed in this book. However, the majority of the POW/MIA activists, when asked, will quickly tell you that the most detested of these government officials is the one that is most prominent: Sen. John McCain. But McCain's activities are only the small tip of a very large cover-up. Co-authored by Father Patrick Bascio and Sgt. John Top Holland—a U.S. veteran of World War II, Korea and Vietnam. Softcover, 225 pages, #PFD, *$25.*

9/11: What Really Happened. The official story of the Sept. 11, 2001 attacks on the United States is well known to most Americans. According to the U.S. government and the mainstream media, a group of 19 members of al Qaeda, a Muslim group led by Osama bin Laden, hijacked four U.S. airliners. Three were flown into buildings (the World Trade Center North and South towers and the Pentagon), and one crashed in Pennsylvania after a heroic effort by the passengers to regain control of the plane. That's the federal story. But what facts are there to support this official scenario? As there was no debris from any airliner found at the Pentagon or at Shanksville, there is little to back up the claims there. And, though most people will admit planes hit the

World Trade Center towers, it is the strange collapse of those buildings and another massive skyscraper nearby that still confounds 9-11 skeptics. In this book author Ed Whitney explains what did and did not happen and presents a much more plausible scenario. Softcover, booklet, saddle-stitched, 61 pages, #EW, *$10.*

Suppressed Science: Radiation, Global Warming, Alternative Health and Healing, Censored Scientists, Global Pandemics & More. Are cures for cancer being suppressed by the mainstream medical profession to protect corporate profits? Is what we are being told about global warming true, or is there a hidden agenda? How many alternative scientific theories and "fringe" practitioners have been suppressed by the power elite to maintain their stranglehold on what the American public is allowed to know? Chemical engineer, climatologist, author, USAR major (ret.) and rocket scientist Jack Phillips delves into these questions and many more as he uncovers the facts behind the facade of lies that fronts for modern science. Topics include: radiation, suppressed cancer cures, suppressed inventors, global warming, Alzheimers, global pandemics, crop circles, chelation therapy, dowsing, hormesis, mercury poisoning and more. Softcover, 176 pages, #SS, *$17.*

THE FUTURE FASTFORWARD TRILOGY

Future FastForward: The Zionist Anglo-American Empire Meltdown. Is the alliance between the United States, the British Empire, and Israel a paper tiger or a mighty empire? Is global "Empire Capitalism" about to come crashing down? Will there be a worldwide "people's war" against the super-capitalists and their Zionist allies? Is nuclear war inevitable? These are just some of the provocative questions addressed in *Future Fastforward*, a no-holds-barred book by Matthias Chang, a former top-level political advisor for Malaysia's longtime prime minister, Dr. Mahathir Mohammad. Softcover, 400 pages, #FFF, *$25.*

Brainwashed for War—Programmed to Kill: How We All Became War Junkies. From the Cold War to Vietnam and now the so-called "War Against Terror," we have been lied to, mind-controlled and duped by president after president (at the behest of America's own intelligence services) with the goal of making us mindless supporters of bloody war. And how many of America's wars have actually been necessary for the defense of the nation? Tracing back four decades and more, *Brainwashed for War* documents the atrocities carried out by the imperialist, Zionist-driven forces whose goal it is to subjugate the peoples of the world. Replete with documentary evidence including detailed appendices of once-classified documents. Softcover, 556 pages, #BW, *$30.*

The Shadow Moneylenders and the Global Financial Tsunami. Untangling the complex structures and the exotic and baffling practices of derivatives trading, high-level financial advisor Matthias Chang has succeeded like no other before in exposing the hidden global loan sharking operations of the "Shadow MoneyLenders." The author reveals for the first time to the public the ultimate secret that has enabled the Shadow MoneyLenders to amass a financial empire greater than the U.S. economy. (The "GDP" of the Shadow MoneyLenders is $500 trillion!) The author is a passionate advocate for the abolition of the Federal Reserve System in the U.S. and a strict policing of the Central Banks controlling the Global Economy. They have all been complicit in allowing the Shadow MoneyLenders to embark on the largest transfer of wealth in history—from the hundreds of millions of hardworking wage earners across the globe to the two percent that comprises the global elite. Softcover, 400 pages, #SL, *$30.*

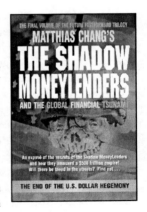

ALL THREE BOOKS IN THE SET FOR $75—save $15!

The Immorality of Illegal Immigration: An Alternative Christian View. A devout Roman Catholic priest, Father Patrick Bascio was quite concerned about the effect illegal immigration was having on America. And, as a Catholic priest, he saw the church participate in making the problem worse by turning a blind eye to illegal immigration, hoping droves of Latinos from Central America would expand the ranks of Christians in America. In *The Immorality of Illegal Immigration* Father Pat rips the veil off the illegal immigration issue, exposing the hidden side of the issue. He makes a devastating case against those who would say it is our duty to welcome in all newcomers through his discussions on the illegal alien component of America's street gangs, the impact on the black community, the fallacy that Americans are "too good" to do tough work, identity theft, the tax drain, national security and the *de facto* Balkanization of America as part of the new world order agenda. Softcover, 175 pages, #IPB, *$25.*

George Washington's Speeches & Letters. A fascinating and revealing look at America's first president and war hero through the personal letters Washington wrote to colleagues and loved ones during the French & Indian War, the American Revolution, early nationhood and his presidency. Perhaps the most telling aspect of a man are those thoughts he pens for posterity. 75 pages, 19 of Washington's letters and speeches re-set in easy-to-read type with a dozen illustrations accentuating key moments in Washington's life. Inside *George Washington's Speeches & Letters* you'll read Washington's innermost thoughts as he quickly writes to his mother to soften the news of a British/American defeat at the hands of the French and her Indian allies in which Washington had two horses shot from beneath him and bullet holes in his uniform. It was during this battle that Braddock was killed and his top aides-de-camp wounded, thrusting Washington into his first command. Or read Washington's letter to Congress begging for supplies, food, clothes and weapons for his army camped in Valley Forge during one of the coldest winters in 100 years. Or how about a letter from Washington to wife Martha informing her he would not be returning to her side for many months as he had been appointed commander-in-chief of the Continental Army. In this letter Washington expresses his regret for leaving her alone and informs her he has drafted a will . . . just in case. There are many more letters plus several speeches including Washington's classic Farewell Address which should be memorized by every U.S. congressman, judge and president. Softcover, 75 pages, #GWS, *$12.50.*

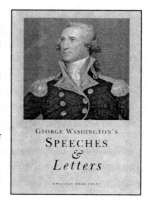

GEORGE WASHINGTON'S
SPEECHES
&
Letters

ORDERING and S&H: Order any of the books listed here from AFP/FAB, 645 Pennsylvania Avenue SE, #100, Washington,D.C. 20003. S&H charges apply: Inside the U.S. add $3 S&H on orders up to $25. Add $5 S&H on orders from $25.01 to $50. Add $8 S&H on orders from $50.01 to $75. Add a flat $10 S&H on orders over $75. Outside the U.S. please email FAB@americanfreepress.net for best S&H to your nation. See more books and videos online at AFP and FAB's website: www.americanfreepress.net.

THE 'HILLARY (AND BILL)' TRILOGY

In *HILLARY (AND BILL): THE SEX VOLUME*—**Part One of the Clinton Trilogy,** Bill and Hillary's meteoric rise to success is chronicled. It's a carefully plotted path that eventually led them to the White House. But along the way, a series of compromises had to be made, including a prearranged marriage, clandestine assignments for the CIA, and Hillary's ultimate role as a "fixer" for her husband's many sexual dalliances. Pulling no punches, investigative journalist Victor Thorn paints a compelling portrait of secrecy, deceit, violence, and betrayal that shatters the myth Mrs. Clinton has tried to create. Softcover, 344 pages, #H1, *$30.*

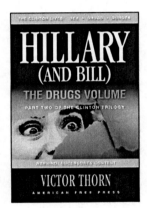

In *HILLARY (AND BILL): THE DRUGS VOLUME*—**Part Two of the Clinton Trilogy,** some of the most damning examples ever put into print of the U.S. government's crimes and corruption are exposed in glaring detail. Beginning with the Clinton family's long-standing ties to the notorious Dixie Mafia, this book illustrates how billions of dollars of cocaine, cash and weapons passed through Arkansas during the 1980s—with the the full knowledge of Bill and Hillary—to finance the illegal war in Nicaragua. (Tons of this CIA-imported coke helped fuel the cocaine epidemic of the 1980s.) In short, Arkansas became nothing less than a narco-republic, with little banks near Mena laundering more money than the big banks in New York City. Softcover, 310 pages, #H2, *$30.*

In *HILLARY (AND BILL): THE MURDER VOLUME*—**Part Three of the Clinton Trilogy**, the "Clinton Body Count" is presented in detail. The most comprehensive study of its kind, nearly 120 mysterious deaths are examined, beginning with the murder of two teenage boys who "knew too much" about the illicit drug trafficking operation in Arkansas. After ascending to the presidency in 1992, more atrocities continued with the nationally televised massacre at Waco. Proof now exists that Hillary directed the attack to destroy evidence of past government crimes. Following this nightmare, the public was confronted with the "suicide" of Vince Foster. Thorn reveals the identity of Foster's killer, as well as the involvement of foreign agents. Also covers the murders of Jerry Parks, Danny Casolaro, and former CIA

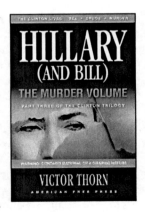

Director William Colby, plus Chinagate and the political assassination of Commerce Secretary Ron Brown. Softcover, 393 pages, #H3, *$30.*

ALL THREE BOOKS IN THE HILLARY SET FOR $75—save $15

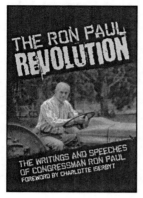

The Ron Paul Revolution: The Speeches and Writings of Congressman Ron Paul. This 278-page assembly of some of Texas Republican Congressman Ron Paul's more significant writings and speeches is all the more timely now that Dr. Paul has brought his principles of liberty, equality, small government and privacy to the world arena. The chapter titles illustrate the broad scope of the material appearing within: Big Government Run Amuck, Freedom From Government, Your Health Privacy, Dollars & Debt, Tax Reform, Immigration and Welfare, Constitutional Foreign Policy, Gun Owner Rights, and, finally, War and Peace. Find out what makes this maverick U.S. legislator so popular in the United States and why the mention of his name sends shivers down the spines of the bankers at the Federal Reserve. Foreword by former Ronald Reagan education director Charlotte Iserbyt. Indexed by subject. Assembled by AFP Executive Editor Christopher Petherick. Softcover, 278 pages, #RP, $25.

Everything They* Ever Told Me Was a Lie—Volume One. Investigative journalist, author and radio show host Pat Shannan has been in pursuit of the truth for nearly half a century. Intrigued by the deception and on-going cover-up of the JFK assassination, he began to notice a similar pattern in the 1968 murders of Martin Luther King and Robert F. Kennedy. Then he found altered and intentionally fabricated FBI official reports regarding these and other cases and began to notice the cooperative news media ignoring blatant and pertinent facts as well. The films of Ronald Reagan exiting the Washington Hilton clearly show Secret Service Agent Tim McCarthy being shot by someone other than John Hinckley, Jr. And what

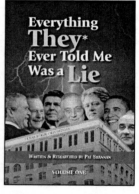

are the odds that the greatest potential beneficiary of Reagan's demise would be the close friend and business associate of John Hinckley, Sr.? Why did the wounded Reagan arrive at the hospital 15 minutes after Jim Brady, when his limo left the scene five minutes before Brady's ambulance? How could Arthur Bremer fire seven shots from a five-shot revolver the day he nearly killed Gov. George Wallace and three innocent bystanders in 1972? Why was Pat Tillman murdered in Afghanistan in 2004? Shannan has long maintained that the hidden power behind the expansion of the central government has been the unconstitutional use of legal tender that is produced at will, and herein proves his case. He also shows that government plots survive because of little or no investigation, and only through the aid of a cooperative news media can such ridiculous conspiracy theories as the 9-11 official story not only survive but thrive. Shannan submitted so much suppressed information from so many historic cases that we have divided it into two books, the second of which we are eagerly compiling for a Volume II publication in the very near future. Softcover, 280 pages, #EAL, $30.

SUBSCRIBE TO *AMERICAN FREE PRESS* NEWSPAPER AND GET FREE GIFTS!

AMERICAN FREE PRESS ORDERING COUPON

Item#	Description/Title	Qty	Cost Ea.	Total
			SUBTOTAL	
	Add shipping and handling. (See below for rates.)			
	Send a 1-year subscription to AFP for $59 plus 1 free book*			
	Send a 2-year subscription to AFP for $99 plus 2 free books**			
			TOTAL	

*NOTE ABOUT FREE GIFTS: For a one-year subscription to *American Free Press* newspaper ($59), we'll send you one free copy of AFP's *CITIZENS HANDBOOK*. **For a two-year subscription we'll send you AFP's *CITIZENS HANDBOOK* PLUS *9/11: WHAT REALLY HAPPENED*—$16 in free publications (domestic USA only).

PAYMENT   ❏ CHECK/MO   ❏ VISA   ❏ MC   ❏ AMEX   ❏ DISCOVER

Card # _____

Expiration Date _____ Signature _____

CUSTOMER INFORMATION: NWA111

NAME _____

ADDRESS _____

CIty/STATE/ZIP _____

U.S. S&H: Add $3 on orders up to $25. Add $5 from $25.01 to $50. Add $8 from $50.01 to $75. Add $10 on orders over $75. Outside U.S. email fab@americanfreepress.net.

RETURN WITH PAYMENT TO: AMERICAN FREE PRESS, 645 Pennsylvania Avenue SE, Suite 100, Washington, D.C. 20003. Call 1-888-699-NEWS (6397) toll free to charge a subscription or books to major credit cards. See also www.americanfreepress.net.

CPSIA information can be obtained
at www.ICGtesting.com
Printed in the USA
FFOW04n0646141115
18450FF